ALL COLOUR

BAKING

By

Annette Wolter

SELECT
EDITIONS

CLB 3489
Published 1994 by CLB Publishing
Exclusively for Selecta Book Ltd, Devizes

Published originally under the title *Backen Köstlich Wie Noch Nie* by
Gräfe und Unzer Verlag GmbH, München – Author Annette Wolter
© 1993 by Gräfe und Unzer Verlag GmbH, München
English translation copyright © 1994 by
Colour Library Books Ltd, Godalming, Surrey

ISBN 1-85833-242-7
Printed and bound in Italy

Introduction

This full-colour cookery book contains a wonderful range of baking recipes carefully selected by a highly-experienced and creative team of cookery writers. A useful reference work containing basic information on many aspects of baking, it includes inspired ideas for cakes, breads, biscuits, savoury pies, quiches and confectionery fit for every occasion.

The reference section at the beginning of the book features basic dough recipes and baking techniques, supported by clearly captioned explanatory step-by-step illustrations that will prove invaluable to both novice and experienced cook. Where more specific information is required, such as how to shape bread into loaves and rolls, how to plait bread dough and how to decorate fancy cakes, biscuits and confectionery, you will find it included within the recipes.

The recipes themselves begin with fruit cakes and tartlets, followed by delicious cakes, cakes for special occasions, popular pastries, sweets and confectionery. A whole chapter is devoted to Christmas baking, then come pizzas, snacks and recipes for delicious loaves and bread rolls.

All the recipes in this book have been tried and tested and are described in simple language to make them as easy as possible to reproduce. There are also plenty of helpful hints to save time and effort, as well as tips about whether the recipe in question is a classic one, a regional dish or a wholefood item. Many cooks will welcome the nutritional information listing the calorie counts, and the protein, fat and carbohydrate content, which is provided with each recipe.

We hope you have fun trying out our varied recipes and that you, your family, guests and friends enjoy them to the full.

Please note: The abbreviations kJ and kcal stand for kilojoules and kilocalories.

The baking temperatures quoted in the recipes may need to be adjusted to suit your oven. Unless otherwise stated, the oven should always be pre-heated to the required temperature before baking.

Contents

Popular Pastries
Pages 102-125

Cakes and Gateaux for Special Occasions
Pages 74-101

Contents

Christmas Fare

Pizzas, Quiches and Savoury Slices

Baking Suggestions for Every Occasion

No coffee morning is complete without a selection of cakes. Whether you want a cream, fruit or nut filling, there are so many recipes to choose from.

Christmas is a good time for biscuit-making and there are also plenty of recipes for teatime, coffee breaks or snacks.

Baking Suggestions for Every Occasion

Home-made bread, fresh rolls and croissants are perfect for breakfast on any day of the week

Appetisers and Late-night Snacks

Satisfying Party Favourites

Just Right for Children's Parties

Savoury and sweet pastries help parties to go with a swing. They are a satisfying way to start an evening if wine or beer are to follow.

Getting Started

Victoria sponge

To make a good Victoria sponge, all ingredients have to be stirred together evenly over a lengthy period until a runny, homogeneous mixture forms. Traditional recipes suggest that the butter, sugar and eggs should be beaten for at least 30 minutes, sometimes even for 1 hour, and always in the same direction. Using highly refined sugar nowadays can reduce stirring time by 10 to 20 minutes. To make a lighter sponge mix, separate the eggs and then whisk the egg whites until they form stiff peaks. If the quantities of butter and sugar stated in our basic recipe are reduced, then add 2 teaspoons of baking powder.

Heat the oven to 180°C/350°F/Gas Mark 4. Grease the cake tin with butter and sprinkle a few bread or sponge cake crumbs on top. Separate 4 eggs and whisk the egg whites until they form soft peaks. Gradually add 75g/3oz sugar and whisk until firm but not dry.

Sweet shortcrust or biscuit dough

Shortcrust pastry is quick and easy to make, but the dough needs to be thoroughly chilled before rolling out. Sweetened shortcrust is known as sweet shortcrust dough or biscuit dough. Shortcrust pastry can be used as a pie shell, a base for fruit flans and tarts, patisserie and mince pies. The usual formula for the main ingredients is one, two or three parts sugar, depending on the sweetness desired, to two parts fat to three parts flour. Eggs or other liquids are not essential but are added in some variations.

To make the dough, sift 225g/8oz plain flour onto worktop; make a well in the centre for an egg yolk and then sprinkle 75g/3oz sugar and a pinch of salt over the flour. Cut 125g/5oz chilled butter into dice and sprinkle them around the egg yolk.

Curd cheese and oil dough

This dough is easy and straightforward to make and has a neutral flavour. It handles well and can be used in many different recipes. The dough should be slightly sweetened for sweet fillings. It is delicious when used to make a plait stuffed with nuts, or without sugar and using olive oil, as a pizza base. Pastry made with this dough should, if possible, be eaten on the day it is baked and is at its best when eaten hot. The cheese used can be any kind of unmatured cheese, from quark and low-fat curd cheese to mascarpone and similar full-fat soft cheeses.

To make apple turnovers with sweet curd cheese and oil dough, sift 300g/10oz self-raising flour onto a worktop. Make a well in the flour and pour in 6 tablespoons of flavourless oil, 5 tablespoons milk, 50g/2oz sugar and 50g/2oz vanilla sugar. Mix well and then add 150g/5½oz well-drained curd cheese, a tablespoon at a time. Knead thoroughly.

Choux paste

Eclairs and profiteroles are the best known examples of choux paste patisserie. The mixture is usually referred to as a paste because, unusually for a dough, it is cooked before baking. Fat, water and flour are combined to make a smooth, virtually flavourless paste. Sugar is not usually added, so choux pastry can be combined with sweet or savoury fillings. Choux paste is soft and sticky, so it is normally piped or spooned onto a baking sheet. Cream puff pastries or éclairs should be cut open or pierced from the underside when they come out of the oven to release the trapped air.

To make choux paste, pour 250ml/8 fl oz water and a pinch of salt into a large saucepan. Add 50g/2oz butter and bring rapidly to the boil. Remove from the heat and add 200g/7oz flour. Stir and then beat with a wooden spoon over a low heat until the dough comes away cleanly from the sides of the saucepan.

Beat 200g/7oz softened butter with 100g/4oz sugar, 1 tablespoon vanilla sugar and a pinch of salt and stir until the sugar has been fully absorbed. Slowly add the egg yolks, 300g/10oz sifted flour, a tablespoon at a time, and 4 tablespoons rum or arak.

Fold in the whisked egg whites and then transfer the mixture to the oven and bake on the middle shelf for 50 to 60 minutes. When it is ready, a skewer inserted into the centre should come out clean. Switch off the oven and leave the cake to stand for 10 minutes.

With cold hands, or in a food processor, knead to a smooth, workable dough. Roll into a ball, cover with clingfilm and refrigerate for at least 30 minutes, preferably 1 hour.

Dust a little flour over the worktop and roll out the dough. Keep the dusting flour to a minimum as too much can affect the quality of the pastry. Line a flan tin with the sheet of dough, trimming off any excess. Bake for 20 minutes at 200°C/400°F/Gas Mark 6, until golden brown.

Roll out the smooth dough to a thickness of about $\frac{1}{2}$cm/$\frac{1}{4}$in. Use a glass to cut out circles 10cm/4in in diameter. Spoon on a little prepared apple filling, brush the edges with water and fold, pressing down the edges with a fork.

Heat the oven to 200°C/400°F/Gas Mark 6 and bake the turnovers on the middle shelf for about 20 minutes, or until golden brown. Brush with a thin icing sugar glaze.

Transfer the dough to a mixing bowl and use the kneading attachment on the food mixer to beat in one egg. Leave to cool. Add three more eggs, one at a time, but with the last egg add a generous pinch of baking powder. The dough should be smooth and shiny.

Fill a piping bag with the dough and pipe whirls onto a baking sheet. Heat the oven to 220°/450°F/Gas Mark 7 and bake for 20 minutes. Do not open the oven door during this period. Before baking, sprinkle 125ml/4 fl oz water over the baking sheet. Allow plenty of room between each whirl as choux paste swells during baking.

Sponge cake

The smooth foaming mixture made from eggs, sugar and flour is more of a batter than a dough. Whether the eggs are used whole or separated, the mixture has to be beaten for a long time and the tiny air bubbles thus formed substantially increase the volume of the mixture. Ground hazelnuts, walnuts or almonds can be added to the flour at this stage. Every utensil must be kept absolutely free from fat. Madeira, Victoria sponge and sand cake are made in exactly the same way, but cooled, melted butter is added to the aerated mixture. It is vital that the oven is pre-heated to the required temperature as sponge mixtures can collapse easily.

Grease only the bottom of a springform tin and sprinkle a thin layer of fine, dry breadcrumbs or cake crumbs over it. Heat the oven to 180°C/350°F/Gas Mark 4. Carefully separate 6 eggs. Mix 125g/5oz sugar, 1 tablespoon vanilla sugar and 2 tablespoons warm water or orange juice with the egg yolks and whisk until foaming.

Swiss roll

Making a basic Swiss roll is quick and much easier than you imagine. Bake a sponge cake in an oblong tin with a raised edge, known as a Swiss roll tin. Turn it out onto a clean, damp tea towel laid flat on the work surface. Remove the baking paper if it is still stuck to the sponge (if you use a magic baking sheet it will not adhere). While the sponge is still warm, brush it with hot apricot jam, roll it up and dust with icing sugar. Other fillings include whipped cream mixed with fruit purée, buttercream or cream cheese slightly diluted with cream or yogurt. Other ideas for delicious fillings are given in the recipe section in this book.

Combine 8 egg yolks, 100g/4oz sugar, a pinch of salt, 1 tablespoon vanilla sugar, 4 egg whites, plus 50g/2oz each cornflour, plain white flour and cocoa powder. Cover a Swiss roll tin. Pour the mixture into the tin and smooth the top.

Meringue

Meringue consists simply of whipped egg whites and a high proportion of sugar. Many different flavourings, such as instant coffee powder, flaked chocolate, ground nuts or almonds, can be added. A variety of small cakes and even large ones can be made from the basic meringue mixture. To make meringue nests to hold fruit and/or cream mixtures, pipe 6cm/2½in meringue whirls onto non-stick baking paper, using a large star nozzle. Or use a small star nozzle and pipe a larger meringue base in a spiral pattern. It is helpful to draw circles of the correct size on the baking paper beforehand. Plain meringues without flavourings can be made well in advance and stored in an airtight tin.

To make the meringue mixture, take a spotlessly clean bowl and add 250ml/8 fl oz egg whites (about 8 eggs) which are free of any trace of egg yolk. Beat them into soft peaks with a pinch of cream of tartar. Add 200g/7oz caster sugar, whisking with a hand beater or an electric beater set at the slowest speed. As soon as soft peaks form, turn the whisk to the highest speed

Fritter batter

A basic fritter batter should be slightly thicker than a pancake batter. Such items as apple rings or bread dough filled with jam can be dipped in batter and deep-fried in hot fat or oil. The best fat for deep-frying is a flavourless cooking oil, such as corn oil. Clarified butter and coconut oil are also good, since they contain no water and will not burn or smoke at high temperatures. For deep-frying, the temperature of the fat should be somewhere between 175C°/350°F and 190°C/375°F which means that a 2.5cm/1in cube of bread dropped into the oil will brown in about 60 seconds Use a frying thermometer if a temperature-controlled deep-fryer is not available.

To make a cream batter, beat 200ml/6 fl oz whipping cream with a pinch of salt until it forms stiff peaks and mix in 2 eggs. Sift 200g/7oz flour into the mixture and beat until smooth. Cover with clingfilm and leave to stand for 1 hour.

Whisk the egg whites and a pinch of salt with a clean whisk until soft peaks form. Slowly sprinkle in 75g/3oz sugar and continue to whisk until the peaks are stiff but not dry. Fold the whisked egg white into the egg yolk mixture. Sift 125g/5oz flour and 75g/3oz cornflour over the mixture and stir gently.

Pour the mixture into the prepared tin, smooth the top with a spatula or palette knife and bake in the oven for 30 minutes. Do not open the oven door during the first 15 minutes.

Heat the oven to 220°C/450°F/ Gas Mark 7 and bake on the top shelf for 8 to 10 minutes.

For a chocolate sponge, prepare a simple buttercream or cream cheese filling. Drizzle Cointreau over the sponge, cover with an even layer of filling and roll up. Spread a thin layer of cream over the surface and decorate by piping whirls of cream. Finish with segments of mandarin orange.

and continue to whisk until the whites are stiff and dry.

Combine 200g/7oz icing sugar with 30g/1oz cornflour. Sift this over the egg whites and fold in with a metal spoon. Line two baking tins with non-stick baking paper. Heat the oven to 100°C/212°F/Gas Mark 1/4. Fill a piping bag with the whisked egg white mixture and create the shapes of your choice.

Bake the meringues in a very cool oven for 2 to 6 hours, depending on the size of the meringues. Wedge the oven door slightly ajar with a wooden spoon handle. The bases of the meringues can be dipped in melted chocolate and left to dry. Meringue nests can be filled with a mixture of cream, fresh fruit and/or ice cream.

Heat 1l/1³/4 pints oil or 1kg/2¹/4 lbs fat such as clarified butter or coconut fat in a deep-fryer or a heavy saucepan. A rough way to gauge the temperature of the fat, is to dip the handle of a wooden spoon into the fat. If tiny bubbles quickly form around the wood, then the fat should be hot enough.

Give the batter a good stir and then dip the fruit portions or prepared bread rolls in the mixture. Fry for a few minutes until golden brown. Lift the fritters out of the hot fat with a slotted spoon; drain and serve.

Getting Started

Yeast doughs

A yeast dough is not particularly difficult to make. It is important, however, to create a warm and moist environment and to allow sufficient time for the live yeast to start working. The process by which yeast rises is usually divided into three phases – the sponge, the rising and the proving. There is also another method, the 'cold' method, as the experts call it, in which all the dry ingredients are first mixed together, then the liquid added. The dough is then left to rise, covered, for 12 hours in a cool place. In the example shown here, a wholemeal flour plait is being made using the 'cold' method.

Dissolve some crumbled fresh yeast into 125ml/4 fl oz of warm milk. Cream 100g/4oz butter with 3 egg yolks, 5 tbsps maple syrup and a pinch of salt. Add a teaspoon of grated lemon rind and then add 500g/1lb 2oz wholemeal flour and the yeast mixture.

Starter dough

To make a successful starter dough, it is important that all ingredients should be at room temperature. It is therefore advisable to weigh out the required quantities and leave them for at least 30 minutes. The yeast, whether fresh or dried, should have been bought recently, so that the micro-organisms can be activated at an even rate. When using the new kind of dried yeast there is no need to leave the yeast to rise three times, as it is mixed with the dry ingredients first before liquid is added. Most professional pastry chefs use fresh yeast, however, as they prefer the slightly sour taste. Fresh yeast is available at healthfood shops.

In this case, a yeast dough, using a starter dough, is being used for a large flan. Sift 500g/1lb 2oz flour into a bowl and add 42g/1½oz crumbled yeast. Sprinkle 1 teaspoon of sugar on top, together with 125ml/4 fl oz lukewarm milk. Stir a little flour in with the yeast. Cover and leave to rise in a warm place for 15 to 30 minutes.

Yeast puff dough

Rolls have all sorts of different names, there are bridge rolls and kaiser rolls, sandwich and cloverleaf rolls, caraway and salt fingers. They usually consist of a yeast dough, made with milk, water or salt; sometimes eggs are added. If you want a golden-brown crust, brush the rolls prior to baking with lukewarm water, milk, beaten egg or egg yolk. Rolls made with refined flour, wholegrain flour and combined flours can be sprinkled with poppy seeds or sesame seeds, ground coriander, caraway, sunflower and pumpkin seeds, linseed, or coarse salt, or a mixture of these. Rye rolls are good topped with chopped walnuts or freshly grated Cheddar cheese.

To make a yeast puff dough, dissolve 30g/1oz yeast in just under 250ml/8 fl oz milk and mix in 500g/1lb 2oz flour, 50g/2oz softened butter, a pinch of salt, 75g/3oz sugar and 2 eggs. Cover and refrigerate for 3 hours.

Turning the dough

The secret of successful croissants and Danish pastry with the distinctive taste of fresh yeast and butter lies in the turning. The dough is rolled, folded and turned in just the same way as for puff dough. Give the sheet of dough three turns, chilling in the refrigerator for 20 minutes after each turn and then rolling out again. For a particularly flaky pastry, four turns are recommended.

Knead the dough well again on a floured surface and roll out a rectangle 25x30cm/10x12in. Place the prepared block of butter and flour (it should be of the same consistency as the yeast dough) in the middle. Brush the edges of the dough with water and fold in the sides over the butter.

Knead the soft dough well, cover and leave in a cool place overnight, but for no longer than 12 hours. By then, the dough should have doubled in bulk. Knead 100g/4oz rum-soaked raisins and 50g/2oz candied lemon peel into the dough and leave the dough to prove for one hour.

On a floured worktop, form the dough into three or four long sausage-shapes and weave these into a plait. Place on a greased baking sheet and brush with a mixture of egg yolk and milk. Sprinkle with flaked almonds and place on the middle shelf of a cold oven. Switch the oven to 200°C/400°F/ Gas Mark 6 and bake for 40 to 50 minutes.

Scatter 50g/2oz softened butter cut into dice, 75g/3oz sugar, a pinch of salt and 1 tablespoon vanilla sugar on the outer ring of flour. Knead these ingredients into the starter dough, adding 125ml/4 fl oz lukewarm milk. Continue until the dough is smooth and workable. Cover again and leave for 30 to 60 minutes, or until the dough has almost doubled in bulk.

Knead the dough again briefly and roll it out on a floured worktop. Line a greased Swiss roll tin with the dough and cover with sliced apples, raisins, chopped hazelnuts and a mixture of sugar and cinnamon. Leave for a further 15 minutes and then bake at 200°C/400°F/Gas Mark 6 for 40 minutes.

Meanwhile, knead together 250g/8oz butter and 50g/2oz flour and then roll into a block about 10x12cm/4x5in. Knead the yeast dough again and roll it out into a 25x30cm/10x12in rectangle.

Wrap the sheet of floured butter in the yeast dough – as described below – and refrigerate for 20 minutes. This part of the process is called 'turning'.

Roll out the dough and butter to its original size, taking care to roll from left to right and from top to bottom. Fold the dough into three. Leave the dough to chill in the refrigerator for 20 minutes, then repeat the process twice.

Leave the dough to stand at room temperature for a few minutes and then roll out and cut into whatever shape is required. To make croissants, slice the dough into 15cm/6in-wide strips and then halve them diagonally to make acute-angled triangles. These can then be rolled into a croissant shape. Brush with beaten egg yolk and bake at 220°C/450°F/Gas Mark 7 for 15 minutes.

Getting Started

Frozen puff dough

As top-quality frozen puff dough can now be bought in the shops, only in exceptional circumstances is it worth taking the time and effort to make it yourself. The same applies to phyllo dough, the paper-thin leaves that are used for making phyllo pastries and strudels. Both puff dough and phyllo dough come in sheets. To defrost them, spread them out and leave them to thaw for 10-15 minutes at room temperature.

Lay the puff dough on a lightly-floured work surface. Always roll it up and down and left to right, i.e. in one direction at a time, rather than backwards and forwards, applying gentle pressure and using a ribbed rolling-pin if possible. Rolling in this way prevents the dough from stretching out of shape.

Macaroon paste

This consists of beaten egg white mixed with sugar, almonds or other nuts, and the optional addition of diced, dried or candied fruit, and/or chocolate. There are, of course, many variations on the macaroon theme. Raw marzipan may also be worked into the mixture. Macaroons are usually baked on circles of rice paper, so that they can be removed from a baking sheet easily and in one piece without breaking. It is therefore best to use non-stick baking paper or a 'magic' non-stick baking sheet..

First beat the egg whites until they form stiff peaks, then gradually sprinkle with the sugar. Continue beating until the egg white is firm and shiny.

Making marzipan

Marzipan is an important ingredient in patisserie. It can be bought as ready-made raw marzipan in supermarkets and health food stores, especially around Christmastime. However, marzipan for special purposes and wholefood marzipan are invariably home-made. Marzipan can be flavoured and coloured, and used in a variety of ways. It can be moulded into fancy shapes for decoration. Marzipan can be made from nuts other than almonds, such as hazelnuts and brazil nuts and for healthier eating it can be sweetened with honey or with raw cane sugar.

To make classic marzipan, grind 350g/10oz blanched almonds in a spice grinder, clean coffee grinder or food processor. You may need to mill them twice to get the right texture.

Marzipan confectionery

Marzipan can be flavoured and can also be coloured for making marzipan sweets. You can either use shop-bought edible food colourings or make your own natural colours which may also impart a delicate flavour to the marzipan. Marzipan can also be coloured by adding cocoa powder or strong coffee. Pink or red can be obtained by adding beetroot juice. Use saffron or turmeric for a yellow colour and concentrated spinach juice, which will not impair the taste, for green.

Real marzipan, as opposed to almond paste, is cooked. To make real marzipan, heat three parts honey in a bain-marie or double boiler with four parts very finely ground almonds and 2-3 drops rosewater.

When cutting out shapes from puff dough or phyllo dough, use a very sharp, thin knife or biscuit cutters. Do not press the edges of the dough firmly together, as this will prevent it from rising evenly. Phyllo dough sheets need to be spread with melted butter before filling and baking. Never brush the edges of cut shapes with egg white or glaze, as this, too, will prevent puff or phyllo dough from rising during baking

Lay any remaining offcuts of dough on top of each other, press them together lightly and roll them out once again. Cut out biscuit shapes and brush with melted butter if the dough is a phyllo dough. Rinse a baking sheet with cold water, or rinse moulds and arrange the biscuits on them. Leave to stand for about 10 minutes in a cool place before baking.

Take the blanched, ground or chopped almonds and/or the remaining ingredients listed in the recipe which should have been prepared for immediate use. Fold them lightly into the egg white, using a metal spoon.

Using two moist teaspoons, place little mounds of paste on the baking sheet or on rice paper circles cut to the correct size. Leave enough space between the mounds, as they will spread while baking. Bake them at 190°/375°F/Gas Mark 5 for about 12 minutes on the centre shelf of the oven.

Combine the almonds with an equal quantity of sifted icing sugar, 2-3 drops of almond essence and the same amount of rosewater. Knead to an elastic paste but do not overknead, otherwise the marzipan will become sticky. Dip your hands into a bowl of icing sugar several times, while kneading.

Dust a work surface with icing sugar and place the marzipan on it. Dust a rolling-pin with icing sugar and use it to roll out the marzipan to the desired size and thickness. Process further as directed in the recipe.

To colour marzipan, divide the block of marzipan into as many pieces as required. Use your thumb to make a well in the centre of each, pour in the colour and knead it into the mass. Roll out the coloured marzipan pieces. Layers of different colours can be superimposed and cut or moulded into shapes.

Marzipan sweets can be coated with chocolate, caramel or fondant, as desired.

Getting Started

Yeast starter

Breads made from yeast doughs are often light breads containing refined or mixed grain flours. Yeast dough must be allowed to rise twice and prove once to prevent the crumb from becoming too soft and aerated. You should plan the timing of your bread baking carefully, as yeast breads taste best when freshly made (however, yeast bread can be frozen fresh from the oven and any leftover slices toasted). If you are working with fresh yeast or active dry yeast, which are both good sources of the vitamin B complex, you first have to make a starter or leaven. This procedure is not necessary if you are using the type of dried yeast that can be mixed directly with the dry ingredients. All the ingredients for the dough must be at room temperature but no hotter than blood heat. Try and ensure that the kitchen is as dry as possible. Even the weather outside makes a difference; bread will rise better on a sunny day than on a wet one.

One way a making the yeast starter or leaven, which is widely used on the Continent, is to weigh all the flour used in the recipe and sift it into a large bowl. Make a well in the centre. Crumble fresh yeast into the well and sprinkle with a teaspoon of sugar. Add 100 ml/4 fl oz of the liquid used in the recipe and mix in a little of the flour.

Kneading the yeast dough

In general, the longer and more thoroughly a yeast dough is kneaded, the lighter the bread, although it can be overkneaded. You should never knead for longer than 20 minutes. The gluten present in wheat is essential for this process as it makes the dough light and elastic. The yeast gives off carbon dioxide, causing a considerable increase in the volume of the dough. Flours such as rye and barley have a much lower gluten content, and cornmeal has no gluten at all. Rye is often mixed with wheat to make rye bread that is lighter and rises more quickly. The other flours must be mixed with wheat to make a yeast-risen bread or, as in the case or cornbread, they are risen with baking powder and sour milk or buttermilk. Kneading a heavy dough by hand is time-consuming and hard work. If you find it too strenuous, use a food processor, or a mixer with a dough hook, though hand-kneading is best.

If other ingredients are to be added, these must also be at room temperature. Add them at the edge of the bowl. Add the remaining lukewarm liquid and mix it in, either with the dough hook of an electric hand mixer, or with a wooden spoon.

Using baking powder as a raising agent

Bread made with baking powder is made rather like sourdough bread. It is a fairly simple process, but takes time. Baking powder is particularly useful as a raising agent for breads made from grains such as rye, oats and barley, which are low or lacking in gluten. The dough rises mainly because of the effect of warmth during long standing periods rather than due to intensive kneading. In summer, leave the dough to rise in a warm, shady place; in winter use the oven, with the pilot light or interior light switched on, maintaining a constant temperature of 24°C/75°F to 28°C/82°F. Like sourdough bread, bread made with baking powder should not be sliced until one day after baking. If it is stored in a cool, dry place, it will stay fresh for up to 14 days.

Combine 250g/8oz freshly ground wholemeal rye flour in a bowl with 1 tsp baking powder, 1 tsp tartaric acid, 500ml/18 fl oz lukewarm water and 2 tbsps liquid honey. Cover and leave to rise in a warm place for 24 hours at 24°C /75°F (min.). The surface should then be light and foaming.

Making your own sourdough

Sourdough bread is usually made from rye or a mixture of wholegrain flours. It has a slightly sour taste and stays fresh for a long time. Healthfood shops stock sourdough starter. To make your own natural sourdough, use sourdough extract or liquid sourdough as a starter. With time and patience, however, you can even make your own sourdough from wheat or rye flour. Although making a sourdough is time-consuming, it can be used over and over. After making the first batch of bread, keep back some of the dough and refrigerate it (it will keep for up to six months). Use it as the basis for the next batch of sourdough bread. In this way, you can go on making sourdough breads indefinitely from one original sourdough fermentation.

On the first day, mix 200g/7oz finely ground wheat or rye flour with 250ml/9 fl oz lukewarm water and 2 to 3 tbsps buttermilk in a large, tall earthenware pot or crock. Cover with a damp cloth and leave to stand at a temperature of at least 24°C/75°F.

Alternatively, crumble the fresh yeast or pour the active dry yeast into a small bowl, add a teaspoon of sugar and about 100ml/4 fl oz of lukewarm liquid. Cover and stand for 15 minutes. If the mixture is frothy, the yeast is working and this starter can be mixed with the dry ingredients This is a very good way to ensure that your yeast is active; if the liquid does not froth, the yeast is not working and you will have to throw it away and start again.

Dust the dough with flour, cover with a damp cloth or clingfilm and leave to rise for 15 to 30 minutes in a warm, draught-free place at room temperature (approx. 22°C/70°F). Make sure there is plenty of room in the bowl for the dough to rise. The surface of the flour will now have fine cracks across it.

Now knead the dough by hand just until it leaves the bowl clean. Transfer the dough to a floured work surface and knead it thoroughly with the heel of your hand for about 10 minutes, folding and turning it slightly with each movement. By the end it should be elastic and springy.

Shape the dough into a ball and cover it with a damp cloth or clingfilm. Leave in a warm place until it has doubled in bulk – this should take between 45 minutes and one hour. Knead again and then mould into the shape required by the recipe or put into a loaf tin. The second rising that most breads need, after the dough has been shaped is called proving. The dough should be proved for at least 30 minutes. Some yeast dough recipes call for second and even third provings.

Into this starter, stir the same quantity of wholegrain flour and 250ml/9 fl oz lukewarm water. Cover and leave to rise for 12 more hours at 24°C/75°F (min.). Fermentation should be even more obvious by now: the foam will have subsided and the dough will have a yeasty smell.

Add about 700g/1lb 10oz mixed wholegrain flour and/or coarsely ground grains (depending on the recipe), salt and spices to the starter dough and knead to make an elastic, slightly sticky dough. Put the dough into the greased loaf tin and leave to rise for a further 2 hours or until it has increased in bulk by one third.

On the second day, stir in 100g/4oz wholemeal wheat or rye flour and 250ml/9 fl oz warm water. On the third day, add 100g/4oz wholemeal wheat or rye flour and 125ml/4 fl oz warm water. Keep the container at a constant, warm temperature and keep covered with a cloth.

On the fourth day, add a further 100g/4oz wholemeal wheat or rye flour and 125ml/4 fl oz warm water. Cover and leave to stand. During fermentation the sourdough should foam and rise each time.
If the sourdough is reddish in colour at this time or has not risen, it is no good and must be discarded.

Getting Started

Starter from bread dough

You can make a starter again and again in a much less time-consuming process than the one just described if you put aside a little raw bread dough from one batch to use as a basis for making the next batch of dough. This works with both yeast-based and baking powder doughs. You can freeze the dough for up to 14 days. To defrost it, leave it for an hour in lukewarm water, press it down with a wooden spoon, leave for another hour and then beat with a whisk. Then use the method illustrated and described to make the starter dough in about 18 hours:

Place 200g/7oz raw dough in a large bowl and cover with 500ml/18 fl oz lukewarm water. Cover and leave to rise in a warm place (min. 24°C) for 30 minutes. Using a wooden spoon, cut the dough into pieces and leave for a further 30 minutes.

Savoury shortcrust pastry

Savoury shortcrust pastry is usually used for the sort of light dough crust required for a pie, tart or quiche, and for many other savoury pastries with cheese, vegetable and meat fillings. Unlike a yeast dough, the ingredients for shortcrust pastry must be cold and should be incorporated quickly. Once the dough has been kneaded, leave it in the refrigerator for 30 minutes to an hour. Shortcrust dough should be firm enough to be rolled out easily and made into the shapes required by the recipe. Shortcrust dough basically consists of flour, a pinch of salt and fat; adding 1 small egg or an egg yolk will stop the dough from becoming too crumbly.

Sift 250g/8oz flour on to a work surface, make a well in the centre and break the egg yolk into it. Cut 125g/5oz chilled butter into cubes and add to the flour with 2 tbsps ice-cold water and 1/2 tsp salt. Cut the ingredients together, using a dough scraper or a pastry cutter.

Bread dough with vegetables

Vegetables can enhance the taste, colour and texture of bread. Try using grated courgettes, beetroot or carrots, diced onions fried gently in butter, cooked and puréed pumpkin, tomato purée or steamed, mashed potatoes. The amount of water used in the basic bread recipe should be reduced as vegetables contain fluid, but otherwise the process of making the dough is the same. Cooked vegetables should be cooled slightly so that they are lukewarm when mixed in with the starter, seasoning and flour.

Knead the yeast mixture with wholewheat flour, salt, 250g/8oz grated courgettes, dried thyme and as much lukewarm buttermilk as required to form an elastic dough. Cover and leave to rise at room temperature for 1 hour.

Flatbreads

This special bread is made all over the world. Flatbreads come in squares, rounds and ovals, can be made of wheat or rye flour or a combination of the two, or even of other flours. They may be leavened or unleavened. If unleavened they may be baked immediately or left for the natural enzymes in flour to soften them. sprinkled with poppy seeds, sesame or caraway seeds or coarse salt, or simply dusted with flour. Some are cooked in a heavy pan or griddle on the hob, others are baked in the oven and a few on hot stones over an open fire. If they are baked for a long time they are wonderfully crisp; those baked for a shorter time are softer and thinner. When spread with garlic paste, herb butter or pâté they are delicious rolled or folded up.

Make a basic yeast bread dough with wholewheat flour. When it has proved, divide it into equal-sized pieces and, with floured hands, shape into balls. On a floured work surface roll these out into oval shapes 1cm/1/2in thick

Stir the dough and add 250g/8oz wholewheat flour. Leave in a warm place (at least 24°C/75°F) for 12 hours.

Stir in a further 250g/8oz wholewheat flour and 250ml/9 fl oz lukewarm water; cover and leave to rise for a further 6 hours. The sourdough is now ready for use.

Mix rapidly together to form an elastic dough. Shape into a ball and refrigerate for 30 minutes to an hour, either covered or wrapped in aluminium foil or clingfilm. In the meantime, prepare any filling required by the recipe.

Roll the pastry out on a lightly floured work surface and process according to the recipe. For example, you could make pasties by cutting the dough into 12x12cm/5x5in squares, spooning on the prepared filling on each square and folding the corners together to make a triangle. Brush with egg yolk and press the edges firmly.

Knead the dough again thoroughly and shape into an oval loaf. Place on an oiled baking sheet, cover and leave to rise for 30 minutes. Using a razor blade, make three diagonal incisions on the surface, brush with olive oil and bake on the centre shelf of the oven until golden-brown.

Test whether the bread is done by turning it out onto a cloth and tapping the underside. If it sounds hollow, it is done. Leave the courgette bread to cool on a wire rack before slicing.

Brush the flatbreads with melted butter, sprinkle with sesame seeds and place immediately on a heated, greased baking sheet. Bake on the centre shelf of a hot oven for 10 to 20 minutes, or cook under a hot grill, turning half-way through cooking, until lightly browned.

Serve warm with a topping of your choice. These breads are especially popular in the Middle East, where toppings include cooked, diced lamb, garlic, fresh coriander onion, red peppers and chillies, feta cheese puréed with olive oil and mixed with chopped mint and parsley.

Fruit Tartlets and Cakes

For best results use fresh home-grown fruit – lots of ideas for a variety of fruit fillings and toppings

Strawberry Almond Tarlets

So easy to prepare – the empty cases will stay fresh for days

Quantities for 12 12cm/5in tartlet tins

250g/8oz flour
Generous pinch of baking powder
100g/4oz ground almonds
150g/5¹/₂oz butter, diced
100g/4oz sugar
Pinch of salt
1 egg yolk
750g/1lb 11oz strawberries
5 tbsps strawberry jam
1 tbsp raspberry liqueur or peach schnapps
200ml/6 fl oz whipping cream
100g/4oz plain chocolate
2 tbsps whipping cream
1 tbsp chopped pistachio nuts

Preparation time: 1¹/₂ hours
Baking time: 15-20 minutes
Nutritional value:
Analysis per tartlet, approx:
- 1890kJ/450kcal
- 7g protein
- 27g fat • 44g carbohydrate

Mix together the flour, baking powder, almonds, butter, sugar, salt and egg yolk. Knead to a workable dough. Wrap the dough in clingfilm and refrigerate for 1 hour. • Heat the oven to 180°C/350°F/Gas Mark 4. • Rinse, dry and hull the strawberries. Halve any large fruit. Strain the jam and mix it with the liqueur. Heat through gently. Whisk the cream until stiff. • Roll out the dough into a thin sheet and use it to line the greased tartlet tins. Bake the pastry blind for 15 to 20 minutes until golden brown. • Melt the chocolate in a bain-marie and mix with the cream. When the pastry cases have cooled, fill them with the chocolate cream. Arrange the strawberries on top and glaze with the jam and liqueur mixture. Top with a whirl of whipped cream and a pinch of chopped pistachios.

Strawberry Meringues

These taste out of this world if made with wild strawberries

Quantities for 8 meringues

3 egg whites
200g/7oz sugar
¹/₂ tsp lemon juice
500g/1lb 2oz small strawberries
20g/¹/₂oz plain chocolate
250ml/8 fl oz whipping cream
1 tbsp vanilla sugar

Preparation time: 30 minutes
Baking time: 2 hours
Nutritional value:
Analysis per meringue, approx:
- 1210kJ/290kcal
- 6g protein
- 12g fat
- 36g carbohydrate

In a bowl which is free of any trace of grease, whisk the egg whites until stiff. Sprinkle them with 150g/5¹/₂oz sugar. Add the lemon juice and beat until the sugar has dissolved. Whisk the meringue mixture again until it forms stiff peaks. Quickly fold in the rest of the sugar. • Line a baking sheet with non-stick baking paper. Use a pencil to mark out eight circles about 8cm/3ins in diameter. Spoon the meringue mixture into a piping bag fitted with a star nozzle. Pipe a spiral base starting from the centre of each circle and then finish with a ring of whirls around the rim. Repeat for the other circles. • Place the meringues in a cold oven on the middle shelf. Dry rather than bake them for 2 hours at 80°C/180°F to 100°C/212°F or Gas Mark ¹/₄. • Remove the non-stick baking paper. • Rinse, dry, hull and halve the strawberries. Grate the chocolate. Whip the cream with the vanilla sugar until stiff and add the grated chocolate. Attach a star nozzle to a piping bag. Fill the bag with the chocolate cream and pipe a cream base on to the meringues. Arrange the halved strawberries in a circle on the cream.

Strawberry Cheesecake

An elegant cake, but allow plenty of time for the preparation

Quantities for 1 28cm/11in springform tin
FOR THE SHORTCRUST PASTRY:
200g/7oz flour
Large pinch baking powder
100g/4oz sugar
1 tbsp vanilla sugar
1 egg yolk
100g/4oz butter, diced
FOR THE FILLING:
500g/1lb 2oz quark, drained
3 eggs • 1 egg white
100g/4oz butter
150g/5¹/₂oz sugar • ¹/₂ lemon
150g/5¹/₂oz crème fraîche
50g/2oz cornflour
500g/1lb 2oz strawberries
1 packet red jelly glaze
125ml/4 fl oz cream
1 tbsp vanilla sugar

Preparation time: 1 hour
Baking time: 1¹/₄ hours
Nutritional value:
Analysis per slice, approx, if divided into 16 slices:
• 1590kJ/380kcal • 9g protein
• 22g fat • 32g carbohydrate

Knead the shortcrust dough ingredients, wrap in clingfilm and leave to chill in the refrigerator. • Separate the eggs. Cream the butter and sugar and add the egg yolks. Grate the lemon rind into the creamed butter and then squeeze in the juice. Stir in the crème fraîche and quark. Whisk the egg whites until they form stiff peaks and then fold them into the quark mixture. Mix in the cornflour. • Heat the oven to 180°C/350°F/Gas Mark 4. • Butter the springform tin. Roll out the dough and use it to line the tin. Bake blind for 15 minutes. • Pour in the quark mixture and bake on the lower shelf for 1 hour. • Rinse, hull and halve the strawberries. • Prepare the jelly according to the manufacturer's instructions. • Arrange the strawberries on top of the cheesecake and pour the glaze over them. Allow to set. • Whip the cream with the vanilla sugar until stiff, and pipe a whirl of it in the centre of the cake.

Redcurrant Sponge Slices

A shortbread base topped with a light sponge

Quantities for 1 baking sheet
1kg/2¼lbs redcurrants
200g/7oz softened butter
250g/8oz sugar
Zest of ½ lemon
225g/8oz flour
150g/5½oz cornflour
2 tsps baking powder
5 eggs
2 tbsps vanilla sugar
2 tbsps icing sugar

Preparation time: 45 minutes
Baking time: 45 minutes
Nutritional value:
Analysis per slice, approx, if divided into 20 slices:
• 1090kJ/260kcal
• 5g protein
• 11g fat
• 34g carbohydrate

Rinse the redcurrants, drain and remove the tiny stalks. • Cream the butter with 150g/5½oz sugar and the grated lemon rind.

Sift 200g/7oz flour with 100g/4oz cornflour and the baking powder. Add three eggs and the sifted dry ingredients to the creamed butter. • Heat the oven to 200°C/400°F/Gas Mark 6. • Generously butter the baking sheet, spoon the mixture over it and smooth the surface. Arrange the redcurrants evenly on top and bake on the middle shelf of the oven for 30 minutes. • Separate the eggs and whisk the whites into stiff peaks. Beat the yolks with the remaining sugar and vanilla sugar until creamy. Mix the remaining cornflour with the rest of the flour and stir the flour mixture and whisked eggs into the beaten egg yolks. • Cover the biscuit base with the sponge mixture and bake for a further 15 minutes. • Sift icing sugar over the surface and cut into 20 slices.

Redcurrant Chocolate Cake

The sponge base for this 'tipsy cake' can be soaked either in a liqueur or a fruit juice

Quantities for 1 26cm/10in springform tin
100g/4oz softened butter
125g/5oz sugar
4 eggs
125g/5oz plain chocolate
150g/5½oz ground hazelnuts
100g/4oz flour
3 tbsps cocoa powder
2 tsps baking powder
500g/1lb 2oz redcurrants
100ml/3 fl oz cassis (blackcurrant liqueur)
2 tbsps sugar
200ml/6 fl oz cream
1 tbsp vanilla sugar
2 tbsps icing sugar

Preparation time: 1 hour
Baking time: 40 minutes
Nutritional value:
Analysis per slice, approx, if cake is divided into 12 slices:
• 1890kJ/450kcal
• 8g protein
• 27g fat • 39g carbohydrate

Cream the butter with the sugar. Separate the eggs and whisk the egg whites until they stand in stiff peaks. Melt the chocolate in a bain-marie and then stir into the creamed butter with the egg yolks. Add the nuts and then stir in the flour, cocoa and baking powder. • Heat the oven to 180°C/350°F/Gas Mark 4. Butter the tin and sprinkle with breadcrumbs. • Spoon the mixture into the tin, smooth the surface and bake for 40 minutes. • Wash the redcurrants, dry well and remove the tiny stalks. • When the cake has cooled down, cut off a thin slice of cake with a sharp knife and crumble. Drip the liqueur over the base and then spread an even layer of berries and a dusting of sugar on top. Whip the cream with the vanilla sugar until stiff and spread over the fruit. Top with the crumbled cake and a coating of icing sugar.

Delicious Gooseberry Cakes and Pastries

Serve with whipped cream, to which a little cinnamon sugar has been added

Gooseberry Slices
In the foreground

Quantities for 1 baking sheet

FOR THE DOUGH:

250g/8oz flour • 2 tbsps sugar

Pinch of salt

1 lemon, rind grated

20g/¹/₂oz yeast

125ml/4 fl oz lukewarm milk

1 egg

FOR THE FILLING:

2 digestive biscuits

1kg/2¹/₄lbs gooseberries

FOR THE TOPPING:

150g/5¹/₂oz softened butter

100g/4oz sugar • 4 eggs

50g/2oz flour • pinch of salt

125ml/4 fl oz cream

Preparation time: 1¹/₂ hours
Baking time: 45 minutes
Nutritional value:
Analysis per slice, approx, if divided into 20 slices:
• 1000kJ/240kcal • 6g protein
• 13g fat • 26g carbohydrate

Sift the flour into a bowl and make a well in the middle. Spread the sugar, salt and grated lemon rind around the outside of the well. Stir the yeast and a little milk into the well. Leave to rise in a warm place for 30 minutes. • Place the digestive biscuits in a polythene bag and crush with a rolling pin. Rinse the gooseberries and drain well. • To make the topping, cream the butter, sugar and eggs. Add the flour, salt and cream. • Knead the starter dough with flour, the remaining milk and the egg. Leave for 15 minutes. • Butter a large baking sheet. Roll out the dough, lay it on the baking sheet and leave for a further 15 minutes. • Heat the oven to 200°C/400°F/Gas Mark 6. • Sprinkle first the biscuit crumbs and then the gooseberries over the dough. Pour on the topping. • Bake for 45 minutes on the lower shelf.

Apricot and Gooseberry Tart
In the background

Quantities for 1 28cm/11in springform tart tin

150g/5¹/₂oz quark (20% fat)

125g/5oz sugar

1 lemon, rind grated

Pinch of salt

6 tbsps oil

4 tbsps milk

300g/10oz flour

1 tsp baking powder

2 digestive biscuits, crushed

500g/1lb 2oz ripe apricots

250g/8oz gooseberries

Preparation time: 30 minutes
Baking time: 45 minutes
Nutritional value:
Analysis per slice, approx, if divided into 16 slices:
• 670kJ/160kcal
• 4g protein
• 4g fat
• 27g carbohydrate

Leave the quark to drain well and then beat in the sugar, grated lemon rind, salt, oil and milk. Mix the flour with the baking powder, add to the quark mixture, a tbsp at a time and then knead well. • Heat the oven to 200°C/400°F/Gas Mark 6. • Butter the tin and sprinkle with digestive biscuit crumbs. • Roll out the dough on a floured worktop and lay it in the tin, allowing for a rim of 2cm/1in. • Rinse, drain, halve and stone the apricots. • Place the apricot halves cut-side down on the dough base. Rinse and drain the gooseberries and use them to fill the gaps between the apricots, pressing down firmly. • Bake for 45 minutes.

Tartlets as a Snack or a Dessert

These sweetened shortcrust pastry bases can be prepared separately and kept for several weeks in a well-sealed container

Tarte aux Pommes Alsacienne

In the foreground

Quantities for 12 12cm/5in tartlet tins

FOR THE SWEETENED SHORTCRUST DOUGH:

250g/8oz flour	
125g/5oz butter	
100g/4oz icing sugar	
Pinch of salt	
¹/₂ lemon, rind grated	
50g/2oz ground hazelnuts	
1 egg yolk	

FOR THE FILLING:

500g/1lb 2oz small tart apples	
150g/5¹/₂oz crème fraîche	
2 eggs	
50g/2oz sugar	
1 tbsp vanilla sugar	
2 tbsps lemon juice	
2 tbsps icing sugar	

Preparation time: 1¹/₂ hours
Baking time: 25 minutes

Nutritional value:
Analysis per tartlet, approx:
- 1510kJ/360kcal
- 7g protein
- 20g fat
- 37g carbohydrate

Knead the dough ingredients briefly until smooth. Roll into a ball, cover with clingfilm and refrigerate for 1 hour to chill. • Peel, quarter and core the apples. Cut into thin wedges. • Mix the crème fraîche with the eggs, sugar, vanilla sugar and lemon juice. • Heat the oven to 220°C/450°F/Gas Mark 7. Lightly butter the tartlet tins. • Roll out a thin sheet of dough and use it to line the tins. Arrange the apples on the dough cases. Bake for 5 minutes. Reduce the heat to 180°C/350°F/Gas Mark 4. Pour the cream mixture over the apples and bake for a further 20 minutes. • Sift a little icing sugar over the tartlets.

Rhubarb Tartlets

In the background

Quantities for 8 12cm/5in tartlet tins

125g/5oz flour	
150g/5¹/₂oz sugar	
1 tsp vanilla sugar	
2 pinches salt	
1 egg yolk	
50g/2oz cold butter	
250g/8oz rhubarb	
Generous pinch of ground cinnamon	
¹/₂ packet unflavoured gelatine	
5 drops red food colouring	
100g/4oz plain chocolate icing	
250ml/8 fl oz whipping cream	
1 tbsp chopped pistachio nuts	

Preparation time: 1¹/₄ hours
Baking time: 20 minutes
Nutritional value:
Analysis per tartlet, approx:
- 1680kJ/400kcal
- 7g protein
- 24g fat • 40g carbohydrate

Mix the flour, 50g/2oz sugar, vanilla sugar, pinch of salt, egg yolk and butter, and knead to a smooth dough. Refrigerate for 1 hour to chill. • Rinse and trim the rhubarb, stripping off the stringy fibres. Chop the rhubarb into short lengths and simmer in 3 tbsps water with the remaining sugar, a pinch of salt and cinnamon. • Dissolve the gelatine in 125ml/4fl oz hot water for 10 minutes and add it to the hot stewed rhubarb, with the red colouring. Leave the fruit to cool. • Heat the oven to 220°C/450°F/Gas Mark 7. Roll out a sheet of dough 3mm/¹/₈in thick and use it to line the tartlet tins. Prick the dough with a fork. • Bake the cases blind on the lower shelf for 20 minutes. • Melt the chocolate in a bain-marie and brush it over the pastry. Whip the cream until stiff and fold it into the partially-set rhubarb mixture. Spoon the cream into the tartlets and sprinkle with pistachios.

Apple Pie with Ginger

Try this British favourite either hot with vanilla ice-cream or custard or cold with whipped cream

Quantities for 1 24cm/9¹/₂in pie
250g/8oz flour
150g/5¹/₂oz cold butter
2 tbsps sugar
Pinch of salt
750g/1lb 11oz Bramley apples
1 lemon
25g/1oz crystallised ginger
1 tsp ground cinnamon
3 tbsps sugar
1 tbsp cornflour
3 tbsps apricot jam

Preparation time: 1¹/₄ hours
Baking time: 45 minutes
Nutritional value:
Analysis per slice, approx, if divided into 8 slices:
- 1380kJ/330kcal
- 4g protein
- 16g fat
- 45g carbohydrate

Cut the butter into pieces and mix with the flour, sugar, salt and 2 to 3 tbsps of ice-cold water. Knead into a workable shortcrust dough. Cover and leave in a cool place for 1 hour. • Peel, quarter and core the apples and cut into thin slices. Rinse the lemon in warm water, dry and then grate the lemon. Add grated rind and juice to the apples. Chop the ginger and stir into the apples, together with the cinnamon, sugar and cornflour. • Heat the oven to 200°C/400°F/Gas Mark 6. • Divide the dough into two pieces, one twice the size of the other. Roll out the larger piece to fit the pie dish and prick it several times with a fork. Cut off any excess and brush the pastry border with cold water. Spoon the apples onto the pie base. Roll out the smaller portion of pastry and use it to cover the apple filling. Seal the two layers of dough by pinching them together with thumb and forefinger. Brush cold water over the lid and decorate with shapes cut from the dough trimmings. Cut a hole in the lid to allow steam to escape. • Bake the pie for 45 minutes or until golden-brown. • Warm the apricot jam and brush it over the hot surface of the pie before serving.

Cherry Cakes Made with Wholewheat Flour

Leave overnight for the full flavour to emerge – these cakes will stay fresh for two or three days

Chocolate Cherry Cake

Illustrated left

Quantities for 1 28cm/11in springform tin

150g/5¹/₂oz wholewheat flour
50g/2oz wholemeal rye flour
25g/1oz cocoa powder
1 tsp baking powder
¹/₂ tsp each ground cinnamon and ground coriander
200g/7oz ground almonds
200g/7oz softened butter
200g/7oz clear honey
4 eggs
2 tbsps rum
500g/1lb 2oz sour cherries
200g/7oz honey-sweetened chocolate
50g/2oz flaked almonds

Preparation time: 30 minutes
Baking time: 45 minutes
Nutritional value:
Analysis per slice, approx, if divided into 12 slices:
- 2310kJ/550kcal
- 12g protein
- 35g fat
- 44g carbohydrate

Mix the flours with the cocoa powder, baking powder, cinnamon and coriander. Add the ground almonds. • Cream the butter and honey. Add the flour mixture, eggs and rum a little at a time to the creamed butter. • Heat the oven to 180°C/350°F/Gas Mark 4. Butter the tin. • Pour the mixture into the tin and smooth the surface. • Rinse the cherries and remove the stalks. Dry well and remove the stones. Press the cherries lightly into the mixture. • Bake the cake on the middle shelf for 45 minutes. Switch off the oven and leave for 10 minutes. • Melt the chocolate in a basin over hot water. Pour an even layer of melted chocolate over the cake and sprinkle with the flaked almonds.

Cherry Oat Slices

Illustrated right

Quantities for 1 baking sheet

1kg/2¹/₄lbs sweet cherries
300g/10oz softened butter
200g/7oz sugar
1 tbsp vanilla sugar
4 eggs
1 lemon, rind grated
250g/8oz pinhead oatmeal
200g/7oz wholewheat flour
1 tsp baking powder
4 tsps rum
2 tbsps coarse oatflakes
50g/2oz sugar
50g/2oz desiccated coconut

TO SERVE:

250ml/8 fl oz whipped cream flavoured with 2 tbsps vanilla sugar

Preparation time: 15 minutes
Baking time: 35-40 minutes
Nutritional value:
Analysis per slice, approx, if divided into 20 slices:
- 1630kJ/390kcal • 13g protein
- 36g fat • 59g carbohydrate

Heat the oven to 200°C/400°F/Gas Mark 6. • Butter a baking sheet. Wash, dry and stone the cherries. • Cream the butter with the sugar and vanilla sugar. Add the eggs one at a time to the creamed butter, together with the grated lemon rind and rum. Mix the oatflakes with the flour and baking powder. Add to the butter and egg mixture, a spoonful at a time. • Pour the mixture over the baking sheet and smooth the surface. Arrange the cherries on top. Combine the oatflakes, sugar and desiccated coconut and sprinkle over the cherries. • Bake the cake on the middle shelf for 35 to 40 minutes until golden brown. • Cut the cake into 20 slices using a knife dipped in cold water. Leave the slices to cool on a wire rack. • Serve with whipped vanilla cream.

Cherry and Nut Cake

This cake contains no flour or baking powder

Quantities for 1 28cm/11in springform tin

500g/1lb 2oz cherries	
150g/5½oz softened butter	
150g/5½oz sugar	
4 eggs	
100g/4oz plain chocolate	
200g/7oz ground hazelnuts	
4 tbsps sponge cake crumbs or digestive biscuit crumbs	
1 tbsp icing sugar	

Preparation time: 25 minutes
Baking time: 1 hour
Nutritional value:
Analysis per slice, approx, if divided into 12 slices:
- 1590kJ/380kcal
- 7g protein
- 27g fat
- 26g carbohydrate

Rinse, dry and stone the cherries. • Cream the butter and sugar. Separate the eggs. Grate the chocolate. Whisk the egg whites until they form stiff peaks. Add the egg yolks one at a time to the creamed butter. Add the chocolate and ground hazelnuts. Fold in the whisked egg whites. • Heat the oven to 180°C/350°F/Gas Mark 4. Grease the tin and sprinkle with sponge crumbs or digestive biscuit crumbs. • Spoon the mixture into the tin and arrange the cherries on top. Bake the cake on the lower shelf for 1 hour. • Switch the oven off and leave the cake in the oven for a further 10 minutes. • When cool, sift icing sugar onto the surface of the cake.

Our tip: To make sponge cake crumbs, take some leftover sponge cake bases and leave to dry out in an open tin. Crush with a rolling pin between two sheets of clingfilm.

Cherry and Kiwi Fruit Cake

Leave to cool for at least two hours before serving

Quantities for 1 28cm/11in springform tin

500g/1lb 2oz cherries	
1 tbsp lemon juice • 2 eggs	
75g/3oz sugar • 1 tbsp vanilla sugar	
50g/2oz each flour and cornflour	
½ packet unflavoured gelatine	
150g/5½oz crème fraîche	
2 tbsps warm milk	
50g/2oz sugar • 3-4 kiwi fruit	
1 packet lemon jelly glaze	
2 tbsps sugar	
250ml/8 fl oz apple juice	

Preparation time: 20 minutes
Baking time: 20 minutes
Final preparations: 35 minutes
Nutritional value:
Analysis per slice, approx, if divided into 12 slices:
- 880kJ/210kcal • 4g protein
- 7g fat • 31g carbohydrate

Stone the cherries and cook gently in 250ml/8fl oz water and lemon juice for 5 minutes. Leave to drain. • Separate the eggs. • Beat the yolks with 2 tbsps warm water, sugar and vanilla sugar. Whisk the whites until they form stiff peaks. Fold into the yolk mixture, together with the flour and cornflour. • Heat the oven to 180°C/350°F/Gas Mark 4. • Pour the mixture into a tin and bake for 20 minutes. Switch off the oven and leave for a further 10 minutes. • Soften the gelatine in 125ml/4fl oz hot water. Mix the crème fraîche with the milk and sugar and stir in the gelatine until it has dissolved. Add the crème fraîche, a spoonful at a time. Smooth this cream over the sponge base. Arrange the cherries around the rim of the cake. Peel the kiwi fruit, cut them into slices and arrange them inside the ring of cherries. • Add the glaze powder to the sugar and apple juice, bring to the boil and then pour over the fruit.

More Cherry Cakes

Sweet cherries appear on the market stalls at the beginning of June – sour cherries are available a few weeks later

Cherry Cheesecake

Illustrated left

Quantities for 1 28cm/11in cake

FOR THE CAKE BASE:

100g/4oz softened butter	
125g/5oz sugar	
1 tbsp vanilla sugar • 2 eggs	
150g/5½oz flour	
50g/2oz cornflour	
1 tsp baking powder	

FOR THE TOPPING:

500g/1lb 2oz sweet cherries	
4 eggs	
150g/5½oz softened butter	
150g/5½oz sugar	
2 tbsps vanilla sugar	
750g/1lb 11oz low-fat quark	
100g/4oz cornflour	

Preparation time: 45 minutes
Baking time: 1 hour
Nutritional value:
Analysis per slice, approx, if divided into 12 slices:

- 2010kJ/480kcal
- 17g protein
- 22g fat
- 53g carbohydrate

Heat the oven to 180°C/350°F/Gas Mark 4. Butter the springform tin. • Cream the butter, sugar and vanilla sugar. Add the eggs. Mix the flour, cornflour and baking powder and add to the egg and butter mixture. • Pour the mixture into the tin and bake for 20 minutes. • To make the topping, rinse, drain and stone the cherries. Separate the eggs. • Cream the butter, sugar, vanilla sugar and egg yolks. Whisk the egg whites until they form stiff peaks. Stir the quark into the creamed butter. Fold in the whisked egg whites, cornflour and cherries. • Pour the quark mixture over the base and bake for a further 50 minutes. Switch off the oven and leave to stand for 10 more minutes.

Cherry Crumble Pie

Illustrated right

Quantities for 1 26cm/10in springform tin

300g/10oz butter	
500g/1lb 2oz cherries	
225g/8oz sugar	
500g/1lb 2oz self-raising flour	
½ tsp grated lemon rind	
Pinch of salt	
1 tsp ground cinnamon	
1 egg	
50g/2oz ground, blanched almonds	

Preparation time: 30 minutes
Baking time: 40 minutes
Nutritional value:
Analysis per slice, approx, if divided into 12 slices:

- 1380kJ/330kcal
- 3g protein
- 24g fat
- 27g carbohydrate

Melt the butter over a low heat and then leave to cool. • Rinse, drain and stone the cherries. Sprinkle them with 25g/1oz sugar. • Mix the flour, baking powder, remaining sugar, grated lemon rind, salt and cinnamon in a bowl. Add the melted butter and egg. Use a food mixer or food processor to work the mixture to a crumbly dough. • Heat the oven to 200°C/400°F/Gas Mark 6. Butter the springform tin. • Place half the dough in the tin and press down. Sprinkle with ground almonds and then spread the cherries evenly over the base. Crumble the rest of the dough on top. • Bake on the middle shelf for 40 minutes, until golden brown. • Release the side of the springform tin. Leave the cake to cool. • This cake is best eaten fresh, but will last for one or two days.

Redcurrant Meringue Cake

A cake which is quick to make – ideal for the unexpected visitor

3 eggs
150g/5¹/₂oz sugar
1 tbsp vanilla sugar
250g/8oz flour
2 tsps baking powder
50g/2oz butter
5 tbsps milk
Pinch of salt
1kg/2¹/₄lbs redcurrants
200g/7oz sugar

Preparation time: 30 minutes
Baking time: 30-35 minutes
Nutritional value:
Analysis per slice, approx, if
divided into 20 slices:
- 710kJ/170kcal
- 4g protein
- 4g fat
- 30g carbohydrate

Separate the eggs. To make the base, beat 3 tbsps hot water into the egg yolks. Gradually add the sugar and sprinkle with the vanilla sugar. Combine the flour and baking powder. Melt the butter and, when it is lukewarm, add it to the whisked egg yolk mixture together with the milk and flour. • Heat the oven to 200°C/400°F/Gas Mark 6. Butter a large baking sheet . • Spread the sponge mixture over the sheet with a spatula. Bake for 15 minutes. • Meanwhile, rinse the redcurrants and leave to drain, removing the tiny stalks. Whisk the egg whites with the salt until they form stiff peaks and then gradually add the sugar. Stir in the redcurrants. • Reduce the oven temperature to 150°C/300°F/Gas Mark 2. • Spread the whisked egg white and redcurrant mixture over the sponge and bake on the middle shelf for 15 to 20 minutes, until the surface of the meringue becomes crispy. • Cool, cut into 20 slices and serve.

Our tip: Try mixing bilberries, gooseberries or stoned sweet cherries into the meringue, instead of redcurrants.

Damson Flan

Crispy shortcrust pastry with succulent fruit and a mouthwatering cream topping

Quantities for 1 28cm/11in springform tin

250g/8oz flour
50g/2oz sugar
Generous pinch of salt
100g/4oz butter, diced
8 tbsps cold water
2 tsps vinegar
1kg/2¼lbs damsons
125ml/4 fl oz cream
2 eggs
Generous pinch of ground cinnamon

Preparation time: 50 minutes
Baking time: 35 minutes
Nutritional value:

Analysis per slice, approx, if divided into 12 slices:
- 1090kJ/260kcal
- 5g protein
- 12g fat
- 33g carbohydrate

Mix the flour with 1 tbsp sugar, the salt, butter, water and vinegar. Make a dough using a food mixer or food processor, then use cold hands to make a smooth shortcrust dough. Wrap in clingfilm and leave in the refrigerator for 30 minutes to chill. • Rinse, drain, halve and stone the damsons. • Butter the tin. Heat the oven to 220°/450°F/Gas Mark 7. • Roll out the dough into a circle on a floured work top. Line the tin with the dough, pinching up a 2cm/1in rim. Arrange the damsons close together in a circular pattern on the dough, cut sides upwards. • Bake on the middle shelf of the oven for 10 minutes. • Stir the remaining sugar and cinnamon into the eggs and cream and pour this over the damsons. Bake for a further 25 minutes. If required, sprinkle a few sugar crystals over the cooled surface before serving.

Grapes and Cream in Crispy Pastry

Smooth fillings made from whisked egg white or full-fat cream cheese

Wholewheat Grape Tart
Illustrated left

Quantities for 1 26cm/10in springform tin

75g/3oz softened butter
3 tbsps honey
2 egg yolks
200g/7oz wholewheat flour
75g/3oz ground hazelnuts
2 tbsps sesame seeds
500g/1lb 2oz green grapes
4 eggs
250g/8oz mascarpone or full-fat soft cheese
1 tbsp semolina
100g/4oz black treacle
1 lemon, juice squeezed, rind grated

Preparation time: 1¼ hours
Baking time: 50 minutes
Nutritional value:
Analysis per slice, approx, if divided into 12 slices:
- 1510kJ/360kcal
- 10g protein
- 22g fat
- 29g carbohydrate

Cream the butter with the honey and egg yolks. Mix the flour with the nuts and sesame seeds. Add the flour to the creamed butter a tablespoon at a time and then knead to a firm, workable dough. Cover the dough and leave in a cool place for 1 hour. • Wash and dry the grapes and remove any seeds and stalks. • Separate the eggs. Beat the egg yolks with the mascarpone, semolina, treacle, lemon juice and zest. Whisk the egg whites until they form stiff peaks. Fold into the egg and mascarpone mixture. • Heat the oven to 180°C/350°F/Gas Mark 4. Lightly butter the tin. • Roll out the dough and line the tin. Pour the cream filling over the dough and add the grapes. Bake for 50 minutes.

Grape and Almond Tart
Illustrated right

Quantities for 1 26cm/10in springform tin

FOR THE SWEET SHORTCRUST DOUGH:
225g/8oz flour
125g/5oz butter
1 egg yolk
75g/3oz sugar
½ lemon, rind grated
1 tbsp rum

FOR THE FILLING:
500g/1lb 2oz green grapes
5 egg yolks
50g/2oz sugar
1 vanilla pod
150g/5½oz ground almonds
6 egg whites
50g/2oz flour

Preparation time: 1½ hours
Baking time: 1 hour
Nutritional value:
Analysis per slice, approx, if divided into 12 slices:
- 1890kJ/450kcal
- 12g protein
- 23g fat
- 46g carbohydrate

Quickly knead together the ingredients for the dough. Roll into a ball and refrigerate for 1 hour. • Wash, halve and seed the grapes. • Whisk the egg yolks and sugar. Slit open the vanilla pod and scrape out the pulp. Add the pulp to the egg yolks together with the almonds and flour. Whisk the egg whites until they form stiff peaks and then fold into the egg mixture. • Heat the oven to 180°C/350°F/Gas Mark 4. • Roll out the dough on a floured work top, and line the tin with it. • Mix the grapes into the egg mixture and pour over the dough. Bake on the middle shelf for 1 hour. • If required, ice the tart and decorate with grapes dipped in fondant.

Delicious Damson and Plum Cakes

Early autumn is the time to enjoy fresh plums and damsons

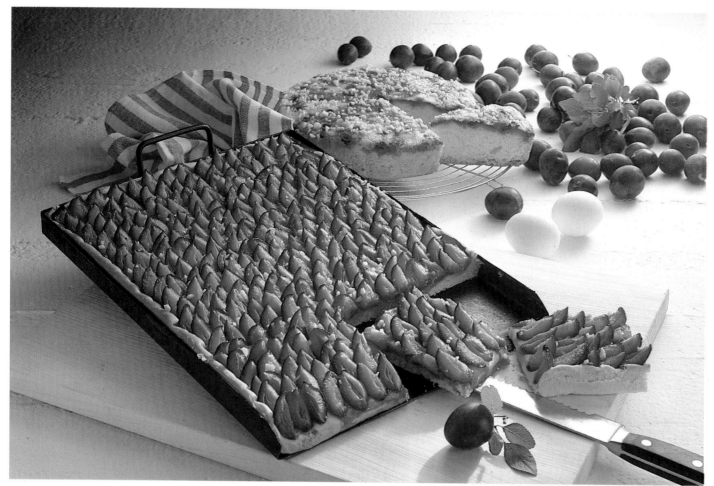

Plum Datschi
Illustrated left

Quantities for 1 baking sheet
20g/¹/₂oz fresh yeast
1 tbsp sugar
200g/7oz lukewarm milk
400g/14oz flour
Pinch of salt
1 egg
100g/4oz sugar
75g/3oz butter, melted
1.25kg/2³/₄lbs plums
50g/2oz chopped almonds
¹/₂ tsp ground cinnamon

Preparation time: 45 minutes
Rising time: 45 minutes
Baking time: 30 minutes
Nutritional value:
Analysis per slice, approx, if
divided into 20 slices:
- 790kJ/190kcal
- 4g protein
- 6g fat
- 31g carbohydrate

Mix the sugar, yeast and milk in a bowl, cover and leave to rise in a warm place for 15 minutes. • Mix the salt, egg, 75g/3oz sugar and half the flour with the yeast and milk mixture. Add the melted butter and then knead in the rest of the flour. The dough should come away cleanly from the side of the bowl when ready. If it is still sticky, add a little more flour. Cover and leave for a further 30 minutes. • Rinse, dry and stone the damsons. Make two cuts in the flesh of each damson. • Knead the dough well. Butter a baking sheet and line with a layer of dough. • Arrange the damsons on the dough and sprinkle with chopped almonds. • Heat the oven to 220°C/450°F/Gas Mark 7. • Bake the Plum Datschi on the lower shelf for 30 minutes. • Mix the remaining sugar with the ground cinnamon and sprinkle evenly over the surface. • Serve with sweetened whipped cream.

Upside-down Plum Cake
Illustrated right

Quantities for 1 26cm/10in springform tin
500g/1lb 2oz plums
100g/4oz softened butter
150g/5¹/₂oz sugar
1 tbsp vanilla sugar
3 eggs
100g/4oz each flour and cornflour
3 tsps baking powder
50g/2oz chopped almonds
3 tbsps coarse sugar crystals

Preparation time: 30 minutes
Baking time: 1 hour
Nutritional value:
Analysis per slice, approx, if
divided into 12 slices, approx:
- 1210kJ/290kcal
- 5g protein
- 12g fat
- 36g carbohydrate

Rinse, dry, halve and stone the plums. • Heat the oven to 180°C/350°F/Gas Mark 4. Line the tin with a sheet of aluminium foil and fold over any protruding edges. Butter well. • Cream the butter with the sugar and vanilla sugar. Add the eggs one at a time. Mix the flour, baking powder and cornflour and add to the egg and butter mixture a spoonful at a time. • Arrange the plums in the tin with the cut sides facing upwards. Pour in the cake batter and smooth the surface. Bake on the middle shelf of the oven for 1 hour. • Open the springform tin and leave the cake to cool for 10 minutes. Invert the tin on to a serving dish. Remove the foil. • Toast the chopped almonds in a dry frying pan until golden-brown. Cool and then sprinkle over the plums with the sugar crystals.

Summer Berries in Shortcrust or Yeast Pastry

Enjoy the taste of summer out of season – bilberries and blackberries freeze well

Bilberry Pie
In the foreground

Quantities for 1 24cm/9¹/₂in pie

FOR THE SWEET SHORTCRUST DOUGH:

250g/8oz flour
125g/5oz butter, diced
50g/2oz sugar
Pinch of salt •1 egg yolk

FOR THE FILLING:

2 egg whites •1 banana
2 tbsps lemon juice
500g/1lb 2oz bilberries
50g/2oz flaked almonds
50g/2oz sugar
¹/₂tsp ground cinnamon

FOR THE GLAZE:

1 egg yolk •2 tbsps milk

Preparation time: 1¹/₂ hours
Baking time: 40 minutes
Nutritional value:
Analysis per slice, approx, if divided into 8 slices:
• 1680kJ/400kcal • 8g protein
• 20g fat • 50g carbohydrate

Knead the flour with the butter, sugar, salt and egg yolk, and chill in the refrigerator for 1 hour. • Whisk the egg whites until they form stiff peaks. Peel the banana, cut into thin slices and sprinkle with lemon juice. Rinse the bilberries. Stir the flaked almonds, sugar, cinnamon, banana slices and whisked egg whites into the berries. • Heat the oven to 200°C/400°F/Gas Mark 6. • Divide the dough into a larger and a smaller portion. Roll out the larger portion and line the base of the tin. Brush cold water over the rims and then spoon in the fruit mixture. Roll out the lid, place on top of the filling and press the rims together firmly. Prick the lid with a fork. Beat the milk and egg yolk. Roll out any leftover dough and cut out a few decorative shapes with a pastry cutter. Brush the pie with milk and egg yolk, and bake on the lower shelf for 40 minutes until golden brown.

Blackberry Cake
In the background

Quantities for 1 baking sheet

FOR THE YEAST DOUGH:

400g/14oz flour
Sachet of dried yeast
50g/2oz each butter and sugar
1 egg
Pinch of salt
¹/₂ lemon, rind grated

FOR THE TOPPING:

1kg/2¹/₄lbs blackberries
5 eggs
500g/1lb 2oz low-fat quark
150g/5¹/₂oz crème fraîche
150g/5¹/₂oz sugar
Sachet of custard powder
50g/2oz flaked almonds
2 tbsps icing sugar
¹/₂ tsp ground cinnamon

Preparation time: 1¹/₂ hours
Baking time: 1 hour
Nutritional value:
Analysis per slice, approx, if divided into 20 slices:
• 1210kJ/290kcal
• 11g protein
• 11g fat
• 34g carbohydrate

Knead together all the ingredients for the yeast dough and leave to rise in a warm place for 30 minutes. Rinse the blackberries and pat dry. • Roll out the dough onto a buttered baking sheet and arrange the blackberries on top. • Separate the eggs. Stir the egg yolks into the quark, crème fraîche, sugar and pudding powder. Whisk the egg whites until stiff peaks are formed and fold into the quark mixture. Spread the mixture on top of the blackberries. • Heat the oven to 180°C/350°F/Gas Mark 4. • Sprinkle the flaked almonds on top of the quark and bake for 1 hour. • Mix the icing sugar with the ground cinnamon and sift over the surface.

Apple Tarts and Pies

Mouth-watering cakes, which cost very little – just allow plenty of time for making them

Apple Tart with Almonds
Illustrated left

Quantities for 1 26cm/10in springform tin

150g/5¹/₂oz flour
¹/₂ tsp baking powder
50g/2oz sugar • 1 egg yolk
Pinch of salt
100g/4oz cold butter, diced
750g/1lb 11oz cooking apples
2 tbsps lemon juice
375ml/14 fl oz milk
1 packet custard powder
2 tbsps sugar
150g/5¹/₂oz redcurrant jelly
40g/2oz flaked almonds
3 tbsps apricot jam

Preparation time: 1¹/₄ hours
Baking time: 45 minutes
Nutritional value:
Analysis per slice, approx, if divided into 12 slices:
• 1170kJ/280kcal • 4g protein
• 14g fat • 39g carbohydrate

Knead the flour, baking powder, sugar, yolk, salt and butter to make a smooth dough. Cover with clingfilm and leave in a cool place for 1 hour. • Peel, halve and core the apples and then make a series of parallel cuts on the surface. Sprinkle with lemon juice. • Make up the custard with the milk and sugar. • Roll out a circle of dough and use it to line the tin. Raise the rim by about 2cm/1in. • Heat the oven to 200°C/400°F/Gas Mark 6. • Bake the pastry blind for 10 minutes. • Brush redcurrant jelly over the surface of the pastry and then spoon in the custard. Arrange the halved apples cut-side down on the surface. Bake for 35 minutes.
• Toast the flaked almonds in a dry pan until golden brown. Heat the apricot jam, sieve it and brush it over the apples. Sprinkle with the almonds.

Apple and Nut Pie
Illustrated right

Quantities for 1 24cm/9¹/₂in springform tin

100g/4oz ground hazelnuts
400g/14oz plain flour
250g/8oz butter
200g/7oz sugar
3 tbsps vanilla sugar
Pinch of salt
2 egg yolks
100g/4oz raisins
4 tbsps rum
750g/1lb 11oz cooking apples
75g/3oz toasted, flaked almonds
100g/4oz icing sugar
3 tbsps calvados

Preparation time: 1¹/₄ hours
Baking time: 1 hour
Nutritional value:
Analysis per slice, approx, if divided into 8 slices:
• 2640kJ/630kcal
• 9g protein
• 32g fat
• 73g carbohydrate

Knead the ground hazelnuts, flour, butter, 150g/5¹/₂oz sugar, 1 tbsp vanilla sugar, salt and egg yolks into a dough and chill in the refrigerator for 1 hour.
• Rinse the raisins in hot water and soak them in the rum. Quarter, peel and core the apples. Dice and mix them with 50g/2oz toasted almonds, the soaked raisins and remaining sugar and vanilla sugar. • Heat the oven to 200°C/400°F/Gas Mark 6. • Break the dough into a larger and smaller portion. Roll out both portions. Line the lightly buttered tin with the larger circle and spoon in the apple filling. Cover with the smaller pastry circle and crimp the two borders together. • Bake the pie for 1 hour. • Stir the icing sugar into the calvados. • Brush this icing on to the pie and sprinkle with the remaining almonds.

Polish Apple Meringue

A delicious apple filling coated with an almond meringue

Quantities for 1 baking sheet
200g/7oz softened butter
250g/8oz sugar
1 vanilla pod • 3 eggs
4 tbsps milk
225g/8oz flour
50g/2oz cornflour
2 tsps baking powder
50g/2oz each raisins and currants
3 tbsps rum
750g/1lb 11oz cooking apples
½ lemon
½ tsp ground cinnamon
Generous pinch of ground cloves
100g/4oz chopped almonds

Preparation time: 1¼ hours
Baking time: 45 minutes
Nutritional value:
Analysis per slice, approx, if divided into 20 slices:
• 1090kJ/260kcal • 4g protein
• 13g fat • 32g carbohydrate

Cream the butter with 100g/4oz sugar. Separate the eggs. Cut the vanilla pod in half lengthways and scrape out the pith. Stir half of it into the egg yolks and milk and then mix this with the creamed butter. Combine the flour, cornflour and baking powder and then stir into the butter mixture, a spoonful at a time. • Wash the raisins and currants in hot water, drain and soak in the rum. Peel, quarter and core the apples and slice them thinly. Wash the lemon in warm water, scrape off the rind with a zester and sprinkle over the apples. Squeeze the juice from the lemon and mix with the apples, together with the rum-soaked dried fruit, spices and 50g/2oz sugar.• Heat the oven to 200°C/400°F/Gas Mark 6. Butter the baking sheet. • Roll out the dough and lay it on the buttered baking sheet. Spoon an even layer of apple mixture over it. Bake for 25 minutes on the middle shelf of the oven. • Beat the egg whites with the remaining sugar and vanilla until they form stiff peaks. Add the almonds. Spread an even coating of whisked egg white on top of the apples and bake for a further 20 minutes on the bottom shelf.

Raspberry Sponge Cake

Something for the calorie-counters

Strawberry Cheese Shortcake

A scrumptious cake for summer – and one for beginners to try

Raspberry Sponge Cake

Quantities for 1 28cm/11in springform tin
2 eggs • 75g/3oz sugar
1 tbsp vanilla sugar • Pinch of salt
50g/2oz each flour and cornflour
4 tbsps dry breadcrumbs
400g/14oz raspberries
200ml/6 fl oz whipping cream
3 tbsps sugar
1 packet red jelly glaze
250ml/8 fl oz water

Preparation time: 40 minutes
Baking time: 20 minutes
Nutritional value:
Analysis per slice, approx, if cake is divided into 12 slices:
• 670kJ/160kcal • 3g protein
• 7g fat • 20g carbohydrate

Separate the eggs and whisk 2 tbsps warm water into the egg yolks. Gradually add the sugar and vanilla sugar. Whisk the egg whites with the salt until they form stiff peaks. Mix the flour and cornflour and add to the yolk mixture. Fold in the whisked egg whites. • Heat the oven to 180°C/350°F/Gas Mark 4. Grease the springform tin well and sprinkle the base with bread-crumbs. Pour in the mix and bake on the lower shelf for 20 minutes, until golden brown. Switch off the oven. Leave the tin to stand in the oven for a further 15 minutes and then invert the cake over a plate. • Rinse the raspberries and drain well. Whisk the cream with the sugar. Spoon about a quarter of the whipped cream into a piping bag fitted with a star nozzle and leave to chill in the refrigerator. • Cover the cooled base with the remaining cream and arrange the raspberries on top. • Mix the jelly glaze powder with the remaining sugar and water, according to the manufacturer's instructions. Starting from the middle, pour the cooled glaze over the fruit. Allow about 30 minutes to set. Pipe cream around the rim and serve.

Strawberry Cheese Shortcake

Quantities for 1 28cm/11in springform tin
75g/3oz each butter and sugar
1 tbsp vanilla sugar
2 eggs
150g/5¹/₂oz flour
1 tsp baking powder
Pinch of salt • 4 tbsps milk
¹/₂ packet unflavoured gelatine
125g/5oz quark (20% fat content), at room temperature
5 tbsps sugar
200ml/6 fl oz whipping cream
500g/1lb 2oz strawberries

Preparation time: 15 minutes
Baking time: 20 minutes
Final preparations: 30 minutes
Nutritional value:
Analysis per slice, approx, if divided into 12 slices:
• 1000kJ/240kcal
• 6g protein
• 13g fat
• 24g carbohydrate

Cream the butter with the sugar, vanilla sugar and eggs. Combine the flour, baking powder and salt. Slowly add the flour and milk to the creamed butter. • Heat the oven to 200°C/400°F/Gas Mark 6. • Pour the mixture into a tin and bake on the lower shelf of the oven for 20 minutes. Cool and invert onto a plate. • Soak the gelatine in 125ml/4fl oz hot water. • Beat 3 tbsps sugar into the quark. Add the gelatine and warm through over a pan of hot water, stirring until it has dissolved, and then mix in the quark, adding a tbsp at a time. • Whip the cream with the rest of the sugar until stiff, and fold half into the quark. • Rinse and hull the strawberries. Dry well, halving any larger fruit. • Cover the cake base with the quark mixture and arrange the strawberries on top. Finish with a border of piped whipped cream.

Summer Fruit Flans

You can rely on rhubarb and berries for refreshing desserts

Summer Fruit Flan
Illustrated left

Quantities for 1 24cm/9¹/₂in flan
250g/8oz self-raising flour
1 egg • 75g/3oz sugar
Pinch of salt
125g/5oz butter, diced
100g/4oz marzipan
75g/3oz icing sugar
250g/8oz strawberries
200g/7oz raspberries
125g/5oz each blackberries and redcurrants
100g/4oz blackcurrants
2 packets lemon jelly glaze
250ml/8 fl oz each red fruit juice and water • 4 tbsps sugar

Preparation time: 45 minutes
Baking time: 25 minutes
Nutritional value:
Analysis per slice, approx, if
divided into 8 slices:
• 1890kJ/450kcal • 8g protein
• 18g fat • 65g carbohydrate

Mix the flour with the egg, sugar, salt and butter to make a smooth dough. Leave to stand for 30 minutes. • Knead the marzipan with 50g/2oz icing sugar. Roll out a circle of marzipan the size of the tin on a surface dusted with the remaining icing sugar, • Wash all the berries and leave to drain; halve any large strawberries and remove the tiny stalks from the redcurrants. Mix the fruits. • Heat the oven to 200°C/400°F/Gas Mark 6. • Roll out a circle of dough and use it to line the tin. Prick all over with a fork. Trim off any excess dough. Sprinkle with dried beans and bake blind for 25 minutes, or until lightly browned. When cool, place on a tray and line with the marzipan. Arrange the fruit on top. • Prepare the jelly glaze with the remaining ingredients, pour this over the fruit and leave to set. in a cool place.

Rhubarb Cake with an Almond Meringue
Illustrated right

Quantities for 1 26cm/10in springform tin
150g/5¹/₂oz softened butter
300g/11oz sugar
1 tbsp vanilla sugar • 5 eggs
150g/5¹/₂oz flour
75g/3oz cornflour
1¹/₂ tsps baking powder
600g/1lb 6oz rhubarb
Pinch of salt
50g/2oz ground almonds
1 tbsp lemon juice

Preparation time: 30 minutes
Baking time: 45 minutes
Nutritional value:
Analysis per slice, approx, if
divided into 12 slices:
• 1380kJ/330kcal
• 7g protein
• 15g fat
• 43g carbohydrate

Cream the butter with 125g/5oz of the sugar and the vanilla sugar. Separate 3 of the eggs. Beat the 2 remaining whole eggs with the egg yolks and gradually add to the creamed butter. Mix the baking powder and cornflour with the flour and add to the egg and butter mixture. • Heat the oven to 180°C/350°F/Gas Mark 4. Butter the tin. • Rinse the rhubarb, trim the ends and strip off the stringy fibres. Cut the sticks into 4cm/1¹/₂in lengths. • Lay the dough in the tin and arrange the rhubarb lengths on top, pressing each piece down a little into the dough. Bake for 25 minutes on the middle shelf. Whisk the egg whites with the salt until they form soft peaks. Add the rest of the sugar and whisk for a little longer until it stands in stiff peaks. • Add the ground almonds and lemon juice. • Pipe or spoon the whisked egg mixture over the cake. • Bake for a further 20 minutes.

Fruit Desserts to all Tastes

Marzipan cream and almonds combine perfectly with a fruit filling

Apricot and Marzipan Slices

In the background

Quantities for 1 baking sheet
125g/5oz low-fat quark
5 tbsps milk
5 tbsps oil
75g/3oz sugar
250g/8oz flour
3 tsps baking powder
250ml/8 fl oz milk
½ packet custard powder
1 tsp cornflour
50g/2oz marzipan
750g/1lb 11oz apricots
100g/4oz apricot jam
50g/2oz flaked almonds

Preparation time: 45 minutes
Baking time: 40 minutes
Nutritional value:
Analysis per slice, approx, if divided into 20 slices:
• 710kJ/170kcal
• 4g protein
• 5g fat
• 20g carbohydrate

Drain the quark well and blend with the milk, oil and all but 1 tbsp of the sugar. Mix the flour with the baking powder and stir half into the quark mixture, gradually kneading in the rest. • Mix the custard powder, cornflour and remaining sugar with 4 tbsps milk. Bring the rest of the milk to the boil, stir in the custard mixture, bring back to the boil and remove from the heat. Add the marzipan, stirring well until it dissolves. • Heat the oven to 200°C/400°F/Gas Mark 6. Brush the baking sheet with oil. • Roll out the dough and place on the baking sheet. Cover with the cooled pudding. • Stone the apricots and arrange on the pudding. Bake for 45 minutes on the lower shelf. • Brush the cake with warmed apricot jam and sprinkle with the flaked almonds.

Cherry Tart with Almonds

In the foreground

Quantities for 1 24cm/9½in flan
300g/10oz flour
1 tsp baking powder
150g/5½oz softened butter
150g/5½oz sugar
1 tbsp vanilla sugar
750g/1lb 11oz sweet cherries
2 tbsps cornflour
375ml/14 fl oz cherry juice
2 tbsps kirsch
100g/4oz chopped almonds
1 egg yolk

Preparation time: 1½ hours
Baking time: 45 minutes
Nutritional value:
Analysis per slice, approx, if divided into 12 slices:
• 1590kJ/380kcal • 7g protein
• 18g fat • 50g carbohydrate

Knead together the flour, baking powder, butter, 100g/4oz sugar and vanilla sugar to make a workable dough. Wrap in clingfilm and chill in the refrigerator for 1 hour. • Rinse and stone the cherries. Blend the cornflour and the remaining sugar with 5 tbsps of the cherry juice. Bring the remaining juice to the boil, remove from the heat and stir in the cornflour and cherries. Cook for 1 minute, stirring well. Leave to cool. • Heat the oven to 200°C/400°F/Gas Mark 6. • Roll out the dough and use it to line the buttered flan tin. Prick the dough well with a fork. Bake blind for 20 minutes. • Mix the kirsch with the cherries and then pour this into the pastry base. Sprinkle with the chopped almonds. Roll out the rest of the dough and cut it into 1½cm/½in strips. Arrange them in a lattice pattern over the cherry filling and brush with the beaten egg yolk. • Bake for a further 25 minutes or until golden brown. • Leave to stand for at least 4 hours before serving.

Peach Cake with Almonds

If required, sift a little icing sugar onto the surface of the cake just before serving

Quantities for 1 26cm/10in springform tin
250g/8oz flour
100g/4oz cornflour
50g/2oz ground almonds
3 eggs
175g/6oz softened butter
Pinch of salt
250g/8oz sugar
2 tbsps vanilla sugar
1kg/2¼lbs peaches
50g/2oz flaked almonds
200g/7oz crème fraîche
½ lemon, rind grated

Preparation time: 1 hour
Baking time: 40 minutes
Nutritional value:
Analysis per slice, approx, if divided into 12 slices:
- 2100kJ/500kcal
- 8g protein
- 26g fat
- 54g carbohydrate

Place the flour, almonds and 50g/2oz cornflour in a bowl. Add one egg, butter, salt, 100g/4oz sugar and 1 tbsp vanilla sugar. Quickly knead to a smooth dough and refrigerate for 30 minutes • Dip the peaches in boiling water, remove the skins, halve and stone them. Bring 250ml/8 fl oz water and 50g/2oz sugar to the boil and simmer the peaches for 15 minutes. • Heat the oven to 180°C/350°F/Gas Mark 4. • Grease the tin. • Cover the base of the tin with the dough, making a 2cm/1in rim. Bake blind for 15 minutes. • Fill the pastry case with the peach halves and sprinkle with almonds. Separate the remaining eggs. Beat the egg yolks with the remaining sugar and vanilla sugar. Stir in the crème fraîche, grated lemon rind and the remaining cornflour. Whisk the egg whites until they form stiff peaks and fold into the egg and cream mixture. • Pour the liquid over the peach halves, smooth the surface and bake for a further 25 minutes. • Leave the cake to cool completely before removing it from the tin. Cool on a wire rack.

Peach Fillings for Light Pastries

Try apricots, kiwi fruit or mangos instead of peachs

Peach Pie
Illustrated left

Quantities for 1 24cm/9¹/₂in fruit flan tin

3 eggs	
250g/8oz flour	
Generous pinch of baking powder	
150g/5¹/₂oz butter	
125g/5oz sugar	
100g/4oz ground almonds	
1 tbsp lemon juice	
3 tbsps rum	
500g/1lb 2oz ripe peaches	
50g/2oz chopped almonds	
3 tbsps apricot jam	

Preparation time: 50 minutes
Baking time: 1 hour
Nutritional value:

Analysis per slice, approx, if divided into 8 slices:
• 2310kJ/550kcal
• 12g protein
• 30g fat
• 52g carbohydrate

Separate the eggs. • Combine the flour with the baking powder, butter, 50g/2oz sugar and 1 egg yolk. Knead to a workable dough. Wrap in clingfilm and refrigerate for 30 minutes. • Whisk the egg whites to form stiff peaks. Combine the ground almonds, lemon juice, 2 tbsps rum and the remaining egg yolks and sugar. Fold in the whisked egg whites. • Heat the oven to 180°C/ 350°F/Gas Mark 4. Butter the tin. • Roll out the shortcrust dough and use it to line the tin. Bake blind for 25 minutes. • Peel, halve and stone the peaches. • Pour the almond mixture into the tin and bake for 15 minutes. • Press the peach halves lightly onto the surface and bake for a further 15 minutes. • Toast the almonds in a dry frying pan until golden brown. • Combine the remaining rum and apricot jam. Warm through, stirring well, and then brush over the warm pie. Sprinkle with chopped almonds.

Peach Cake with Quark
Illustrated right

Quantities for 1 26cm/10in springform tin

500g/1lb 2oz quark	
3 tbsps each milk and oil	
125g/5oz sugar • 200g/7oz flour	
2 tsps baking powder	
100ml/3 fl oz cream	
2 tbsps vanilla sugar • 3 eggs	
1 tbsp cornflour	
2 tbsps semolina	
500g/1lb 2oz peaches	
2 tbsps icing sugar	

Preparation time: 1 hour
Baking time: 1 hour
Nutritional value:

Analysis per slice, approx, if divided into 12 slices:
• 1090kJ/260kcal • 11g protein
• 10g fat • 34g carbohydrate

Drain the quark. Combine 75g/3oz quark with the milk, oil and 25g/1oz sugar. Stir the baking powder into the flour, add to the quark mixture and knead well. • Oil the tin and line it with the quark dough, making a 3-cm/1-in rim • Mix the remaining sugar and vanilla sugar into the cream. • Separate the eggs. Beat the egg yolks into the cream. Whisk the egg whites into stiff peaks. Mix the cornflour with the semolina and add to the egg yolk mixture, together with the remaining quark. Fold in the whisked egg whites. • Heat the oven to 200°C/400°F/Gas Mark 6. • Dip the peaches into boiling water, remove the skins, halve and stone. • Pour one third of the quark mixture into the tin. • Place the peach halves on top and cover with the remaining quark mixture. • Bake the cake on the lower shelf for 1 hour. Switch off the oven and leave for a further 10 minutes. • When cooled, sprinkle with sifted icing sugar.

Pineapple Tart with Cream Icing

The thin quark pastry case contains a delicious fruit filling

Quantities for 1 26cm/10in fruit flan tin
75g/3oz low-fat quark
2 tbsps milk
3 tbsps oil
125g/5oz sugar
Pinch of salt
200g/7oz flour
2 tsps baking powder
1 fresh pineapple
2 eggs
$\frac{1}{2}$ tsp grated lemon rind
250ml/8 fl oz sour cream

Preparation time: 30 minutes
Baking time: 40 minutes
Nutritional value:
Analysis per slice, approx, if divided into 12 slices:
- 920kJ/220kcal
- 6g protein
- 6g fat
- 35g carbohydrate

Heat the oven to 200°C/400°F/Gas Mark 6. Butter the tin. • Drain the quark and then mix with the milk, oil, 50g/2oz sugar, salt, 150g/5½oz flour and baking powder. First use a kneading hook on a food mixer, finishing by hand to make a smooth dough. • Roll out two-thirds of the dough on a floured surface and use it to line the tin. Roll out the rest into a long strip and use it to line the sides of the tin. • Quarter the pineapple and remove the outer skin. Remove the tough, inner core and cut the fruit into wedges. • Separate the eggs. Beat the egg yolks with the remaining sugar and grated lemon rind and then add the remaining flour and sour cream, a little at a time. Whisk the egg whites until they form stiff peaks and then fold them into the egg yolk mixture. • Arrange the pineapple wedges on the dough and pour in the filling. • Bake the tart on the middle shelf for 40 minutes. • Leave for 5 minutes before releasing from the tin and then allow to cool on a wire rack.

Apple and Rhubarb Slices with Vanilla Cream

Rhubarb makes a delicious, moist cake filling

Quantities for 1 baking sheet
FOR THE DOUGH:
400g/14oz flour
1 tsp baking powder • 1 egg
125g/5oz sugar
Pinch of salt
250g/8oz butter, diced
FOR THE TOPPING:
1 tbsp dry breadcrumbs
2kg/4½lbs rhubarb
1kg/2¼lbs apples
250g/8oz sugar
½ tsp each ground cinnamon and ground coriander
125ml/4 fl oz water
FOR THE GLAZE:
2 packets red jelly glaze
4 level tbsps sugar
FOR THE VANILLA CREAM:
½ packet unflavoured gelatine
500ml/18 fl oz milk
1½ packets custard powder
3 tbsps sugar
250ml/8 fl oz whipping cream

Preparation time: 1½ hours
Baking time: 35 minutes
Final preparations: 1 hour
Nutritional value:
Analysis per slice, approx, if divided into 24 slices:
- 1200kJ/290kcal
- 4g protein
- 12g fat
- 43g carbohydrate

Mix the flour, baking powder, egg, sugar, salt and butter, and knead in a food mixer or food processor. Finally, knead by hand to create a smooth workable dough. Roll into a ball, wrap in clingfilm and refrigerate for 1 hour. • Trim the rhubarb and strip off the stringy fibres. Wash and cut into 2cm/1in lengths. Quarter, peel and core the apples. • Place the prepared fruit, sugar, cinnamon, coriander and water in a saucepan. Cover and cook gently for 5 minutes. • Strain the fruit and collect the liquid. • Butter a baking sheet. Heat the oven to 220°C/450°F/Gas Mark 7. • Roll out the dough into a sheet about the same size as the baking sheet. Dust with a little flour, wrap around a rolling pin and unroll onto the baking sheet. Prick the dough with a fork. Fold a strip of aluminium foil twice and place at the open end of the pastry to keep the rim even. Bake the dough on the middle shelf of the oven for 5 minutes and then sprinkle with the breadcrumbs. Spread the stewed fruit over the dough. • Bake on the middle shelf of the oven for about 30 minutes and leave to cool. Top the reserved fruit juice up to 500ml/18 fl oz with water. Make up the glaze following the manufacturer's instructions using the reserved liquid and sugar. • Pour this over the fruit and leave to set. • To make the vanilla cream, soak the gelatine in 2 tbsps cold water for 10 minutes. • Mix the sugar and custard powder with 6 tbsps milk. Bring the rest of the milk to the boil and then add the custard mixture. Return to the boil, then leave to cool, stirring frequently. Whip the cream until stiff. Dissolve the gelatine in 125ml/4fl oz hot water. Stir well. Add 2 tbsps whipped cream to the gelatine and then stir this mixture into the remaining whipped cream. • Fold the whipped cream into the custard with a whisk. Fit a star nozzle onto a piping bag and create a lattice pattern. Cut into 24 slices.

Tartlets with Summer Fruit Fillings

The cases are made with a quark or a wholewheat shortcrust dough

Raspberry Tartlets with Pistachio Cream

Illustrated left

Quantities for 8 tartlets

250g/8oz low-fat quark
5 tbsps milk • 5 tbsps oil
100g/4oz sugar
1 tbsp vanilla sugar
Pinch of salt
250g/8oz flour
3 tsps baking powder
1/2 packet unflavoured gelatine
1 egg yolk
200ml/6 fl oz whipping cream
400g/14oz raspberries
2 tbsps chopped pistachio nuts

Preparation time: 20 minutes
Baking time: 20 minutes
Final preparations: 30 minutes
Nutritional value:
Analysis per tartlet, approx:
• 1680kJ/400kcal • 12g protein
• 19g fat • 43g carbohydrate

Drain the quark. Mix half with the milk, oil, 50g/2oz sugar, vanilla sugar and salt. Stir to a smooth paste. Add the flour and baking powder and knead to a smooth dough. Roll out the dough into a sheet about 1/2cm/1/4in thick. Cut out eight circles 10cm/4ins in diameter. • Heat the oven to 200°C/400°F/Gas Mark 6. Bake the pastry cases blind in buttered tartlet tins for 20 minutes until brown. • Soak the gelatine in 125ml/4 fl oz hot water to dissolve. Beat the egg yolk with the remaining sugar and add the remaining quark. Put 2 tbsps of the quark mixture in the gelatine liquid and stir well. Return this mixture to the quark. • Whip the cream until stiff and stir half of it into quark. Fill the pastry cases with the quark and cream. Arrange the raspberries in the middle and then surround with whirls of whipped cream. Sprinkle with pistachio nuts.

Redcurrant Tartlets

Illustrated right

Quantities for 8 tartlets

200g/7oz wholewheat flour
25g/1oz buckwheat flour
25g/1oz barley flour
1 tsp baking powder
Generous pinch of ground cinnamon
100g/4oz cold butter, diced
175g/6oz clear honey
1 egg
250g/8oz redcurrants
50g/2oz chocolate nut paste
200g/7oz whipping cream

Preparation time: 25 minutes
Baking time: 15-20 minutes
Final preparations: 20 minutes
Nutritional value:
Analysis per tartlet, approx:
• 1680kJ/400kcal
• 7g protein
• 23g fat • 42g carbohydrate

To make the dough, combine the flours, baking powder, cinnamon and butter with 100g/4oz of the honey and the egg. Leave to rest for 15 minutes. • Heat the oven to 200°C/400°F/Gas Mark 6. • Butter the tartlet tins. • Divide the dough into eight equal parts and roll them out. Use them to line each tin, and trim off any excess. • Bake blind for 15 to 20 minutes, or until golden brown. • Rinse the redcurrants and remove all the tiny stalks. Mix together the remaining honey and the nut paste and then fold in the redcurrants, reserving a few for the final decoration. Whip the cream until stiff and add three-quarters of it to the berries. • Fill the pastry cases with the redcurrant cream and top each tartlet with a whirl of whipped cream and a redcurrant.

Citrus and Raspberry Delights

These little cakes are delicious with freshly-made coffee

Orange Slices
Illustrated left

Quantities for 1 baking sheet
200g/7oz softened butter
150g/5½oz sugar
1 tbsp vanilla sugar
Pinch of salt
3 eggs
250g/8oz flour
2 tsps baking powder
1 orange
1 lemon
200g/7oz icing sugar

Preparation time: 40 minutes
Baking time: 20 minutes
Nutritional value:
Analysis per slice, approx, if
divided into 24 slices:
- 630kJ/150kcal
- 2g protein
- 8g fat
- 17g carbohydrate

Cream the butter, gradually adding the sugar, vanilla sugar, salt and eggs. Mix the flour and baking powder. Wash the lemon in lukewarm water. Grate the rind with a zester and squeeze out the juice. • Stir the juice and rind into the flour and then add the creamed butter. • Heat the oven to 200°C/400°F/Gas Mark 6. Butter a baking sheet. • Cover three quarters of the baking sheet with the mixture. Fold a strip of aluminium foil twice and place it at the open end of the dough, so that the mixture does not run. • Bake the cake on the middle shelf of the oven for 20 minutes or until golden brown. • Rinse the orange in lukewarm water, dry and grate the rind with a zester. Squeeze out the juice. • Mix the icing sugar with the orange juice and brush it over the warm cake. Sprinkle with orange zest. Leave the icing to dry. • Cut the cake into 24 bars or diamonds.

Raspberry Boats
Illustrated right

Quantities for 12 boats
FOR THE SWEET SHORTCRUST DOUGH:
250g/8oz flour
100g/4oz icing sugar
50g/2oz ground almonds
100g/4oz butter • egg yolk
FOR THE FILLING:
250g/8oz raspberries
125ml/4 fl oz milk
2 tsp cornflour • 1½ tbsps sugar
2 egg yolks • ½ vanilla pod
3 tbsps Advocaat or egg nog
125ml/4 fl oz whipping cream

Preparation time: 10 minutes
Cooling time: 1 hour
Baking time: 15-20 minutes
Final preparations: 1 hour
Nutritional value:
Analysis per boat, approx:
- 1510kJ/360kcal • 7g protein
- 20g fat • 33g carbohydrate

Work the shortcrust ingredients into a smooth dough. Cover with clingfilm and chill for 1 hour. • Wash the raspberries and pat dry. • Heat the oven to 180°C/350°F/Gas Mark 4. • Roll out a thin sheet of dough. Lightly grease the boat-shaped moulds. Line them with the dough and bake blind for 15 to 20 minutes, or until golden brown. • Bring the milk to the boil. Mix the cornflour with a little cold milk and 1 tbsp of sugar and add to the milk. Bring to the boil again, remove from the heat and then add the egg yolks. Slit the vanilla pod lengthways and scrape out the pulp. Stir the pulp into the custard, together with the advocaat. Leave the custard to cool. • Whip the cream and remaining sugar until stiff. Fill the boats with the cream and raspberries. Top with a whirl of whipped cream.

Grape Tartlets

Butter the tins thickly as the pastry cases are very brittle

Quantities for 8 12cm/5in tartlets

FOR THE SWEET SHORTCRUST DOUGH:

300g/10oz flour

150g/5½oz butter

100g/4oz sugar

1 tbsp vanilla sugar

Pinch of salt

1 egg yolk

FOR THE FILLING:

1 packet unflavoured gelatine

3 eggs

100g/4oz icing sugar

125ml/4 fl oz marsala

2 tbsps lemon juice

300g/10oz each green and black grapes

50g/2oz toasted, flaked almonds

Preparation time: 1¾ hours
Baking time: 20 minutes
Nutritional value:
Analysis per tartlet, approx:
- 2310kJ/550kcal
- 12g protein
- 25g fat
- 68g carbohydrate

Mix together the ingredients for the dough. Knead well, cover with clingfilm and chill for 1 hour. • Dissolve the gelatine in 125ml/4 fl oz hot water. Separate the eggs. Pour sufficient water into a large saucepan for it to come 5cm/2in up the sides. Put the egg yolks and icing sugar into a mixing bowl and beat them over the water . Stir in the marsala. Warm the lemon juice and add it to the yolks. Add the gelatine and mix well. Whisk the egg whites until stiff but not dry and then fold into the egg yolk mixture with a spoon. Leave this custard in the refrigerator for 1 hour to set, stirring occasionally. • Heat the oven to 200°C/ 400°F/Gas Mark 6. • Butter the tartlet tins. Divide the dough into eight equal parts. Roll it into thin sheets and use them to line the tins. Prick the dough with a fork and trim off any excess. Bake the tartlets blind for 20 minutes or until golden brown. • Wash the grapes and remove any stalks. • Spoon the wine custard into the tartlets. Top with grapes and sprinkle flaked almonds around the rims.

Sheet Cakes and Cakes Baked in the Tin

Famous cakes and favourite cakes,
but also something new to try

More Cakes for Coffee Mornings

These attractive moulds are now available from good kitchenware shops

Chocolate Madeira Cake
Illustrated left

Quantities for 1 Continental ring mould

175g/6oz softened butter	
200g/7oz sugar	
1 tbsp vanilla sugar	
2 tbsps rum	
Pinch of salt	
5 eggs	
250g/8oz flour	
50g/2oz cornflour	
2 tsps baking powder	
100g/4oz cocoa powder	
2 tbsps apricot jam	
150g/5$\frac{1}{2}$oz plain chocolate icing	
Sprinkling of breadcrumbs	

Preparation time: 20 minutes
Baking time: 1 hour
Nutritional value:
Analysis per slice, approx, if divided into 16 slices:
• 1380kJ/330kcal
• 7g protein
• 18g fat
• 37g carbohydrate

Heat the oven to 180°C/350°F/Gas Mark 4. Butter the mould and sprinkle with breadcrumbs. • Cream the butter. Add the sugar, vanilla sugar, rum, salt and the eggs, one at a time. Stir well. Mix the flour, cornflour, baking powder and cocoa powder and add to the mixture, a spoonful at a time. • Pour the mixture into the mould and bake for 1 hour. • Warm the apricot jam. • Unmould the cake, brush it with jam and leave to cool on a wire rack. • Melt the chocolate icing in a bain-marie and pour it over the cake.

Kugelhopf
Illustrated right

Quantities for 1 large kugelhopf mould

500g/1lb 2oz flour	
42g/1$\frac{1}{2}$oz fresh yeast or 1 sachet dried yeast • 125g/5oz sugar	
125ml/4 fl oz lukewarm milk	
375g/13oz butter • 5 eggs	
Pinch of salt • 1 lemon, rind grated	
100g/4oz raisins	
50g/2oz currants	
50g/2oz chopped almonds	
50g/2oz chopped candied citron	
2 tbsps icing sugar	

Preparation time: 40 minutes
Rising time: 50 minutes
Baking time: 1 hour minutes
Nutritional value:
Analysis per slice, approx, if divided into 20 slices:
• 1510kJ/360kcal
• 7g protein
• 22g fat • 33g carbohydrate

Put the flour in a bowl and make a well in the centre. Crumble in the yeast and mix with about 4 tbsps of the flour, 1 tsp of the sugar and half the milk. Cover and leave to rise in a warm place for 20 minutes. • Melt the butter. Add the rest of the milk and sugar, the eggs, salt and grated lemon rind. • Beat the butter mixture and starter yeast into the rest of the flour and knead well. Rinse the currants and raisins in hot water and drain well. Mix together with the almonds and candied citron and add to the yeast dough. • Butter the mould well and then place the dough inside. Cover and leave to rise to the top. • Heat the oven to 180°C/350°F/Gas Mark 4. • Bake the kugelhopf on the lower shelf for 1 hour. • Switch off the oven and leave for 10 minutes. • Invert the mould and cover it with a damp cloth. After 10 minutes remove the mould. • Dust with icing sugar.

Countess Cake

This elegant cake looks most attractive when baked in a triangular mould, otherwise use a loaf tin

Quantities for 1 30cm/12in loaf
1 orange
250g/8oz softened butter
200g/7oz sugar
5 eggs
250g/8oz flour
100g/4oz cornflour
3 tsps baking powder
4 tbsps apricot liqueur or Cointreau
200g/7oz plain cooking chocolate
100g/4oz plain chocolate cake covering or icing
Sprinkling of breadcrumbs

Preparation time: 1 hour
Baking time: 1 hour
Resting time: 1 day
Nutritional value:
Analysis per slice, approx, if divided into 20 slices:
- 1300kJ/310kcal
- 5g protein
- 17g fat
- 31g carbohydrate

Heat the oven to 200°C/ 400°F/Gas Mark 6. Butter the tin well and sprinkle with breadcrumbs. • Wash the orange in hot water and grate the rind. Cream the butter and add the sugar, orange rind and eggs, one at a time. Sift the flour with the baking powder and cornflour and add to the creamed butter mixture, a spoonful at a time. • Pour the cake mixture into the tin, smooth the surface and bake on the lower shelf for 1 hour. • Unmould the cake and leave it on a wire rack for 24 hours. • Squeeze the juice from the orange and mix with the liqueur. • With a sharp knife, cut the cake into five longitudinal slices. Sprinkle with the liqueur and allow to soak in. • Melt the cooking chocolate and the cake covering in a bain-marie. Coat each slice with the melted chocolate. Re-assemble the cake and cover with the rest of the chocolate mixture. Lay the cake on one side until the icing has set.

Tyrolean Chocolate Cake

A delicious sponge cake requiring very little flour

Quantities for 1 30cm/12in loaf
200g/7oz almonds
150g/5½oz plain cooking chocolate
200g/7oz softened butter
200g/7oz sugar
6 eggs
125g/5oz flour
1 tsp baking powder
2 tbsps rum
200g/7oz chocolate cake covering or icing
Sprinkling of breadcrumbs

Preparation time: 45 minutes
Baking time: 1 hour
Nutritional value:
Analysis per slice, approx, if divided into 15 slices:
- 1800kJ/430kcal
- 9g protein
- 30g fat
- 29g carbohydrate

Grind the almonds in a mill. Grate the chocolate. • Cream the butter and slowly add the sugar. Separate the eggs. Add the yolks, one at a time, to the creamed butter. Mix the flour and baking powder and sift into the creamed butter, together with the ground almonds and grated chocolate. Whisk the egg whites until they form stiff peaks and fold into the cake mixture, together with the rum. • Heat the oven to 180°C/350°F/Gas Mark 4. • Butter the tin and sprinkle a few breadcrumbs on top. • Pour the cake mixture into the tin, smooth the surface and bake on the middle shelf for 1 hour. Test the centre of the cake with a skewer; if it doesn't come out cleanly, bake the cake for another 10 minutes. Switch off the oven and allow the cake to stand for a further 10 minutes. • Unmould the cake and leave it to cool on a wire rack. Melt the chocolate cake covering and pour over the cake.

Marble Cakes

These cakes can be baked either in a fancy mould or in a loaf tin. Poppy seeds should be ground in a spice grinder or coffee grinder

Poppyseed Marble Cake
Illustrated left

Quantities for 1 26cm/10in loaf
300g/10oz wholewheat flour
2 tsps baking powder
¹/₂ tsp vanilla essence
200g/7oz softened butter
175g/6oz honey
4 eggs
50g/2oz diced candied peel
150g/5¹/₂oz freshly ground poppyseeds
1 tbsp rosewater
¹/₂ tsp ground cinnamon
2 tsps cocoa powder
2 tbsps each rum and lemon juice

Preparation time: 45 minutes
Baking time: 1 hour
Nutritional value:
Analysis per slice, approx, if divided into 12 slices:
• 1590kJ/380kcal
• 10g protein
• 23g fat
• 29g carbohydrate

Sift the flour and baking powder. Cream the butter and 150g/5¹/₂oz honey with the vanilla. Add the flour and the eggs a little at a time, stirring well. Add the candied peel. • Heat the oven to 180°C/350°F/Gas Mark 4. Butter the loaf tin and add half the mixture. Add the poppyseeds, rosewater, cinnamon, cocoa powder and the remaining honey to the other half. Pour the dark mixture over the lighter mixture and swirl the two together lightly with a palette knife. • Bake the marble cake on the middle shelf for 1 hour. Switch off the oven and leave the cake for a further 5 minutes. • Mix the rum with lemon juice and sprinkle over the cake before unmoulding. Leave the marble cake to cool in the tin.
• The cake should be left a full two days to allow the flavours to develop.

Classic Marble Cake
Illustrated right

Quantities for 1 kugelhopf tin
250g/8oz softened butter
250g/8oz sugar
1 tbsp vanilla sugar
4 eggs
400g/14oz self-raising flour
100g/4oz cornflour
Pinch of salt
100ml/3 fl oz milk
30g/1oz cocoa powder
1 tbsp icing sugar

Preparation time: 30 minutes
Baking time: 1 hour
Nutritional value:
Analysis per slice, approx, if divided into 20 slices:
• 1210kJ/290kcal
• 5g protein
• 13g fat
• 33g carbohydrate

Cream the butter, gradually adding the sugar and vanilla sugar. Beat the eggs into the creamed butter one at a time. Mix together the flour, cornflour, baking powder and salt. Add the flour and milk to the creamed butter, stirring well. • Heat the oven to 180°C/350°F/Gas Mark 4. Butter the tin and pour half of the mixture into it. • Add the cocoa powder to the remaining mixture and pour over the first half. Swirl together lightly with a fork, to create a marbled effect. • Bake on the middle shelf of the oven for 1 hour. To test if the cake is done, insert a skewer into the centre. If the skewer does not come out clean, the cake will require a little longer in the oven. • When the cake has cooled, invert the tin over a rack. Sift a little icing sugar over the cake before serving.

Aniseed Cake

A simple sponge cake, but flavoured with sweet spices and herbs

Quantities for 1 26cm/10in loaf tin
200g/7oz wholewheat flour
25g/1oz soya flour
25g/1oz cocoa powder
2 tsps baking powder
½ tsp each ground cinnamon, ground ginger and ground anise
1 orange
2 tbsps raw whole cane sugar
150g/5½oz softened butter
225g/8oz honey
3 eggs
3 tbsps arak or aniseed liqueur

Preparation time: 30 minutes
Baking time: 50 minutes
Nutritional value:
Analysis per slice, approx, if divided into 12 slices:
- 1210kJ/290kcal
- 7g protein
- 18g fat
- 30g carbohydrate

Mix the flours with the cocoa, baking powder, cinnamon and ginger. Wash the orange in warm water, dry and grate the rind with a zester. Mix the grated rind and cane sugar with the flour. • Cream the butter with 150g/5½oz of the honey. Add the eggs and half the arak to the flour mixture, a little at a time. • Heat the oven to 180°C/350°F/Gas Mark 4. Butter the tin. • Pour the mix into the tin and smooth the surface. Bake on the middle shelf of the oven for about 50 minutes. Test the centre of the cake with a skewer to see if it is done. • Switch off the oven and leave for a further 10 minutes. • Squeeze the juice from the orange and mix with the remaining honey and arak. • Pour the liquid evenly over the cake and leave to cool in the tin. • Leave the aniseed cake for a day for the full flavour to develop. It will stay fresh for two or three days.

Spice Cake

If preferred, use wholewheat flour for this traditional cake

Quantities for 1 30cm/12in loaf tin
Sprinkling of breadcrumbs
200g/7oz softened butter
250g/8oz sugar
2 tbsps vanilla sugar
4 eggs
200g/7oz ground hazelnuts
1 tsp ground cinnamon
Generous pinch each ground cloves, ground ginger and ground allspice
250g/8oz flour
3 tsps baking powder
2 tbsps rum

Preparation time: 20 minutes
Baking time: 1 hour
Nutritional value:
Analysis per slice, approx, if divided into 20 slices:
- 960kJ/230kcal
- 4g protein
- 17g fat
- 15g carbohydrate

Heat the oven to 200°C/ 400°F/Gas Mark 6. Grease the tin and sprinkle with breadcrumbs. • Cream the butter with the sugar and vanilla sugar. Add the eggs, ground hazelnuts and spices, a little at a time. Add the rum. Mix the flour with the baking powder and add to the mixture a tablespoonful at a time. • Pour the mixture into the tin, smooth the surface, and bake on the middle shelf of the oven for 1 hour. • The flavour will improve if the cake is left for a day before being cut.

Our tip: Spice cake has a long shelf life. Uncut, it will keep for up to a fortnight if wrapped in aluminium foil and stored in a well-sealed container.

Nut Ring

This is a traditional Easter Cake in central Europe

Quantities for 1 ring
250g/8oz cream cheese
6 tbsps milk
1 egg
125ml/4 fl oz oil
100g/4oz sugar
1 tbsp vanilla sugar
Pinch of salt
425g/15oz self-raising flour
100g/4oz candied orange peel
250g/8oz chopped hazelnuts
Zest of ½ lemon
50g/2oz sugar
5 tbsps cream
100g/4oz marzipan
1 egg yolk

Preparation time: 40 minutes
Baking time: 50 minutes
Nutritional value:
Analysis per slice, approx, if divided into 16 slices:
- 1590kJ/380kcal
- 9g protein
- 24g fat
- 39g carbohydrate

Drain the cheese well and mix it with the milk, egg, oil, sugar, salt and vanilla sugar. Combine the flour and baking powder and then spoon it into the quark mixture, kneading well. • For the filling, chop the candied peel and mix with the hazelnuts, grated lemon rind, sugar and 4 tbsps cream. Cut the marzipan into thin slices. • Heat the oven to 180°C/ 350°F/Gas Mark 4. Butter a ring mould. • Roll the dough out on a floured work top into a rectangular strip 80x20cm/30x8ins. Place the marzipan slices along the centre of the dough strip, together with the fruit and nut mixture. Fold the rims of the dough over the filling and press down. Turn the roll over so that the seam faces downwards, place in the ring mould and shape into a circle. Link the two ends, pressing the pastry rims together firmly. Whisk the egg yolk with the remaining cream and brush over the surface. Cut a zigzag pattern in the dough with a pair of kitchen scissors. • Bake the nut ring on the middle shelf of the oven for about 50 minutes, or until golden brown.

Tasty Almond Slices

Wholemeal flour can be substituted for white flour in both these recipes

Butter Cake
In the background

Quantities for 1 baking sheet
300g/10oz low-fat soft cheese or quark
6 tbsps milk
7 tbsps oil
50g/2oz sugar
1 tsp grated lemon rind
Pinch of salt
400g/14oz flour
2 tsps baking powder
100ml/3 fl oz single cream
200g/7oz sugar
2 tsps ground cinnamon
100g/4oz butter
100g/4oz flaked almonds

Preparation time: 45 minutes
Baking time: 30 minutes
Nutritional value:
Analysis per slice, approx, if divided into 16 slices:
- 1300kJ/310kcal
- 7g protein
- 14g fat
- 36g carbohydrate

Heat the oven to 200°C/ 400°F/Gas Mark 6. Butter the baking sheet. • Drain the cheese and combine it with the milk, oil, sugar, grated lemon rind and salt. Sift the flour and baking powder into the cheese and oil mixture. Stir well and then knead to a dough. • On a lightly floured surface, roll out the dough to a rectangle the size of the baking sheet. Carefully transfer the dough to the baking sheet. Make a number of hollows at regular intervals in the pastry with the handle of a wooden spoon. Brush the cream over the dough. Mix the sugar and cinnamon and sprinkle on top. Place knobs of butter in the hollows and sprinkle them with the flaked almonds. • Bake on the middle shelf of the oven for 30 minutes. • Cut the cake into 16 slices and leave to cool on a wire rack.

Butter Almond Slices
In the foreground

Quantities for 1 baking sheet
200ml/6 fl oz double cream
100g/4oz sugar
350g/11oz self-raising flour
3 eggs
1 tsp ground cinnamon
FOR THE TOPPING:
200g/7oz butter
150g/5¹/₂oz sugar
6 tbsps double cream
150g/5¹/₂oz flaked almonds

Preparation time: 30 minutes
Baking time: 25 minutes
Nutritional value:
Analysis per slice, approx, if divided into 16 slices:
- 1590kJ/380kcal
- 7g protein
- 23g fat
- 34g carbohydrate

Stir the sugar into the cream until it has almost dissolved. Sift the flour and stir it into the cream and sugar mixture. Stir with a wooden spoon. Add the eggs one at a time, together with the cinnamon. Stir well. • Heat the oven to 180°C/350°F/Gas Mark 4. • Butter the baking sheet. Pour the mixture into the baking sheet and smooth to an even thickness with a spatula. Take a strip of aluminium foil, fold it twice and place it against the "open" side of the dough to keep a clean rim. • Bake the cake base on the middle shelf for 10 minutes. • To make the topping, melt the butter over a low heat. Stir the sugar, cream and flaked almonds into the butter. Spread this mixture over the cake base. • Bake for a further 15 minutes, or until golden brown. • Cut the cake into 16 slices while it is still in the baking sheet. Transfer to a wire rack and leave to cool.

Traditional Cakes from Italy and England

To prevent premature browning, cakes that require long baking times should be covered with aluminium foil until the last 15 minutes

Panettone

In the foreground

Quantities for 1 panettone tin or a 1.4-litre/2¹/₂-pint mould

45g/1¹/₂oz yeast or 1 sachet dried yeast
125g/5oz sugar
125ml/4 fl oz lukewarm milk
500g/1lb 2oz flour • 4 egg yolks
1 tbsp vanilla sugar
1 lemon, rind grated • ¹/₂ tsp salt
125g/5oz softened butter
100g/4oz raisins
100g/4oz diced candied lemon peel • 50g/2oz diced candied orange peel
50g/2oz chopped almonds

Preparation time: 30 minutes
Rising time: 1¹/₄ hours
Baking time: 1¹/₂ hours
Nutritional value:
Analysis per slice, approx, if divided into 12 slices:
• 2010kJ/480kcal • 12g protein
• 23g fat • 54g carbohydrate

Crumble the yeast and mix with 1 tsp of sugar and the milk. Leave to rise in a warm place for 15 minutes. • Add the flour to the fermenting yeast, together with remaining sugar, egg yolks, vanilla sugar, grated lemon rind, butter and salt. Knead for 5 minutes, adding a little more flour if necessary. Leave for 30 minutes. • Wash the raisins in hot water and then add them to the dough, together with the almonds and candied peels. Leave the dough for a further 20 minutes. Line the tin with buttered non-stick baking paper, or butter thickly. Place the dough in the tin and leave for a further 10 minutes. • Heat the oven to 200°C/400°F/Gas Mark 6. • Brush the surface of the dough with melted butter and make a few cuts across the surface with a sharp knife. • Bake on the bottom shelf for 1¹/₂ hours.

English Fruit Cake

In the background

Quantities for 1 30cm/12in loaf tin

250g/8oz softened butter
4 eggs
250g/8oz sugar
1 tsp vanilla essence
2 tbsps rum
50g/2oz each chopped candied orange and lemon peel
¹/₂ lemon, rind grated
2 tbsps lemon juice
Pinch of salt
150g/5¹/₂oz raisins
250g/8oz flour
2 tsps baking powder
125g/5oz cornflour
50g/2oz chopped almonds
100g/4oz icing sugar
2 tbsps lemon juice

Preparation time: 30 minutes
Baking time: 1-1¹/₄ hours
Nutritional value:

Analysis per slice, approx, if divided into 20 slices:
• 1300kJ/310kcal
• 5g protein
• 18g fat
• 41g carbohydrate

Cream the butter. Separate the eggs and add the yolks and sugar to the butter, a little at a time. Whisk the egg whites until they form stiff peaks. Add the vanilla essence, rum, lemon rind and juice, candied peels and salt to the butter mixture. Rinse and drain the raisins and dip in flour. Combine the flour, baking powder and cornflour. Add the whisked egg whites and flour a little at a time to the butter mixture. Add the chopped almonds. • Heat the oven to 180°C/350°F/Gas Mark 4. Butter and flour the cake tin. Pour the mixture into the tin and bake on the lower shelf for 60 to 75 minutes. • Mix the icing sugar and lemon juice and brush over the surface.

Orange Marble Cake

Leave for one or two days for the full flavour to emerge

French Orange Cake

Serve this moist cake with ice-cold whipped cream

Quantities for 1 26cm/10in loaf
250g/8oz wholewheat flour
2 tsps baking powder
150g/5¹/₂oz softened butter
250g/8oz honey
¹/₂ tsp vanilla essence
4 eggs
100g/4oz each hazelnuts and blanched almonds
2 oranges
2 tsps cocoa powder
2 tbsps Cointreau

Preparation time: 45 minutes
Baking time: 1 hour
Nutritional value:
Analysis per slice, approx, if divided into 12 slices:
• 1680kJ/400kcal
• 10g protein
• 24g fat
• 36g carbohydrate

Combine the flour and baking powder. Cream the butter with 100g/4oz honey and the vanilla. Add 3 of the eggs and the flour a little at a time and stir well.
• Heat the oven to 180°C/350°F/Gas Mark 4. • Butter the tin well. • Pour the mixture into the tin and smooth the surface. • Grind the hazelnuts and almonds. Wash the oranges in hot water, dry well and grate the rind with a zester. Mix with the ground nuts, cocoa powder, the remaining honey and egg. Stir well. Pour the nut mixture over the vanilla mixture. Swirl the two mixtures together lightly with a fork. • Bake the cake on the middle shelf of the oven for 1 hour, or until golden-brown. Test the centre of the cake with a skewer to see if it is done. • Switch off the oven and leave the cake to rest for another 5 minutes. • Squeeze the juice from the oranges and mix with the Cointreau. Brush an even coating of the liquid over the cake. Leave to cool in the tin. Orange cake will stay fresh for about a week if stored in a well-sealed container.

Quantities for 1 26cm/10in springform tin
4 eggs
175g/6oz sugar
1 orange
75g/3oz each flour and cornflour
¹/₂ tsp baking powder
75g/3oz butter, melted and cooled
50g/2oz flaked almonds
250ml/8 fl oz freshly squeezed orange juice
Juice of 1 lemon
1 tbsp sugar
2 tbsps icing sugar

Preparation time: 30 minutes
Baking time: 50 minutes
Final preparations: 10 mins
Nutritional value:
Analysis per slice, approx, if divided into 16 slices:
• 750kJ/180kcal
• 4g protein
• 8g fat
• 22g carbohydrate

Separate the eggs. Beat the yolks with the sugar. • Wash the orange in hot water and grate the rind with a zester. Mix with the flour, cornflour and baking powder and combine with the beaten egg yolks. Whisk the whites to form stiff peaks. Fold into the flour and egg mixture, together with the lukewarm butter. • Heat the oven to 180°C/350°F/Gas Mark 4. Line the tin with buttered non-stick baking paper. Sprinkle with the flaked almonds. • Pour the mixture into the tin and smooth the surface. Bake for 50 minutes until golden brown. Switch off the oven and leave the cake to stand for 10 minutes. • Strain the orange juice and mix with the lemon juice and sugar. Warm the liquid through. • Invert the tin and remove the paper. Make a number of holes in the surface of the cake with a thin skewer and pour the juice over it. • Dust with icing sugar prior to serving.

Rich Cheesecakes

Crumble pastry or crushed biscuits or rusks blend well with these mouth-watering fillings

Crumble Cheesecake

Illustrated left

Quantities for 1 28cm/11in springform tin

FOR THE CRUMBLE:

250g/8oz flour

125g/5oz each sugar and butter

1 tbsp vanilla sugar • 1 egg yolk

½ lemon, rind grated

FOR THE CHEESE FILLING:

1kg/2¼lbs curd cheese, cottage cheese or quark

125g/5oz softened butter

150g/5½oz sugar • 4 eggs

1 egg white

1 tbsp vanilla sugar

½ lemon, rind grated

2 tbsps semolina

Sprinkling of semolina for tin

Preparation time: 50 minutes
Baking time: 1 hour
Nutritional value:
Analysis per slice, approx, if 1

cake is divided into 12 slices:
• 2100kJ/500kcal • 19g protein
• 23g fat • 52g carbohydrate

To make the crumble, rub the butter into the sugar, flour, vanilla sugar, egg yolk and grated lemon rind . • Heat the oven to 200°C/400°F/Gas Mark 6. Butter the springform tin and sprinkle with semolina. • Place two thirds of the crumble in the tin and press down lightly. Chill the remaining crumble mix until you are ready to use it. • Squeeze any liquid from the curd cheese, cottage cheese or quark. Cream the butter with the sugar. Separate the eggs. Mix the egg yolks with creamed butter. Whisk the egg whites until they form stiff peaks. Stir the vanilla sugar, grated lemon rind, quark and semolina into the butter and egg mixture. Fold in the stiff egg whites and pour into the tin. Smooth the surface and sprinkle with the rest of the crumble. • Bake for 1 hour.

American-style Cheesecake

Illustrated right

Quantities for 1 26cm/10in springform tin

10 rusks or 5 digestive biscuits (100g/4oz) • 2 tbsps sugar

40g/1½oz butter

600g/1lb 6oz full fat cream cheese • 200g/7oz sour cream

5 eggs • 175g/6oz sugar

½ lemon, rind grated

2 tbsps lemon juice

50g/2oz cornflour

1 tsp baking powder

Preparation time: 45 minutes
Baking time: 1½ hours
Nutritional value:
Analysis per slice, approx, if divided into 12 slices:
• 1680kJ/400kcal • 12g protein
• 25g fat • 28g carbohydrate

Wrap the rusks or digestives in clingfilm and crush them

with a rolling pin. Rub in with the sugar and butter to make a crumbly mixture. Press the mixture into the base of a tin and smooth the surface. • Combine the cream cheese and sour cream. Separate the eggs. Stir the egg yolks into the cream cheese mixture, together with the sugar, grated lemon rind and juice. Whisk the egg whites to form stiff peaks. Combine the cornflour and baking powder and sift over the cheese mixture. Fold in the beaten egg whites. • Heat the oven to 150°C/300°F/Gas Mark 2. • Spoon the cheesecake mixture over the rusk base, smooth the surface and bake on the bottom shelf for 1½ hours, until golden brown. • Leave in the oven for 30 minutes, then for another 30 minutes with the door wedged ajar. Open the springform tin and loosen the rim of the cake with the blade of a knife. Do not unmould until ready to serve.

Yeast Doughs Flavoured with Almonds

Two similar cakes, one traditional German recipe and the other a wholefood variation. Try them both to see which you prefer!

Bee Stings

Illustrated left

Quantities for 1 baking sheet

FOR THE DOUGH:

45g/1½oz fresh yeast or 1 sachet dried yeast • 75g/3oz sugar	
250ml/8 fl oz lukewarm milk	
500g/1lb 2oz flour	
50g/2oz softened butter	
Pinch of salt	

FOR THE ALMOND TOPPING:

100g/4oz butter, melted	
200g/7oz flaked almonds	
150g/5½oz sugar • 3 tbsps milk	

FOR THE CREAM FILLING:

½ packet unflavoured gelatine	
500ml/18 fl oz milk	
75g/3oz sugar • 1 tbsp vanilla sugar	
50g/2oz cornflour • 1 egg	

Preparation time: 90 minutes
Baking time: 30 minutes
Nutritional value:
Analysis per slice, approx, if divided into 16 slices:

• 1590kJ/380kcal • 8g protein
• 17g fat • 50g carbohydrate

Mix yeast with 1 tsp sugar and 2 tbsps milk. Leave until foaming. • Knead the flour with the butter, salt and remaining milk and sugar. Add yeast mixture and leave to rise in a warm place for 45 minutes. • Combine the butter, almonds, sugar and milk. • Roll out the yeast dough on a lightly-greased baking sheet. Spread with the topping and leave for 15 minutes. • Heat oven to 200°C/ 400°F/Gas Mark 6. • Bake for 30 minutes. • Dissolve gelatine in 125ml/4 fl oz hot water. Combine all the cream filling ingredients except the egg. Mix the egg yolk with the dissolved gelatine. Whisk the egg white until stiff, and fold into the yolk and gelatine. • Cut the pastry base into four and slice each in half crossways. Spread filling on one half of each slice and cover with the other half. Cut each slice into four.

Honey Bee Stings

Illustrated right

Quantities for 1 baking sheet

FOR THE DOUGH:

600g/1lb 6oz wholewheat flour	
50g/2oz soya flour	
½ tsp ground cinnamon	
45g/1½oz fresh yeast or 1 sachet dried yeast	
375ml/14 fl oz lukewarm milk	
50g/2oz clear honey	
50g/2oz softened butter	

FOR THE ALMOND TOPPING:

200g/7oz flaked almonds	
200g/7oz honey • 100g/4oz butter	

FOR THE CREAM FILLING:

75g/3oz honey	
500ml/18 fl oz milk	
40g/1½oz cornflour or arrowroot	
½ tsp vanilla essence	
250g/8oz softened butter	

Preparation time: 90 minutes
Baking time: 25 minutes
Nutritional value:
Analysis per slice, approx, if divided into 16 slices:
• 2180kJ/520kcal • 10g protein
• 30g fat • 48g carbohydrate

Mix the flour and cinnamon. Make a well in the centre and add the yeast, milk, honey and 4 tbsps of the flour. Leave to rise in a warm place for 15 minutes. • Knead the dough with the yeast mixture and butter, and leave for 30 minutes. • Roll the dough and place on a buttered baking sheet; leave for a further 15 minutes. • Combine almonds, honey and butter, and heat until dissolved. Spread mixture over the dough. • Heat oven to 220°C/450°F/Gas Mark 7. • Bake for 25 minutes. • Heat the honey. Stir the milk with vanilla essence and cornflour or arrowroot. Add to the honey, bring to the boil and allow to cool. Remove from heat and mix with the butter, a spoonful at a time. • To assemble, follow instructions for the preceding recipe.

Chestnut Cake

If made with canned chestnut purée this cake can be enjoyed all the year round

Quantities for 1 24cm/9¹/₂in springform tin

FOR THE SWEET SHORTCRUST DOUGH:

200g/7oz flour

100g/4oz butter

75g/3oz icing sugar • 1 egg yolk

FOR THE FILLING:

750g/1lb 11oz chestnuts

150g/5¹/₂oz softened butter

150g/5¹/₂oz sugar

2 tbsps vanilla sugar

1 tsp ground cinnamon

2 eggs • 2 egg whites

2 tbsps amaretto (almond liqueur)

125ml/4fl oz sweetened, whipped cream, to serve

Preparation time: 1 hour
Baking time: 1 hour
Nutritional value:
Analysis per slice, approx, if divided into 12 slices:
• 2100kJ/500kcal • 8g protein
• 24g fat • 62g carbohydrate

Use cold hands to knead the flour, butter, icing sugar and egg yolk to a smooth dough. Cover with clingfilm and leave to rest for 1 hour. • Heat the oven to 200°C/400°F/Gas Mark 6. • Slit the pointed ends of the chestnuts with a sharp knife, place on a baking sheet and roast for 10 minutes. • Shell the cooled chestnuts and remove the brown inner skin. Bring 500ml/16 fl oz water to the boil and simmer the chestnuts for 20 minutes. • Cream the butter with the sugar, vanilla sugar and cinnamon. Separate the eggs. Mix the egg yolks with the creamed butter. Whisk all the egg whites until they form stiff peaks. • Strain the chestnuts, leave to cool and then purée them in a liquidiser. Add the chestnut purée to the creamed butter and then fold in the beaten egg whites. • Heat the oven to 180°C/350°F/Gas Mark 4. • Roll out the dough and use it to line the springform tin, pinning up a 3cm/1in rim at the sides. Bake blind for 10 minutes. • Spoon in the chestnut mixture and bake for a further 50 minutes. • Drizzle the amaretto over the surface of the cake. Serve when cold with sweetened whipped cream.

Special Nut Cakes

Hazelnuts and walnuts are the predominant flavours in these two cakes – one containing flour and one without

Madeira Nut Cake

In the foreground

Quantities for 1 30cm/12in loaf
175g/6oz softened butter
250g/8oz sugar
1 tbsp vanilla sugar
4 eggs • 150g/5¹/₂oz flour
100g/4oz cornflour
1 tsp baking powder
100g/4oz ground hazelnuts
75g/3oz ground walnuts
1 tbsp lemon juice

Preparation time: 30 minutes
Baking time: 70 minutes
Nutritional value:
Analysis per slice, approx, if divided into 15 slices:
• 1380kJ/330kcal
• 6g protein
• 20g fat
• 32g carbohydrate

Cream the butter. Stir in 150g/5¹/₂oz sugar and the vanilla sugar. Separate two of the eggs. Sift together the flour, cornflour and baking powder. Combine the egg yolks with the two whole eggs and add to the creamed butter, together with the flour mixture. Heat the oven to 180°C/350°F/Gas Mark 4. Line the tin with non-stick baking paper. • Pour in the sponge mixture. • Whisk the egg whites into stiff peaks and then sprinkle in the remaining sugar. Add the ground nuts and lemon juice. • Cut a wide groove in the top of the sponge mixture and spoon the nut mixture into it. • Bake the cake on the bottom shelf of the oven for 70 minutes. It may be necessary to cover the cake with aluminium foil for the last 45 minutes to prevent it from browning. • Test the centre of the cake with a skewer to see if it is done. Switch off the oven and leave for 10 minutes to cool. Remove the cake from the tin and cool on a wire rack.

Swiss Nut Cake

In the background

Quantities for 1 30cm/12in loaf
250g/8oz walnuts
¹/₂ tbsp butter
200g/7oz sugar
150g/5¹/₂oz hazelnuts
50g/2oz rusks or digestive biscuits
6 eggs
2 level tsps baking powder
1 jar hazelnut chocolate paste

Preparation time: 50 minutes
Baking time: 50 minutes
Nutritional value:
Analysis per slice, approx, if divided into 15 slices:
• 1510kJ/360kcal • 10g protein
• 24g fat • 23g carbohydrate

Set aside eight walnuts for the decoration. Chop 100g/4oz of the walnuts. Melt the butter in a frying pan, add the chopped walnuts and brown, stirring frequently. Sprinkle with 2 tsps sugar and caramelise lightly. Remove from the pan and leave to cool. • Grind the remaining walnuts and hazelnuts. Use a rolling pin to crush the rusks or digestive biscuits between two sheets of aluminium foil. • Line the tin with non-stick baking paper. Heat the oven to 180°C/350°F/Gas Mark 4. • Whisk the eggs and sprinkle with the remaining sugar and ground nuts. Mix the crushed rusks or biscuits with the baking powder and chopped walnuts. Add to the whisked egg and ground nut mixture. Pour into the loaf tin and smooth the surface. Bake the cake on the middle shelf for 50 minutes. Test the centre of the cake with a skewer to see if it is done. • Switch off the oven and leave for 10 minutes. Invert the tin, remove and leave the cake to cool. • Melt the chocolate paste in a bowl over hot water. Use it to ice the cake, and top with the reserved whole walnuts.

Delicious Cakes for Unexpected Guests

Sponge cake bases with magical toppings

Marzipan and Almond Slices

In the foreground

Quantities for 1 Swiss roll tin

FOR THE SPONGE MIXTURE:

6 eggs

150g/5½oz butter, melted

250g/8oz sugar

Pinch of salt

1 lemon, rind grated

350g/11oz self-raising flour

6 tbsps milk

FOR THE TOPPING:

150g/5½oz butter

100g/4oz crème fraîche

150g/5½oz sugar

1 tbsp vanilla sugar

200g/7oz marzipan

2 tbsps cognac

400g/14oz flaked almonds

Preparation time: 45 minutes
Baking time: 30 minutes
Nutritional value:
Analysis per slice, approx, if

divided into 24 slices:
- 1800kJ/430kcal
- 9g protein
- 26g fat
- 36g carbohydrate

Beat the eggs with the melted butter, sugar, salt and grated lemon rind. Stir in the butter, flour, baking powder and milk. • Heat the oven to 200°C/400°F/Gas Mark 6. • Butter a large Swiss roll tin and cover with an even layer of the sponge mixture. Bake for 15 minutes. • Combine the crème fraîche, butter, sugar, vanilla sugar and salt and bring to the boil. Cut the marzipan into pieces and add the cognac. First stir the butter and sugar mixture into the marzipan then add the flaked almonds. • Spread the topping over the sponge base and cook for a further 15 minutes. • Leave the cake to cool, and cut into 24 slices.

White Wine Cake

In the background

Quantities for 1 24cm/9½in springform tin

Sprinkling of breadcrumbs

200g/7oz softened butter

200g/7oz sugar

1 tbsp vanilla sugar

3 eggs

1 lemon, rind grated, juice squeezed

200ml/6 fl oz white wine

3 tbsps white rum

300g/10oz flour

50g/2oz cornflour

1 tbsp baking powder

FOR THE ICING:

150g/5½oz icing sugar

3 tbsps lemon juice

Preparation time: 15 minutes
Baking time: 45 minutes
Final preparations: 10 minutes
Nutritional value:
Analysis per slice, approx,

if divided into 12 slices:
- 1450kJ/345kcal
- 6g protein
- 12g fat
- 52g carbohydrate

Heat the oven to 180°C/350°F/Gas Mark 4. • Butter the tin and sprinkle with breadcrumbs. • Cream the butter with the sugar and vanilla sugar. Add the eggs one at a time. Add the grated lemon rind and juice to the creamed butter and mix well. Combine the flour, baking powder and cornflour and add to the creamed mixture, a tablespoonful at a time, together with the rum and half the white wine. • Pour the sponge mixture into the tin and bake on the middle shelf of the oven for 45 minutes. • Make a few holes in the surface of the cake with a skewer and pour the rest of the wine over it. Leave the cake to cool. Combine the icing sugar and lemon juice. • Pour the icing over the cake.

Children's Favourites

Fun to make and fun to eat

Cold Dog

Illustrated left

Quantities for 1 26cm/10in loaf
250g/8oz creamed coconut
2 eggs
100g/4oz sugar
1 tbsp vanilla sugar
50g/2oz instant cocoa powder
4 tbsps milk
50g/2oz coarsely ground almonds
300g/10oz thin shortbread or digestive biscuits

Preparation time: 45 minutes
Cooling time: 4 hours
Nutritional value:
Analysis per slice, approx, divided into 26 slices:
• 750kJ/180kcal
• 4g protein
• 13g fat
• 13g carbohydrate

Warm the creamed coconut over a low heat. Whisk the eggs and add the sugar, vanilla sugar, cocoa powder and milk. Mix the almonds with the lukewarm creamed coconut and stir into the cocoa mixture. • Line the loaf tin with aluminium foil or non-stick baking paper. Cover the base with a coating of the cocoa mixture, followed by a layer of biscuits. Add another layer of the cocoa mixture and then a layer of biscuits. Continue until all the ingredients have been used. Place a plate on top of the cake to compress the layers and leave for 4 hours in the refrigerator to chill. • Remove the cake from the tin and discard the foil or baking paper. Cut the 'cold dog' into 1cm/1/2in slices. • Store the cake in the refrigerator, where it will stay fresh for at least a week.

Our tip: If the cake is to be served to adults, then rum may substituted for milk. You can also use 200g/7oz icing sugar instead of granulated sugar and leave out the almonds.

Birthday Tree Cake

Illustrated right

3 eggs • Pinch of salt	
100g/4oz sugar	
1 tbsp vanilla sugar	
75g/3oz flour • 50g/2oz cornflour	
250g/8oz raspberry jam	
1 egg white	
200g/7oz icing sugar	
125ml/4fl oz chocolate icing	
Hundreds and thousands	

Preparation time: 1 hour
Baking time: 12-15 minutes
Nutritional value:
Analysis per slice, approx, if divided into 8 slices:
• 1510kJ/360kcal • 8g protein
• 5g fat • 73g carbohydrate

Heat the oven to 180°C/350°F/Gas Mark 4. • Separate the eggs. Whisk the egg whites with the salt and 50g/2oz sugar, until they form stiff peaks. Beat the egg yolks with the remaining sugar and vanilla sugar. Stir the flour, cornflour and beaten egg whites into the egg yolk mixture. • Line a baking sheet with buttered non-stick baking paper. Pour the mixture onto the baking sheet and smooth the surface. • Bake the sponge base for 15 minutes, leave to cool and remove the paper. • Meanwhile, cut a template for the 'tree' out of non-stick baking paper. Make a circular top and a thick 'trunk'. Use a sharp knife to cut two tree shapes out of the sponge. Coat one tree with raspberry jam and use biscuit cutters to cut small holes in the tree top of the other. Turn the second tree over and place it on top of the first tree. Fill the holes with raspberry jam. • Mix the egg white with the icing sugar. Brush this over the tree and sprinkle with hundreds and thousands. Pipe chocolate icing over the trunk.

Ottilie's Cake

A classic Continental chocolate cake

Saddle of Venison Cake

The special tin shown in the picture is used for this cake. It is stocked by specialist kitchen equipment shops

Quantities for 1 30cm/12in loaf
250g/8oz softened butter
200g/7oz sugar
1 tbsp vanilla sugar
Pinch of salt
4 eggs
1 tbsp rum
200g/7oz flour
50g/2oz cornflour
1 level tsp baking powder
100g/4oz plain chocolate
100g/4oz chopped almonds
50g/2oz candied lemon peel
3 tbsps apricot jam
100g/4oz chocolate cake covering
2 tbsps flaked almonds
Sprinkling of breadcrumbs

Preparation time: 40 minutes
Baking time: 1 hour
Final preparations: 15 minutes
Nutritional value:
Analysis per slice, approx, if divided into 20 slices:
• 1300kJ/310kcal
• 6g protein
• 21g fat • 30g carbohydrate

Cream the butter and gradually add the sugar, vanilla sugar, salt, eggs and rum. Sift the flour with the baking powder and cornflour and combine with the creamed butter mixture. Stir well. • Heat the oven to 180°C/ 350°F/Gas Mark 4. Grease the loaf tin well and sprinkle with a few breadcrumbs. • Grate the chocolate and stir into the mixture, together with the almonds and chopped candied lemon. • Pour the mixture into the tin, smooth the surface and bake on the lower shelf of the oven for 1 hour. • Leave the cake to cool completely before unmoulding it and placing it on a wire rack. • Sieve the apricot jam, warm it and brush it over the surface of the cake. Melt the chocolate cake covering and pour over the cake. While it is still moist, sprinkle with the flaked almonds.

Quantities for 1 saddle of venison tin
100g/4oz almonds
125g/5oz rusks or digestive biscuits
100g/4oz softened butter
150g/5¹/₂oz sugar
4-5 eggs (depending on size)
2 tbsps self-raising flour
200g/7oz plain baking chocolate
2 tbsps rum
25g/1oz creamed coconut
50g/2oz slivered or nibbed almonds
Sprinkling of breadcrumbs

Preparation time: 45 minutes
Baking time: 1 hour
Final preparations: 15 mins
Nutritional value:
Analysis per slice, approx, if divided into 15 slices:
• 1380kJ/330kcal
• 8g protein
• 21g fat
27g carbohydrate

Grind the almonds in a mill. Crush the rusks with a rolling pin between two sheets of foil and then reduce them to a powder in a mill. • Cream the butter and then sprinkle with the sugar. Add the eggs one at a time, followed by the ground almonds and rusks, flour and baking powder. Grate 100g/4oz chocolate and stir into the mixture, together with the rum. • Heat the oven to 180°C/ 350°F/Gas Mark 4. Butter the tin and sprinkle with breadcrumbs. • Pour the mixture into the tin and bake on the middle shelf for 1 hour. Test the centre of the cake with a skewer to see if it is done. Unmould the cake and leave it to cool on a wire rack. • Melt the remaining chocolate with the creamed coconut and pour this over the cake. Stick rows of slivered or nibbed almonds into the icing and leave to set.

Fit for a King

Delicious cakes with the emphasis on wholefood ingredients and plenty of dried fruit

King's Cake
Illustrated left

Quantities for 1 28cm/11in loaf tin

400g/14oz wholewheat flour
2 tsps baking powder
1 lemon, rind grated
200g/7oz softened butter
200g/7oz honey
1/2 tsp vanilla essence
4 eggs
3 tbsps rum
100g/4oz raisins
50g/2oz currants
100g/4oz diced mixed peel

Preparation time: 45 minutes
Baking time: 1 hour 10 minutes
Nutritional value:
Analysis per slice, approx, if divided into 14 slices:
- 1380kJ/330kcal
- 7g protein
- 21g fat
- 41g carbohydrate

Mix the flour, baking powder and grated lemon rind. Cream the butter, honey and vanilla. Slowly add the eggs, rum and flour to the creamed butter, stirring well. • Rinse the currants and raisins in hot water and stir into the mixture, together with the candied peel. Leave the mixture to rest for 30 minutes. • Heat the oven to 180°C/350°F/Gas Mark 4. Butter the tin. • Pour the mixture into the tin, smooth the surface and bake on the middle shelf for 70 minutes. To test if the cake is done, insert a skewer into the centre. If any of the mixture sticks to the skewer, the cake will require 10 more minutes in the oven. • Leave the cake to cool in the tin. • Allow a day for the full flavour of the cake to develop. If the cake is kept cool in a well-sealed tin, it will stay fresh for at least a week.

Emperor's Cake
Illustrated right

Quantities for 1 28cm/11in loaf tin

150g/5 1/2oz stoned prunes
150g/5 1/2oz walnuts
5 tbsps armagnac
75g/3oz diced candied peel
400g/14oz wholewheat flour
2 tsps baking powder
1/2 tsp vanilla essence
7 eggs
125g/5oz cold butter
75g/3oz honey
100g/4oz raw whole cane sugar
50g/2oz butter, melted

Preparation time: 1 hour
Baking time: 50 minutes
Nutritional value:
Analysis per slice, approx, if divided into 12 slices:
- 2100kJ/500kcal
- 14g protein
- 32g fat
- 43g carbohydrate

Chop the prunes and walnuts and soak them in the armagnac, with the candied peel. • Mix 250g/8oz flour with 1 tsp of the baking powder. Separate the eggs. Cut the butter into knobs and mix with the flour mixture, together with the honey, vanilla and 1 egg yolk. Knead well and leave to chill. • Beat the remaining egg yolks with the brown sugar and 2 tbsps warm water. Add the remaining flour and baking powder. Whisk the egg whites until stiff and fold into the cake mixture. • Heat the oven to 180°C/350°F/Gas Mark 4. Butter the tin. • Roll out the dough and use it line the tin, making a 3-cm/1-in rim. Mix the armagnac-soaked fruit and nuts and the melted butter into the cake mixture and pour this over the dough base. Cut the surplus dough into strips to make a lattice pattern. • Bake for 50 minutes.

Spotted Egg Slice

This delicious sheet cake comes from Dresden

Quantities for 1 baking sheet or Swiss roll tin:

FOR THE YEAST DOUGH:

500g/1lb 2oz flour

45g/1½oz fresh yeast or 1 sachet dried yeast • 100g/4oz sugar

250ml/8 fl oz lukewarm milk

100g/4oz softened butter

Pinch of salt

FOR THE TOPPING:

7 eggs • 125g/5oz softened butter

100g/4oz sugar

2 tbsps vanilla sugar

300g/10oz full-fat cream cheese

50g/2oz cornflour

150g/5½oz sultanas, washed

100g/4oz flaked almonds

Zest of ½ lemon

Preparation time: 1 hour
Baking time: 45 minutes
Nutritional value:

Analysis per slice, approx, if divided into 20 slices:
• 1510kJ/360kcal • 11g protein
• 18g fat • 38g carbohydrate

Sift the flour into a bowl and make a well in the centre. Add the crumbled fresh yeast or the dried yeast, 1 tsp sugar, 4 tbsps flour and 4 tbsps milk. Cover the starter dough and leave to rise in a warm place for 15 minutes. • Knead the flour, butter, salt and the remaining sugar and milk with the starter dough. Cover and leave for a further 45 minutes, or until light and fluffy. • Roll out the dough onto a buttered baking sheet or Swiss roll tin. If using a baking sheet, take a strip of aluminium foil, fold it twice and place it against the open side of the dough to keep a clean rim. • Heat the oven to 200°C/ 400°F/Gas Mark 6. • Separate the eggs. Cream the butter with the sugar and vanilla sugar and gradually add the egg yolks, cheese and cornflour. Whisk the egg whites until they form stiff peaks. Add 50g/2oz flaked almonds, the sultanas and grated lemon rind to the quark mixture. • Spread the mixture evenly over the base, and sprinkle with the remaining almonds. Bake on the lower shelf of the oven for 45 minutes, or until golden.

Popular Cakes for Family Gatherings

Crumble toppings on yeast and sponge cake bases

Chocolate Crumble Cake

Illustrated left

Quantities for 1 26cm/10in springform tin

75g/3oz butter • 75g/3oz sugar	
1 tbsp vanilla sugar • 1 egg	
1 lemon, rind grated, juiced	
150g/5½oz flour	
50g/2oz cornflour	
2 tsps baking powder	
3-4 tbsps milk	
3 tbsps apricot jam, sieved	
500g/1lb 2oz ripe apricots	

FOR THE CRUMBLE:

150g/5½oz flour	
25g/1oz cocoa powder	
100g/4oz sugar	
1 tbsp vanilla sugar	
100g/4oz softened butter	
1 tbsp icing sugar	

Preparation time: 40 minutes
Baking time: 50 minutes
Nutritional value:

Analysis per slice, approx, if divided into 12 slices:
- 1380kJ/330kcal • 5g protein
- 14g fat • 49g carbohydrate

Cream the butter. Add the sugar, vanilla sugar, egg, grated lemon rind and juice. Mix the flour with the cornflour and baking powder. Stir the milk and flour into the creamed butter and sugar. • Butter the tin and pour in the cake mixture. • Mix the apricot jam with 1 tbsp hot water. Stir well and then spread over the cake mixture. Wash the apricots, dry, halve and stone them and arrange them on top of the mixture. • Heat the oven to 200°C/400°F/Gas Mark 6. • To make the crumble, mix together all the ingredients, apart from the icing sugar. Sprinkle this over the apricots. • Bake for 50 minutes. Switch off the oven and leave the cake for a further 10 minutes. • Sift the icing sugar over the cool cake.

Crumble Cheesecake

Illustrated right

Quantities for 1 baking sheet

20g/½oz fresh yeast or ½ tsp dried yeast • 75g/3oz sugar	
250ml/8 fl oz milk	
500g/1lb 2oz flour	
75g/3oz softened butter	
Pinch of salt • 2 eggs	
500g/1lb 2oz low-fat soft cheese	
100g/4oz sugar	
25g/1oz cornflour	
100g/4oz raisins • 200g/7oz flour	
50g/2oz ground almonds	
100g/4oz sugar	
150g/5½oz butter	

Preparation time: 50 minutes
Rising time: 1 hour
Baking time: 30 minutes
Nutritional value:

Analysis per slice, approx, if divided into 20 slices:
- 1380kJ/330kcal • 10g protein
- 13g fat • 46g carbohydrate

Crumble the yeast and mix with 1 tsp sugar and 4 tbsps milk. Leave to rise in a warm place for 15 minutes. • Add 250g/8oz of the flour, butter, the remaining milk and the salt. Add the rest of the flour and knead well into a firm dough. Use a little more flour if necessary. Cover the dough and leave for 45 minutes. • Separate the eggs. Mix the soft cheese with the sugar, egg yolks and cornflour. Whisk the egg whites until they form stiff peaks and fold them into the quark mixture, together with the raisins. • Knead the yeast dough again and roll it out on a well-buttered baking sheet. Coat with the cheese mixture. • Heat the oven to 200°C/400°F/Gas Mark 6. • Cream the butter with the sugar and rub in the flour and almonds to make the crumble topping. Sprinkle evenly over the quark mixture. • Bake for 30 minutes. Switch off oven and leave cake to cool for 10 minutes.

Traditional Afternoon Tea Cakes

Your guests will enthuse over these two cheesecakes – one with and one without a base

Poppyseed Cheesecake

Illustrated right

Quantities for 1 28cm/11in springform tin

FOR THE SWEET SHORTCRUST DOUGH:

250g/8oz flour

Pinch of baking powder

1 egg yolk • 150g/5½oz butter

50g/2oz sugar • 1 tbsp vanilla sugar

FOR THE POPPYSEED FILLING:

75g/3oz raisins • 2 tbsps rum

250g/8oz ground poppyseeds

125g/5oz sugar • Zest of ½ lemon

½ tsp ground cinnamon

50g/2oz softened butter

125ml/4 fl oz milk

FOR THE CHEESE TOPPING:

500g/1lb 2oz quark (20% fat)

125g/5oz sugar • 2 eggs

2 tbsps lemon juice

100g/4oz crème fraîche

3 tbsps cornflour

1 egg yolk, for glaze

Preparation time: 1 hour
Baking time: 1¼ hours
Nutritional value:

Analysis per slice, approx, if divided into 16 slices:
• 1890kJ/450kcal • 12g protein
• 25g fat • 38g carbohydrate

Mix the flour, baking powder, egg yolk, butter, sugar and vanilla sugar into a workable dough. Cover with clingfilm and refrigerate for at least 30 minutes. • Wash the raisins in hot water, dry them well and soak in rum. • Mix the poppyseeds with the sugar, grated lemon rind, cinnamon and butter. Warm the milk, pour it over the poppyseed mixture, cover and leave to stand. • Mix the sugar into the quark. Separate the eggs. Whisk the egg whites to form stiff peaks. Mix the egg yolks with the lemon juice, crème fraîche and cornflour and add to the cheese. Stir well and then fold in the beaten egg whites. • Heat the oven to 180°C/

350°F/Gas Mark 4. • Roll out a thin sheet of dough. Butter the tin and line it with the dough, making a 3-cm/1-in rim. • Mix the raisins with the poppyseeds and spoon over the pastry base, followed by an even layer of the cheese mixture. • Bake the cake on the lower shelf for 75 minutes. • After 45 minutes, beat the egg yolk with 1 tbsp water and brush it over the surface.

No-base Cheesecake

Illustrated left

Quantities for 1 28cm/11in springform tin

6 eggs • 125g/5oz softened butter

250g/8oz sugar

750g/1lb 11oz low-fat quark

500g/1lb 2oz mascarpone or full-fat cream cheese

Packet of custard powder

3 tbsps cornflour

Sprinkling of breadcrumbs

Preparation time: 20 minutes
Baking time: 1½ hours
Nutritional value:

Analysis per slice, approx, if divided into 12 slices:
• 1890kJ/450kcal
• 20g protein
• 28g fat
• 30g carbohydrate

Separate the eggs. • Cream the butter with the sugar. Add the egg yolks one at a time. Drain the quark. Combine the cheeses with the custard powder and mix this with the butter and egg mixture. Whisk the egg whites into stiff peaks and fold into the cream mixture, together with the cornflour. • Heat the oven to 180°C/350°F/Gas Mark 4. Butter the tin and sprinkle with a few breadcrumbs. • Spoon in the cream mixture and bake for 1 hour 30 minutes, or until golden brown.

Savarin

This famous yeast cake can be soaked in rum or brandy and decorated with a variety of fruits

Quantities for 1 savarin tin

FOR THE RING:

45g/1¹/₂oz fresh yeast or 1 sachet dried yeast • 50g/2oz sugar

125ml/4 fl oz lukewarm milk

125g/5oz softened butter

1 tbsp vanilla sugar • Pinch of salt

4 eggs • 350g/11oz flour

FOR THE PEACH SAVARIN:

750g/1lb 11oz peaches

250ml/8 fl oz passion fruit juice or peach juice • Juice of 1 lemon

125ml/4 fl oz apricot liqueur

125ml/4 fl oz whipping cream ·

4 tbsps advocaat

1 tbsp chopped pistachios

FOR THE CRANBERRY SAVARIN:

100g/4oz sugar

125ml/4 fl oz each Madeira and water • 200g/7oz apricot jam

125ml/4 fl oz whipping cream

1 tsp vanilla essence

1 tsp sugar

400g/14oz cranberry sauce

FOR THE ORANGE SAVARIN:

6 oranges

5 tbsps Cointreau

Juice of 1 lemon

6 tbsps white rum

75g/3oz sugar

125ml/4 fl oz water

200g/7oz clear orange marmalade, strained

125ml/4 fl oz whipping cream

25g/1oz cooking chocolate

Preparation time: 20 minutes
Rising time: 1 hour
Baking time: 40 minutes
Final preparation time: 30 minutes in each case
Nutritional value:
Analysis per slice, approx, if divided into 20 slices:
• 1680kJ/400kcal • 6g protein
• 15g fat • 59g carbohydrate

Crumble the yeast and mix with 1 tsp of sugar and a little milk. Leave to rise in a warm place for 15 minutes. • Cream the butter with the remaining sugar and milk, vanilla sugar, salt and eggs. Add the flour and then combine with the fermenting yeast. Knead the dough thoroughly, cover it with clingfilm and leave for 30 minutes. Pour into a greased tin, cover and leave for a further 15 minutes. • Heat the oven to 200°C/400°F/Gas Mark 6. • Bake on the bottom shelf for 40 minutes. Unmould when completely cooled. • For the peach savarin, dip the peaches in boiling water, skin, quarter and stone them. Bring the passion fruit juice or peach juice to the boil, together with the lemon juice and apricot liqueur. • Pour into the savarin tin and return the cake to the tin. Unmould when all the liquid has been absorbed. • Whip the cream with the advocaat. Place the peach segments in the centre of the cake and pipe the whipped cream on them. Sprinkle with pistachios. • For the cranberry savarin, heat the sugar in a dry frying pan to caramelise it and then add the Madeira and water. Pour the liquid into the bottom of the tin and add the baked cake. Unmould when all the liquid has been absorbed. Brush the surface with warmed apricot jam. Combine the cream, vanilla essence and sugar and whip until stiff. Fill the centre of the cake with the cranberry sauce and pipe the whipped cream on top. • For the orange savarin, peel 4 oranges and remove the pith. Cut into slices, quarter and soak in Cointreau. Squeeze the juice from the remaining oranges. Boil the juice with the lemon juice, rum, sugar and water. Pour the liquid into the tin and add the baked cake. Unmould when all the liquid has been absorbed. Heat the strained marmalade and brush it over the cake. Whip the cream. Grate the chocolate and mix with the cream. Fill the centre of the cake with the oranges and top with the chocolate cream.

Cakes and Gateaux for Special Occasions

A lot easier to make than you think these wonderful cakes are sure to create a festive atmosphere

Icings and Cake Decorations

Chocolate Icing

Chocolate icing can be used as a cake covering or for decoration. The melted chocolate can be brushed onto a greased surface and then scraped into chocolate curls, also known as caraque. Washed rose leaves can be dipped in the liquid chocolate, or painted with it, and then the thin layer of chocolate peeled off when the chocolate has solidified.

1 Warm a little apricot jam, strain it, and then brush it over the surface of the cake base. It may be necessary to dilute the jam with 1 tablespoon of water.

2 Knead 175g/6oz marzipan with 100g/4oz icing sugar, roll out and then position on the cake base with a rolling pin.

3 Break up the chocolate couverture and melt it in a bain-marie. Leave to cool and then reheat to 32°C/90°F. Use it to cover the cake.

4 Mark out portions on the soft glaze. Decorate the cake with glacé cherries and chocolate leaves dusted with icing sugar.

Cream Icings

Buttercream and whipped cream are both ideal for piping with either a star-shaped or a fluted nozzle. Celebration cakes can be topped with rosettes of whipped cream.

1 Cover the cake with the cream and then press chopped hazelnuts, toasted almonds or chocolate strands into the sides.

2 Place a biscuit cutter in the middle of the cake and sprinkle chopped hazelnuts, flaked almonds or chocolate strands inside.

3 Fill a piping bag with cream and decorate the top of the cake with whirls, rosettes, dots and swags.

4 Complete the decoration with whole hazelnuts, candied fruit or coffee powder.

The crowning glory of a cake or gâteau is undoubtedly the decoration. Covering a cake with wafer-thin layers of marzipan or chocolate icing, piping delicate cream garlands or shaping sugar icing needs practice. Patterns are easy to make with the help of templates. Simply dust with icing sugar or cocoa powder.

Decorative Icing

For royal icing, mix 250g/8oz icing sugar with 1 egg white, a little lemon juice or rum and food colouring as necessary.

1 Ice the cake with thick white icing and smooth the surface with a spatula. Leave to set.

2 Mix more sifted icing sugar, cocoa powder or food colouring with the remaining icing. Half-fill a plastic bag with the icing.

3 Snip the tip of the bag, squeeze gently and write a message or make a floral design.

4 Finish with sugared almonds, candied violets, iced garlands or marzipan flowers. Many different types of icing decorations are available commercially.

'Dry' Decorations

Plain cakes or cream-covered gâteaux can be dusted with cocoa or icing sugar. There is no limit to the type of patterns that can be created.

1 Place 1cm/½in-wide cardboard strips over the cake and sift icing sugar over them. Remove the strips carefully.

2 First sift cocoa powder over the surface of the cake. Cover with a cake doily and sift a layer of icing sugar over it. Remove the doily carefully.

3 A cake coated with buttercream can be covered with any cardboard template. Sprinkle with cocoa.

4 Sift a thick layer of icing sugar over the top of the cake. Cover all but the edge with a prepared template to create a garland or star effect. Dust with cocoa and remove the template carefully.

Cool and Refreshing Summer Cakes

Fruity 'frosted' desserts that can easily be prepared in advance

Iced Raspberry Gâteau

Illustrated left

Quantities for 1 24cm/9½in tin
4 eggs • Pinch of salt
300g/10oz sugar
100g/4oz flour
100g/4oz cornflour
1 tsp baking powder
200g/7oz raspberries
4 tsps raspberry liqueur
400ml/15 fl oz whipping cream
1 tbsp icing sugar

Preparation time: 40 minutes
Resting time: 1 day
Baking time: 35 minutes
Setting time: 6 hours
Nutritional value:
Analysis per slice, approx, if divided into 12 slices:
• 1380kJ/330kcal • 6g protein
• 15g fat • 42g carbohydrate

Separate the eggs and whisk the whites with the salt and 50g/2oz sugar until they form stiff peaks. Beat the yolks with 4 tbsps warm water. Gradually add 150g/5½oz sugar. Combine the flour, cornflour and baking powder with the beaten egg whites and fold into the beaten eggs. • Heat the oven to 180°C/350°F/Gas Mark 4. • Bake for 35 minutes. Leave to rest for 24 hours. • Pour the raspberry liqueur over the raspberries. • Slice the cake crossways into two layers and return the bottom layer to the tin. • Whip the cream until stiff, gradually adding the rest of the sugar. Place 4 tbsps whipped cream into a piping bag fitted with a star nozzle. • Drain the raspberries and reserve 12 for the final decorations. Mix the remaining raspberries with the whipped cream and spread them over the bottom layer. • Add the top half and press down gently. Dust with icing sugar and decorate with cream and raspberries. • Freeze for at least 6 hours.

Pineapple Yogurt Cake

Illustrated right

Quantities for 1 28cm/11in tin
225g/8oz flour • 100g/4oz butter
1 egg yolk • Pinch of salt
50g/2oz sugar
1 tbsp vanilla sugar
1 packet unflavoured gelatine
500ml/18 fl oz thick-set yogurt
100g/4oz sugar
Zest of ½ lemon
2 tbsps lemon juice
400ml/15 fl oz whipping cream
1 450g/14oz tin pineapple rings
1 packet lemon jelly glaze
150g/5½oz frozen raspberries

Preparation time: 2 hours
Resting time: about 6 hours
Nutritional value:
Analysis per slice, approx, if divided into 12 slices:
• 1170kJ/280kcal • 5g protein
• 16g fat • 30g carbohydrate

Mix together the flour, butter, egg yolk, salt, sugar and vanilla sugar and knead to a workable dough. Cover with clingfilm and leave to chill for 1 hour in the refrigerator. Roll out the dough and use it to line the tin. Prick the dough all over and bake blind for 20 minutes. • Dissolve the gelatine in 125ml/4 fl oz hot water. • Stir the sugar, grated lemon rind and juice into the yogurt. Whip the cream until stiff. • Drain the pineapple and reserve 6 tbsps of the juice. Heat the juice to below boiling point, add the dissolved gelatine and stir well. Stir this into the yogurt and refrigerate for 20 minutes, or until cooled but not set. Fold in the whipped cream. • Pour the mixture over the pastry base and place in the refrigerator until firm. • Prepare the glaze. • Arrange the pineapple slices and raspberries over the yogurt and coat with the glaze. • Return to the refrigerator and leave to set for 5 hours.

St Honoré Meringue

A variation of the famous St Honoré gâteau, using a meringue base instead of choux pastry

Quantities for 1 26cm/10in flan
FOR THE MERINGUE:
4 egg whites • Pinch of salt
200g/7oz sugar
1 tsp vanilla sugar
FOR THE CHOUX PASTE:
125ml/4 fl oz water
50g/2oz butter • Pinch of salt
75g/3oz flour • 2 eggs
FOR THE CUSTARD TOPPING:
½ packet gelatine
50g/2oz cornflour • 4 egg yolks
500ml/18 fl oz milk
75g/3oz sugar • 1 vanilla pod
200ml/6 fl oz whipping cream
2 tbsps orange liqueur
FOR THE SUGAR SYRUP:
100ml/3 fl oz water
200g/7oz sugar

Preparation time: 2 hours
Drying time: 5 hours
Nutritional value:
Analysis per slice, approx, if
divided into 12 slices:
• 2010kJ/480kcal • 13g protein
• 22g fat • 56g carbohydrate

Heat the oven to 100°C/
212°F/Gas Mark ¼. Line the
tin. • Whisk the egg whites with
the salt, sugar and vanilla sugar,
until stiff. Pipe the egg whites over
the base of the tin. Dry the
meringue in the oven for 5 hours
at the lowest setting with the door
ajar. • Boil the water with the
butter and salt, stirring in the
flour. Add the eggs. • Pipe
walnut-sized whirls of choux paste
onto a buttered tin. Bake for 15
minutes at 200°C/400°F/Gas
Mark 6. • Dissolve the gelatine in
125ml/4 fl oz hot water. Beat the
cornflour with the egg yolks and a
little milk. Bring the rest of the
milk to the boil with the sugar and
vanilla pod. Stir in the egg yolk
mixture and return to the boil.
Remove from the heat and add
the gelatine. Whip the cream until
stiff. Add the liqueur and mix with
the cooled custard and the beaten
egg whites. • Pipe custard into
the choux pastry whirls. Cover the
meringue base with the rest. •
Boil the sugar and water in a pan
for 5 minutes. • Dip the whirls in
the syrup and arrange on the
custard topping.

Sharon Fruit Torte

The bright orange sharon fruit, also known as persimmon or kaki, is in season from November

Quantities for 1 26cm/10in springform tin

175g/6oz flour	
50g/2oz ground almonds	
75g/3oz icing sugar	
100g/4oz cold butter	

FOR THE TOPPING:

100g/4oz softened butter	
2 tbsps advocaat	
1 tbsp icing sugar	
2 tbsps vanilla sugar	
4-5 sharon fruit	
4 tbsps apricot jam	
1 tbsp Cointreau	
200ml/6 fl oz whipping cream	
1 tbsp sugar	
1 tbsp chopped pistachio nuts	

Preparation time: 20 minutes
Resting time: 30 minutes
Baking time: 20 minutes
Final preparations: 30 mins
Nutritional value:
Analysis per slice, approx, if divided into 12 slices:
- 1590kJ/380kcal
- 4g protein
- 22g fat
- 38g carbohydrate

Mix together the flour, almonds and icing sugar. Cut the butter into knobs and add to the flour. Using cold hands, quickly knead to a workable dough. Cover with clingfilm, and place in the refrigerator to chill for 30 minutes. • Heat the oven to 200°C/400°F/Gas Mark 6. • Roll out the dough on a floured worktop. Lightly butter the springform tin. Place the dough inside the tin and pinch up a 2cm/1in rim. • Bake blind on the middle shelf of the oven for 20 minutes. • Leave the pastry case to cool in the tin. • Cream the butter with the advocaat, icing sugar and vanilla sugar. Coat the pastry base with the creamed butter mixture. Peel the sharon fruit, cut into thin slices and arrange it over the cream. Combine the apricot jam and Cointreau, quickly heat through, and allow to cool. Pour this over the sharon fruit as a glaze. • Just prior to serving, whip the cream and sugar until stiff, pipe around the rim of the torte and sprinkle with chopped pistachio nuts.

Shortcrust Pastry Bases with Fruity Fillings

Lightly whipped vanilla cream or rich custard is ideal with dainty fruit flans

Lemon Tart
Illustrated left

Quantities for 1 24cm/9¹/₂in flan

FOR THE DOUGH:

300g/10oz flour	
1 tbsp sugar	
Pinch of salt	
150g/5¹/₂oz cold butter, diced	
1 egg	

FOR THE CREAM FILLING:

1 egg • 75g/3oz sugar	
100g/4oz blanched, finely ground almonds	
Juice of 1¹/₂ lemons	

FOR THE TOPPING:

3 lemons • 1 vanilla pod	
250g/8oz sugar	

Preparation time: 1 hour
Baking time: 30 minutes
Nutritional value:
Analysis per slice, approx, if divided into 12 slices:
• 1680kJ/400kcal • 7g protein
• 21g fat • 50g carbohydrate

Mix the butter with the flour, sugar and egg. Knead to a smooth dough, wrap in clingfilm and refrigerate for at least 30 minutes • Heat the oven to 200°C/400°F/Gas Mark 6. Roll out the dough, line the buttered tin and pinch up a 2cm/1in rim. Bake blind on the lower shelf for 15 minutes. • Beat the egg with the sugar. Add the almonds and lemon juice. Spoon the filling over the pastry case and bake on the middle shelf for 10 to 15 minutes. • Wash the lemons in hot water and cut into thin slices. Slit open the vanilla pod and scrape out the pulp. Mix the pulp and pod with the sugar and 375ml /12 fl oz water. Bring to the boil and simmer the lemon slices in the syrup for 10 to 15 minutes. Drain, reserving the water, and arrange the lemon slices on the cooled topping. Boil the reserved liquid until it turns to a jelly and then spread over the lemon slices.

Orange Tart
Illustrated right

Quantities for 1 24cm/9¹/₂in flan

FOR THE DOUGH:

250g/8oz flour	
100g/4oz icing sugar	
150g/5¹/₂oz butter	
Pinch of salt	
1 lemon, rind grated	

FOR THE CREAM FILLING:

50g/2oz softened butter	
2 eggs	
75g/3oz sugar	
1 orange	
1 tbsp cornflour	

FOR THE TOPPING:

3-4 oranges	
2 tbsps marmalade	
1-2 tbsps orange liqueur	

Preparation time: 1 hour
Baking time: 40-45 minutes
Nutritional value:
Analysis per slice, approx, if divided into 12 slices:
• 1380kJ/330kcal • 5g protein
• 16g fat • 40g carbohydrate

Mix all the dough ingredients with 2 tbsps ice-cold water and quickly knead to a workable dough. Wrap the dough in clingfilm and refrigerate for at least 30 minutes • Heat the oven to 200°C/400°F/Gas Mark 6. • Roll out the dough, line the lightly buttered tin and bake for 15 minutes. • Cream the butter, adding the eggs and sugar. Grate the orange rind with a zester. Squeeze the juice from the orange. Add the grated rind and juice to the creamed butter, together with the cornflour. Pour the filling into the pastry base and bake for a further 15 minutes. • Peel the oranges, discarding all the white pith. Cut the oranges into thin slices and lay them on the cream filling. Place the tart under the grill for 10 to 15 minutes. • Combine the marmalade and orange liqueur and pour over the hot fruit slices.

Devil's Food Kiwi Cake

Kiwi fruit makes an elegant filling and topping for this delicious chocolate sponge which must be made 24 hours in advance

Quantities for 1 26cm/10in springform tin
FOR THE SPONGE:
6 eggs
Pinch of salt
150g/5¹/₂oz sugar
100g/4oz flour
50g/2oz cornflour
75g/3oz cocoa powder
1 tsp baking powder
FOR THE FILLING AND COATING:
1 packet unflavoured gelatine
4-5 kiwi fruit
50g/2oz icing sugar
600ml/1 pint whipping cream
1 tbsp vanilla sugar
25g/1oz flaked almonds
3 tbsps rum
Butter and dry breadcrumbs for the tin

Preparation time: 20 minutes
Baking time: 30 minutes
Resting time: 1 day
Final preparations: 1¹/₂ hours

Nutritional value:
Analysis per slice, approx, if divided into 16 slices:
- 1510kJ/360kcal
- 9g protein
- 22g fat
- 29g carbohydrate

Heat the oven to 180°C/350°F/Gas Mark 4. • Separate the eggs. • Combine the egg yolks with 2 tbsps water and the remaining sugar. Combine the flour, cornflour, cocoa powder and baking powder. Sift this over the egg yolks. Whisk the egg whites with the salt into stiff peaks, slowly adding half the sugar. Fold everything into the egg yolks with a spatula. • Butter the base of the springform tin and sprinkle with breadcrumbs. Pour the mixture into the tin and bake on the middle shelf for 30 minutes. • Release the sponge from the tin and leave to rest for 24 hours, before cutting into slices. • For the cream filling, dissolve the gelatine

in 125ml/4fl oz hot water. Peel the kiwi fruit, reserving one for the decoration. • Chop the other kiwi fruit finely or purée in a liquidiser. Add the icing sugar to the purée and warm through. Whip the cream and vanilla sugar until stiff. Add the whipping cream to the dissolved gelatine a tbsp at a time. Place one third of the cream in the refrigerator to chill. Mix the remainder with the cooled fruit purée. • Chill the fruit cream for 30 minutes. • Toast the flaked almonds in a dry frying pan until golden brown. • Cut the sponge cake twice crossways into three layers. Sprinkle rum over all three layers. Spread the fruit cream on to the bottom and middle layers and then re-assemble the cake. Cover the whole cake with the whipped cream. Attach a star nozzle to a piping bag, fill with the remaining cream and pipe a number of whirls around the top of the cake. Sprinkle the toasted almonds in the centre. Cut the

reserved kiwi fruit into slices and arrange them on top of the cream whirls. • Refrigerate the cake until required, but do not store for too long or the otherwise subtle flavours can become too powerful.

Tropical Cream Cheese Gâteau

Tropical fruits such as mango and kiwi add a special touch

Quantities for 1 28cm/11in tin
3 eggs • 50g/2oz sugar
1 tbsp vanilla sugar
50g/2oz flour • 25g/1oz cornflour
25g/1oz ground hazelnuts
1 packet unflavoured gelatine
500g/1lb 2oz low-fat quark
250g/8oz full-fat cream cheese or mascarpone • 100g/4oz sugar
125ml/4fl oz thick-set yogurt
3 tbsps advocaat
Rind and juice of 1 lemon
400ml/15 fl oz whipping cream
2 tbsps amaretto liqueur
1 large mango • 4 kiwis
125g/4oz flaked almonds
FOR THE TOPPING:
250ml/8 fl oz whipping cream
4 tbsps icing sugar
2 kiwis • 1 medium mango

Preparation time: 6 hours
Baking time: 20 minutes
Nutritional value:
Analysis per slice, approx, if divided into 16 slices:
• 1300kJ/310kcal • 12g protein
• 17g fat • 24g carbohydrate

Heat the oven to 180°C/350°F/Gas Mark 4. • Separate the eggs and whisk the whites until stiff. Beat the yolks with the sugar and vanilla sugar. Fold the flour, cornflour, hazelnuts and whisked whites into the beaten yolks. Bake for 20 minutes. • Dissolve the gelatine in 125ml/4 fl oz hot water. • Drain the quark and then mix with the cream cheese, sugar, yogurt, advocaat and grated lemon rind. • Heat lemon juice with 2 tbsps water. Add the gelatine to the hot lemon water and quark mixture and leave in the refrigerator until partially set. • Whip the cream and stir it into the cheese mixture. • Sprinkle the sponge with amaretto and return to the tin. Line the base and rim of the tin. • Arrange kiwi and mango slices alternately on the sponge base. Spread the cheese mixture over them. Toast the almonds and press them around the cake. Refrigerate for 4 hours until set. Whip cream with icing sugar until stiff, and pipe over cake. Decorate with the kiwi and mango.

Frankfurt Ring

A particularly delicious variation of a traditional layer cake with three different fillings

Quantities for 1 ring

FOR THE DOUGH:

250g/8oz softened butter

150g/5¹/₂oz sugar • 5 eggs

1 tbsp lemon juice

350g/11oz flour

150g/5¹/₂oz cornflour

Sachet of baking powder

FOR THE FILLING:

250g/8oz softened butter

200g/7oz icing sugar

2 egg yolks • 2 tbsps vanilla sugar

200g/7oz marzipan

2 tbsps orange liqueur

225g/8oz marmalade

FOR THE CRUNCHY COATING:

25g/1oz butter

125g/5oz chopped almonds

50g/2oz sugar • 2 mandarins

Preparation time: 15 minutes
Baking time: 50 minutes
Final preparations: 45 mins
Nutritional value:
Analysis per slice, approx, if
divided into 20 slices:
• 2390kJ/570kcal • 9g protein
• 33g fat • 57g carbohydrate

Heat the oven to 180°C/
350°F/Gas Mark 4. • Cream
the butter and sugar. Add the eggs
and lemon juice. Mix the flour,
baking powder and cornflour and
spoon into the butter. Pour the
mixture into the oiled tin and bake
for 50 minutes. • Switch off the
oven and leave to stand for 10
minutes. Allow to cool. • To make
the buttercream, cream the butter
with the icing sugar and then add
the egg yolks and vanilla sugar. •
Add the liqueur and water to the
marzipan and blend until it is of
spreading consistency. • To make
the coating, heat the butter, add
the almonds and sugar and then
caramelise until golden brown.
Leave to cool. • Remove the ring
from the tin and slice it carefully
crossways into three. Cover the
bottom layer with a third of the
filling. Spread marmalade over the
middle layer and cover the top
layer with marzipan. • Re-
assemble the ring and cover first
with the remaining filling and then
with the crunchy coating. • Top
with buttercream whirls and
mandarin segments.

Banana Gâteau

Most of the ingredients are available from health food shops

Quantities for 1 26cm/10in tin
4 eggs
150g/5¹/₂oz raw cane sugar
100g/4oz wholewheat flour
25g/1oz cocoa powder
1 tsp baking powder
1 tsp ground cinnamon
500g/1lb 2oz bananas
50g/2oz butter • 100g/4oz honey
100g/4oz ground rice
¹/₂ tsp ground cinnamon
2 tbsps rum
400ml/15 fl oz whipping cream
1 tsp vanilla essence
50g/2oz banana chips
6 glacé cherries
50g/2oz plain cooking chocolate

Preparation time: 15 minutes
Baking time: 25 minutes
Final preparations: 1¹/₂ hours
Nutritional value:
Analysis per slice, approx, if divided into 12 slices:
• 1800kJ/430kcal • 9g protein
• 21g fat • 48g carbohydrate

Heat oven to 200°C/400°F/ Gas Mark 6. • Separate the eggs and beat yolks with 100g/4oz cane sugar and 2 tbsps warm water. Mix the flour with the cocoa powder, baking powder and cinnamon and stir into the egg yolks. Whisk the whites until they form stiff peaks. Fold into the egg and flour mixture. • Bake for 25 minutes, leave to cool and then cut into two layers. • Peel and slice the bananas. Bring 250ml/8 fl oz water to the boil, together with the butter and honey. Add ground rice and bananas, stirring constantly for 5 minutes. Remove pan from heat and add the cinnamon and rum. Spread the banana mixture over the bottom sponge layer. Leave to cool. • Whip cream with remaining cane sugar and vanilla until stiff. Spread a third of the cream onto the banana mixture. Place the upper cake base on top. Decorate with piped cream, grated chocolate, cherries and banana chips.

Viennese Punch Gâteau

A classic gâteau with an unusual filling

Quantities for 1 24cm/9¹/₂in tin
6 eggs • 125g/5oz sugar
150g/5¹/₂oz flour
75g/3oz cornflour
2 tsps baking powder
4 tbsps rum
300g/10oz apricot jam
Juice of 2 oranges and 1 lemon
200g/7oz icing sugar
¹/₂ tsp cocoa powder

Preparation time: 20 minutes
Baking time: 45 minutes
Resting time: 2 days
Final preparations: 1 hour
Nutritional value:
Analysis per slice, approx, if divided into 12 slices:
• 1380kJ/330kcal • 8g protein
• 6g fat • 58g carbohydrate

Heat oven to 180°C/350°F/ Gas Mark 4. • Separate eggs and whisk whites until stiff. Beat yolks with 100g/4oz sugar. Fold in the whisked whites, flour, cornflour and baking powder. •

Bake mixture for 45 minutes. Leave for 1 day to rest, then slice sponge into three layers. Cut middle layer into 2cm/1in cubes. Sprinkle one third of the rum over the other two layers, and spread with 200g/7oz apricot jam. • Place bottom layer inside the rim of the springform tin. Heat orange and lemon juice, one third of the rum, 50g/2oz jam and remaining sugar and add the sponge cubes. Stir thoroughly. Spoon mixture over the bottom layer and then carefully position upper layer on top. Press lightly. • Leave cake to stand for 1 hour with a weighted board on top. Warm the remaining jam and brush it over the surface of the cake. • Mix icing sugar with remaining rum. Stir the cocoa powder into 2 tbsps of icing sugar. • Glaze cake with white icing and then pipe a spiral of chocolate icing, starting from the middle of the cake. Draw a knife from the middle outwards to create a spider's web effect.

Lemon Gâteau

A delicious, fruity cake with layers of meringue and cream. Preparation start the day before.

Quantities for 1 24cm/9¹/₂in springform tin
FOR THE CREAM FILLING:
2 lemons
125g/5oz sugar
2¹/₂ tsps cornflour
400ml/15 fl oz whipping cream
FOR THE CAKE MIXTURE:
125g/5oz softened butter
125g/5oz sugar
4 egg yolks
1 egg
Pinch of salt
1 tbsp vanilla sugar
2 tsps baking powder
150g/5¹/₂oz flour
2 tbsps milk
FOR THE MERINGUE:
4 egg whites
200g/7oz sugar
TO FINISH:
50g/2oz flaked almonds

Preparation time: 45 minutes
Cooling time: 12 hours

Baking time: 25 minutes
Final preparations: 30 minutes
Resting time: 2 hours
Nutritional value:
Analysis per slice, approx, if divided into 12 slices:
- 2010kJ/480kcal
- 8g protein
- 26g fat
- 51g carbohydrate

First prepare the filling. Grate the rind from one lemon and squeeze the juice from both of them. Combine the grated lemon rind and juice and make the liquid up to 125ml/4 fl oz with water. Add the sugar and bring to the boil. Stir the cornflour into 3 tbsps cold water to make a smooth paste, add to the lemon juice and return to the boil. • Cover the cooled lemon cream and leave overnight in the refrigerator. • For the sponge mixture, cream the butter. Gradually add the sugar, followed by the egg yolks, whole egg, salt and vanilla sugar. Combine the baking powder and flour and stir into the milk. • To make the meringue, whisk the egg whites to make soft peaks. Slowly add the sugar while whisking. • Heat the oven to 180°C/ 350°F/Gas Mark 4. If possible, use two identical springform tins and butter both bases. Divide the cake mixture equally between the two tins. • Cover with the whisked egg whites leaving a margin of 1cm/¹/₂in around the edge of the tin. Sprinkle with a few flaked almonds. • Bake the sponge layers on the middle shelf of the oven for 25 minutes. If only one springform tin is available, then the process simply has to be repeated. Leave the sponge layers to cool on a wire rack. • To make the cream filling, whip the cream until stiff and then add the chilled lemon cream. Place one sponge layer on a board and cover with two thirds of the cream. Place the other layer on top and press down lightly. Spread the rest of the cream around the sides of the cake. • Chill the cake for at least 2 hours for the full flavour to develop. It will keep for several days.

Our tip: For special occasions, the cake can be finished as shown in the illustration with very little extra work. Simply cover the whole cake with the lemon cream and sprinkle with an additional 45g/1¹/₂oz toasted, flaked almonds. Dot the surface with 12 piped whirls of whipped cream. Slice 2 lemons into 12 wafer-thin slices, discarding the ends. Snip each slice and twist into a spiral. Arrange the slices on the whirls of whipped cream.

Malakoff Gâteau

A favourite of General Pelissier, the French Duke of Malakoff

Quantities for 1 24cm/9¹/₂in springform tin
FOR THE CAKE MIX:
3 eggs
50g/2oz sugar
Pinch of salt
75g/3oz flour
Generous pinch of baking powder
1 lemon, rind grated
FOR THE FILLING AND DECORATION:
125ml/4 fl oz dry white wine
125ml/4 fl oz orange juice
3 tbsps sugar
4 tbsps rum
150g/5¹/₂oz flaked almonds
250g/8oz softened butter
125g/5oz icing sugar
5 egg yolks
100g/4oz trifle sponges
1¹/₂ tsps unflavoured gelatine
400ml/15 fl oz whipping cream
Chocolate shapes, to decorate

Preparation time: 20 minutes
Baking time: 15 minutes
Final preparations: 1 hour
Resting time: 2 hours
Nutritional value:
Analysis per slice, approx, if divided into 12 slices:
- 2810kJ/670kcal
- 15g protein
- 51g fat
- 31g carbohydrate

To make the sponge, separate the eggs. • Beat the egg yolks with 3 tbsps hot water, gradually add the sugar and beat until the mixture turns white and has a thick consistency. • Beat the egg whites and salt until stiff. Pour the whisked egg whites over the egg yolk mixture. Combine the flour and baking powder and sift over the egg whites. Fold the flour and egg whites into the egg yolk mixture, together with the grated lemon rind. • Heat the oven to 200°C/400°F/Gas Mark 6. Butter the base of the springform tin. •

Transfer the sponge mixture to the tin and bake for 15 minutes or until golden. Leave to cool on a wire rack. • Meanwhile, boil the white wine with the orange juice and 2 tbsps sugar. Add the rum and leave to cool. • To make the cream filling, toast the flaked almonds in a dry frying pan, stirring constantly. Tip onto a plate and leave to cool. • Cream the butter and gradually add the icing sugar and egg yolks. Grind 100g/4oz flaked almonds finely and mix with the creamed butter. • Line the rim of the springform with non-stick baking paper and place it on a board. Place the sponge base inside it. Spread the cake with 2 tbsps of the buttercream. • Dip the trifle sponges in the wine and juice mixture and place them on top all facing the centre. • Cover with buttercream and add a second layer of trifle sponges, but at right angles to the first layer. Cover with the remaining buttercream. Place

the gâteau in the refrigerator for 2 hours for the liquids to mingle. • Carefully release the cake from the springform rim and the non-stick baking paper. • Dissolve the gelatine in 125ml/4fl oz hot water. Whip the cream with the remaining buttercream until stiff and mix with the dissolved gelatine, adding a tbsp at a time. Attach a star nozzle to a piping bag and fill the bag with a third of the cream. Cover the whole cake with the remaining cream. Decorate with the flaked almonds and piped cream whirls. Top each whirl with a chocolate shape.

Our tip: Use the leftover egg whites to make almond-flavoured meringues or coconut macaroons.

Austrian Cakes Famous the World Over

Not gâteaux in the strictest sense – but both would certainly be the highlights at any coffee morning

Sacher Torte
Illustrated left

Quantities for 1 24cm/9¹/₂in springform tin

150g/5¹/₂oz plain chocolate	
125g/5oz butter	
5 eggs	
125g/5oz sugar	
2 tbsp vanilla sugar	
Pinch of salt	
50g/2oz flour	
50g/2oz cornflour	
1 tsp baking powder	
50g/2oz ground almonds	
¹/₂ vanilla pod	
200g/7oz apricot jam	
200g/7oz plain chocolate couverture or icing	

Preparation time: 20 minutes
Baking time: 45 minutes
Final preparations: 20 minutes
Nutritional value:
Analysis per slice, approx, if divided into 12 slices:
- 1800kJ/430kcal
- 8g protein
- 25g fat
- 45g carbohydrate

Melt the chocolate and butter in a bain-marie. Separate the eggs. • Beat the egg yolks and sugar with the vanilla sugar. • Whisk the egg whites and salt to form stiff peaks. • Combine the flour, cornflour, baking powder and ground almonds. Stir this mixture, the whisked egg whites and the cooled chocolate and butter mixture into the egg yolk mixture. Heat the oven to 180°C/350°F/Gas Mark 4. Butter the tin and sprinkle with breadcrumbs or crumbled sponge. • Pour the mixture into the tin and bake on the lower shelf for 45 minutes. • Switch off the oven and leave for 15 minutes. Warm the jam, pass it through a sieve and brush it over the surface. Melt chocolate icing, spread over the sponge and mark out 12 portions.

Linzer Torte
Illustrated right

Quantities for 1 24cm/9¹/₂in springform tin

200g/7oz flour	
50g/2oz cornflour	
125g/5oz cold butter, diced	
125g/5oz sugar	
2 tbsps vanilla sugar	
1 egg	
3 egg yolks	
1 tsp ground cinnamon	
Generous pinch each ground cloves and cardamom	
150g/5¹/₂oz ground almonds	
¹/₂ lemon, rind grated	
250g/8oz apricot or raspberry jam	
1 tbsp apricot or raspberry liqueur	

Preparation time: 40 minutes
Cooling time: 30 minutes
Baking time: 45 minutes
Nutritional value:
Analysis per slice, approx, if divided into 12 slices:
- 1890kJ/450kcal
- 9g protein
- 25g fat
- 45g carbohydrate

Place the butter in a bowl, together with the flour, cornflour, sugar, vanilla sugar, egg, 2 egg yolks, spices and almonds. Mix the grated lemon rind with the juice. Add to the bowl and then quickly knead into a workable dough. • Leave in the refrigerator to chill for 30 minutes. • Combine the jam and liqueur. • Heat the oven to 180°C/350°F/Gas Mark 4. • Roll out two-thirds of the dough and use it to line a buttered springform tin, pinching up a 1¹/₂cm/³/₄in rim. Brush the jam and liqueur mixture over the dough. Roll out the rest of the dough, cut it into strips and then make a lattice pattern on the surface. Brush with the remaining egg yolk. • Bake for 45 minutes, or until golden brown.

Walnut Gâteau

Try using 200g/7oz melted chocolate sweetened with honey instead of walnut cream

Quantities for 1 28cm/11in tin
FOR THE CAKE MIXTURE:
100g/4oz toasted walnuts
250g/8oz wholewheat flour
25g/1oz cocoa powder
2 tsps baking powder
200g/7oz softened butter
200g/7oz honey
4 eggs • 4 tsps rum
FOR THE FILLING AND TOPPING:
200g/7oz walnuts
100g/4oz wholewheat flour
½ tsp ground cinnamon
½ tsp vanilla essence
100g/4oz honey
100g/4oz butter
250ml/8 fl oz milk
3 tbsps walnut liqueur
400ml/15 fl oz whipping cream
2 tbsps raw whole cane sugar
½ tsp vanilla essence
16 walnut halves

Preparation time: 30 minutes
Baking time: 35 minutes
Final preparations: 1½ hours
Nutritional value:
Analysis per slice, approx, if divided into 16 slices:
• 2010kJ/480kcal • 9g protein
• 33g fat • 33g carbohydrate

Grind the walnuts and mix with the flour, cocoa and baking powder. • Cream the butter and honey. Add the flour mixture, eggs and rum, a little at a time. • Heat the oven to 180°C/350°F/Gas Mark 4. Grease the tin. • Bake the cake for 35 minutes. • Chop 100g/4oz walnuts, and toast with the flour. Add the spices, honey, butter and milk. Stir until the mixture is firm. • Cut the cake into two layers and sprinkle each with half the walnut liqueur. • Add the remaining liqueur to the filling and then spread this over the bottom sponge. Cover with the top layer and press down lightly. • Leave the cake to cool. • Grind the remaining walnuts. Whip the cream with the sugar and vanilla until stiff and then add the chopped nuts. Coat the cake with the walnut cream and score it into 16 segments. Decorate with cream and walnut halves.

Cornflake Cheesecake

This is a classic no-bake, refrigerator cake

Quantities for 1 24cm/9¹/₂in springform tin
100g/4oz butter
150g/5¹/₂oz plain chocolate
150g/5¹/₂oz cornflakes
¹/₂ packet unflavoured gelatine
100g/4oz sugar
2 egg yolks
Juice of 1 lemon
250g/8oz low-fat quark or curd cheese
400ml/15 fl oz whipping cream
350g/11oz stoned sweet cherries
2 tbsps chocolate flake (optional)

Preparation time: 1¹/₄ hours
Resting time: 1 hour
Nutritional value:
Analysis per slice, approx, if divided into 12 slices:
- 1590kJ/380kcal
- 9g protein
- 27g fat
- 25g carbohydrate

Melt the butter and chocolate and mix with the cornflakes. • Butter a sheet of non-stick baking paper. Arrange 12 small clusters of cornflakes on the baking paper. • Line the base and the sides of the tin with baking paper. Spoon the remaining cornflake mixture over the base of the tin and press down. Place the clusters and tin in the refrigerator to chill. • Dissolve the gelatine in 125ml/4 fl oz hot water. • Beat the sugar into the egg yolks and then mix with the lemon juice and quark. • Whisk the cream until stiff. • Add a few tbsps of the quark mixture to the dissolved gelatine, then add to the quark mixture together with the whipped cream. • Cover the cornflake base with one third of the quark mixture. Spread the cherries on top and then add the remaining quark mixture. Refrigerate the cake for at least 2 hours. • Decorate with cornflake clusters and chocolate flake, if liked.

Potato Cake

An unusual recipe that is well worth trying

Quantities for 1 26cm/10in springform tin
300g/10oz day-old boiled potatoes
125g/5oz hazelnuts
75g/3oz raisins
2 tbsps rum
4 eggs
200g/7oz sugar
100g/4oz flour
50g/2oz cornflour
2 tsps baking powder
1 lemon, rind grated
¹/₂ tsp ground cinnamon
200g/7oz icing sugar
2 tbsps rum
3 tbsps redcurrant jelly
8 marzipan balls

Preparation time: 1 hour
Baking time: 50 minutes
Final preparations: 10 mins
Nutritional value:
Analysis per slice, approx, if divided into 16 slices:
- 1300kJ/310kcal • 6g protein
- 10g fat
- 47g carbohydrate

Peel the potatoes and purée or grate them. Grind the nuts. Wash the raisins in hot water and drain well. Soak them in the rum. • Separate the eggs and beat the egg yolks with the sugar. Combine the flour, baking powder, potatoes, cornflour, nuts, grated lemon rind, cinnamon and raisins. Stir into the beaten egg yolks. Whisk the egg whites until they form stiff peaks and then fold into the flour and egg mixture. • Heat the oven to 180°C/350°F/Gas Mark 4. Butter the tin and sprinkle with dry breadcrumbs. • Pour the mixture into the tin and smooth the surface. Bake for 50 minutes. Switch off the oven and leave for 10 minutes. • Mix the icing sugar with the rum and 1 tbsp water and stir to a paste. First brush the cake with redcurrant jelly and then cover with the sugar icing. • Decorate with the marzipan balls.

Cream Gâteaux for Special Family Occasions

The sponge layers for these gâteaux can be baked the day before they are filled and assembled

Chocolate Gâteau

Illustrated left

Quantities for 1 26cm/10in tin
250ml/8 fl oz (8-9) egg whites
350g/11oz sugar
2 tbsps lemon juice
250g/8oz ground hazelnuts
75g/3oz cornflour
400g/14oz chocolate couverture
1/2 packet unflavoured gelatine
400ml/15 fl oz whipping cream
2 tbsps vanilla sugar

Preparation time: 1 hour
Baking time: 1½ hours
Nutritional value:
Analysis per slice, approx, if divided into 12 slices:
• 2100kJ/500kcal • 11g protein
• 27g fat • 51g carbohydrate

Heat the oven to 180°C/ 350°F/Gas Mark 4. • Whisk the egg whites until they form soft peaks. Gradually add the sugar and then whisk until stiff. Fold in the lemon juice, hazelnuts and cornflour. • Cover the lined tin with one fifth of the mixture. Bake on the bottom shelf for 15 minutes. Remove from the tin and repeat four more times with the remaining mixture. • Cut the last sponge layer into 12 segments while still warm. Allow all the sponge layers to cool thoroughly. • Melt the chocolate couverture in a bain-marie. Cover the 12 segments and the other four layers with a thin coating of chocolate. Mark the outline of the 12 segments on one of the bases. • Dissolve the gelatine in 125ml/4 fl oz hot water. Whip the cream with the vanilla sugar until stiff. Add 2 tbsps of whipped cream to the dissolved gelatine. Stir this into the rest of the cream. Use three-quarters of the whipped cream to cover three of the chocolate-coated layers. Place them on top of each other with the marked base last. • Dot each of the segments with a whirl of cream and set the 12 cut pieces on top.

Almond Gâteau

Illustrated right

Quantities for 1 26cm/10in tin
150g/5½oz softened butter
150g/5½oz sugar • 2 eggs
Pinch of salt • 150g/5½oz flour
100g/4oz cornflour
2 tsps baking powder
3 tbsps milk
100g/4oz flaked almonds
1/2 packet unflavoured gelatine
600ml/18 fl oz whipping cream
2 tbsps vanilla sugar
4 tbsps sugar
16 coffee beans

Preparation time: 30 minutes
Baking time: 40 minutes
Final preparations: ½ hour
Nutritional value:
Analysis per slice, approx, if divided into 16 slices:
• 1510kJ/360kcal • 5g protein
• 25g fat • 27g carbohydrate

Cream the butter and sugar. Separate 1 egg and mix the egg yolk with the whole egg, salt, flour, cornflour, baking powder and milk. Stir into the creamed butter. Whisk the egg white. Heat the oven to 240°C/475°F/Gas Mark 9. • Spoon a quarter of the mixture into the tin and cover with a little whisked egg white and 25g/1oz flaked almonds. Bake on the lower shelf for 10 minutes, or until golden. Bake three more sponge layers in the same way. • Cut one of the sponge layers into 16 segments. • Dissolve the gelatine in 125ml/4 fl oz hot water. Whip the cream with the vanilla sugar and sugar until stiff. Stir the dissolved gelatine into the whipped cream. • Cover each sponge layer with whipped cream and arrange them on top of each other. Cover the last layer of cream with the 16 segments. Spread more cream round the outside of the cake. Pipe whirls of cream on top of the cake and decorate with the 16 beans.

Chocolate Vanilla Layer Cake

The cake should be spread with the filling the day before it is to be eaten, but do not decorate with cocoa powder and marzipan until just prior to serving

Quantities for 1 26cm/10in tin

5 eggs • ¹/₂ tsp vanilla essence
150g/5¹/₂oz raw whole cane sugar
100g/4oz wholewheat flour
20g/¹/₂oz cornflour or arrowroot
1 tsp baking powder
100g/4oz coarsely grated plain chocolate
75g/3oz butter, melted
750ml/1¹/₂ pints milk
50g/2oz cornflour
¹/₂ tsp vanilla essence
50g/2oz butter
1 egg yolk

FOR THE DECORATION:

200g/7oz blanched almonds
150g/5¹/₂oz honey
1 tbsp rosewater • 12 currants
50g/2oz cocoa powder

Preparation time: 2 hours
Baking time: 35 minutes
Nutritional value:
Analysis per slice, approx, if divided into 12 slices:
• 2100kJ/500kcal • 14g protein
• 30g fat • 43g carbohydrate

Beat the egg yolks with the vanilla, sugar and 2 tbsps warm water. Mix together the flour, cornflour, baking powder and chocolate and combine with the egg yolks. Whisk the whites until stiff. Fold them into the flour mixture with the butter. • Heat the oven to 180°C/350°F/Gas Mark 4. • Bake for 35 minutes, leave to cool and then slice the cake into three layers. Warm the remaining honey. • Whisk the milk with the cornflour and vanilla. Stir into the honey and boil briefly. • Mix together just under a third of the cooled filling with the butter and egg yolk. Spread the bottom and middle layers with the remaining filling while still warm. Re-assemble the cake. Spread the rest of the filling over the top. • The next day, make the marzipan. Grind the almonds very finely and mix to a paste in a bowl over simmering water with 100g/4oz honey and the rosewater. Sprinkle the top of the cake thickly with cocoa powder. • Roll out half the marzipan to line the side of the cake. Use marzipan and currants to shape 12 flowers.

Flourless Cakes for Entertaining

Delicious cakes made with almonds, chocolate or grated carrots – but without flour

Swiss Carrot Cake
Illustrated left

Quantities for 1 26cm/10in tin
300g/10oz carrots
5 eggs • 200g/7oz sugar
2 tbsps vanilla sugar
300g/10oz ground almonds
1 tsp ground cinnamon
Generous pinch each ground cloves and freshly grated nutmeg
4 tsps rum • 100g/4oz marzipan
250g/8oz icing sugar, sifted
6 pistachio nuts, coarsely chopped or slivered
A few drops of orange food colouring • 2 tbsps lemon juice

Preparation time: 30 minutes
Baking time: 50 minutes
Resting time: 1 day
Final preparations: 30 mins
Nutritional value:
Analysis per slice, approx, if divided into 12 slices:
• 1800kJ/430kcal • 11g protein
• 20g fat • 51g carbohydrate

Peel the carrots and grate them finely. • Separate the eggs. Beat the egg yolks with the sugar and vanilla sugar. Whisk the egg whites until they form stiff peaks. Mix the egg yolks with the carrots, almonds, spices and rum. Fold in the beaten egg whites. • Heat the oven to 200°C/400°F/Gas Mark 6. Butter the springform tin and sprinkle it with breadcrumbs. • Pour the cake mixture into the tin and bake for 50 minutes. Leave to rest for 1 day. • Knead the marzipan with 50g/2oz icing sugar, adding the food colouring a drop at a time. Shape 12 miniature carrots, topping each with a couple of chopped pistachio nuts. • Mix the lemon juice with the remaining icing sugar and use the mixture to ice the cake.

Austrian Chocolate Cake
Illustrated right

Quantities for 1 26cm/10in tin
150g/5¹/₂oz ground almonds
100g/4oz plain chocolate
7 eggs • 125g/5oz sugar
1 tbsp cornflour
1 tsp baking powder
100g/4oz plain chocolate couverture • 2 tbsps rum
¹/₂ packet unflavoured gelatine
500ml/18 fl oz whipping cream
1 tbsp vanilla sugar
12 chocolate leaves

Preparation time: 30 minutes
Baking time: 35 minutes
Resting time: 1 day
Final preparations: ¹/₂ hour
Nutritional value:
Analysis per slice, approx, if divided into 12 slices:
• 2010kJ/480kcal • 12g protein
• 33g fat • 29g carbohydrate

Grate the chocolate finely. • Heat the oven to 180°C/350°F/Gas Mark 4. Line the base and sides of the tin with non-stick baking paper. • Separate 4 eggs. Beat the remaining whole eggs with the egg yolks, adding the sugar, cornflour and baking powder a little at a time. Whisk the egg whites until they form stiff peaks. • Fold the beaten egg whites, almonds and chocolate into the egg yolk mixture. Bake on the lower shelf for 35 minutes. • Place the cake on a cooling rack and leave for 1 day. Cut the cake twice crossways into three layers. • Melt the chocolate icing in a bain-marie and use it to cover the top layer of cake, marking out 12 segments. Sprinkle rum over the other two layers. Dissolve the gelatine in 125ml/4 fl oz hot water. Whip the cream with the vanilla sugar until stiff. Combine the dissolved gelatine with the cream. Spread the cream over the two rum-soaked sponge layers, reserving some for decoration. • Re-assemble the cake and decorate with whirls of whipped cream topped with chocolate leaves.

Cranberry Gâteau

This gâteau must be refrigerated before serving

Quantities for 1 26cm/10in springform tin	
175g/6oz softened butter	
175g/6oz sugar	
1 tbsp vanilla sugar	
4 eggs	
250g/8oz ground hazelnuts	
2 tsps baking powder	
100g/4oz plain chocolate, grated	
2 tbsps cocoa powder	

FOR THE FILLING AND DECORATION:

½ packet unflavoured gelatine	
500ml/16fl oz cranberry sauce	
250ml/8 fl oz whipping cream	

Preparation time: 25 minutes
Baking time: 40 minutes
Final preparations: 40 mins
Nutritional value:
Analysis per slice, approx, if divided into 12 slices:
• 2100kJ/500kcal
• 9g protein
• 39g fat
• 29g carbohydrate

Cream the butter with the sugar and vanilla sugar. Add the eggs, one at a time, followed by the ground hazelnuts, baking powder, 75g/3oz grated chocolate and the cocoa powder. • Heat the oven to 180°C/350°F/Gas Mark 4. Butter the tin. • Bake the cake for 40 minutes. Switch off the oven and leave the cake for 10 minutes. • Allow the cake to cool completely. • Dissolve the gelatine in 125ml/4fl oz hot water and mix with the cranberry sauce. • Whip the cream until stiff. Mix half the whipped cream with the cranberries. • Slice the cake in half crossways into 2 layers. Spread the bottom layer with the cranberry cream. Sandwich the two halves together and spread a thin layer of whipped cream over the whole cake. Press the remaining grated chocolate into the side of the cake and pipe a pattern of cream whirls over the top.

Bilberry Gâteau

Plums, blackberries or blackcurrants can be used instead of bilberries

Quantities for 1 26cm/10in springform tin	
200g/7oz butter	
200g/7oz sugar	
Pinch of salt • 2 eggs	
1 lemon, rind grated	
Generous pinch each ground cloves and ground cinnamon	
200g/7oz ground almonds	
200g/7oz flour	

FOR THE FILLING:

50g/2oz softened butter	
75g/3oz sugar	
2 tbsps raspberry liqueur	
1 tbsp lemon juice	
150g/5½oz ground almonds	
1 egg, separated	
300g/10oz bilberries	
1 egg yolk	
2 tbsps blackcurrant jelly or jam	

Preparation time: 1 hour
Baking time: 40 minutes
Nutritional value:
Analysis per slice, approx, if divided into 12 slices:
• 2310kJ/550kcal • 11g protein
• 36g fat • 45g carbohydrate

Cream the butter with the sugar and salt. Add the eggs one at a time, followed by the lemon rind, spices, almonds and flour. Stir well. • Butter the tin, cover with half the mixture and leave to chill for 30 minutes. • Knead the remaining mixture with a little more flour to make a workable dough. Roll out half to form a thin strip 2cm/1in wide and fit it around the side of the tin. • Cream the butter with the sugar, raspberry liqueur, lemon juice and almonds. Whisk the egg white until stiff. Fold into the mixture. Spread over the base and cover with bilberries. Roll out the rest of the dough, cut it into 1-cm/½-in strips and arrange on top, like the spokes of a wheel. Brush with egg yolk. • Heat the oven to 200°C/400°F/Gas Mark 6. • Bake for 40 minutes. • Glaze with hot blackcurrant jelly.

Marzipan Gâteau

Allow plenty of time for making this many-layered creation, which can be prepared well in advance

Quantities for 1 28cm/11in springform tin

75g/3oz pistachio nuts
300g/10oz almonds
300g/10oz marzipan
650g/1½lbs icing sugar
10 eggs
500g/1lb 2oz softened butter
1 lemon, rind grated
125g/5oz flour
125g/5oz cornflour
200g/7oz lemon curd
200g/7oz plain chocolate couverture or icing

Preparation time: 1 hour
Baking time: 1 hour
Final preparations: 1 hour
Resting time: 7 days
Nutritional value:
Analysis per slice, approx, if divided into 24 slices:
• 2520kJ/600kcal
• 10g protein
• 36g fat
• 56g carbohydrate

Grind two-thirds of the pistachio nuts finely. Dip the almonds into boiling water, leave to cool slightly and then remove the skins. Rub dry and grind finely. • Cut 200g/7oz marzipan into pieces and knead with 100g/4oz icing sugar and the ground pistachios. Divide the marzipan and pistachio mixture into four pieces. • Heat the oven to 250°C/475°F/Gas Mark 9. Butter the springform tin. • Separate the eggs. Cream the butter with 500g/1lb 2oz icing sugar. Add the grated lemon rind and egg yolks one at a time. Combine the flour with the cornflour and ground almonds. Line the tin with non-stick baking paper. Whisk the egg whites to form stiff peaks and fold into the almond and flour mixture. • Use a pastry brush to spread 2 tbsps of the sponge mixture evenly over the tin. Bake on the upper shelf for 5 minutes until golden. • Spread another 2 tbsps of cake

mixture on top of the first layer and bake until golden. Repeat with the third layer. Spread 1 tbsp lemon curd on top. Roll out one of the marzipan and pistachio portions between 2 sheets of clingfilm cut to the same size as the tin. Place on top of the lemon marmalade. Spread 2 more tbsps cake mixture on top. Bake for 5 minutes. • Add another three layers of cake mixture, topped with a layer of lemon curd and marzipan and pistachio mixture. Continue this process until all the cake mixture and marzipan have been used up. When the fourth layer of marzipan and pistachio has been added, bake on the middle shelf of the oven. • Leave to cool and then remove from the tin. Cool on a wire rack. • Brush the surface and sides with lemon curd. • Knead together the remaining marzipan and icing sugar. Roll out a thin layer for the top of the cake and a strip for the sides. Press the marzipan over the

cake. • Melt the chocolate icing in a bain-marie and cover the cake evenly, starting from the middle. • Chop the remaining pistachio nuts and sprinkle them over the chocolate icing. • Wrap the cake loosely in aluminium foil and refrigerate for 7 days.

Our tip: The cake will stay fresh after it has been cut open as long as it is wrapped in foil and kept cool. Its flavour improves with age.

Very Special Cakes

Attractive gâteaux which are easy enough even for novice cake-makers to tackle

Buttercream Gâteau

Illustrated left

Quantities for 1 26cm/10in tin
5 eggs • Pinch of salt
250g/8oz sugar • 125g/5oz flour
125g/5oz cornflour
1 tsp baking powder
50g/2oz toasted flaked almonds
100g/4oz blanched, toasted almonds • 125g/5oz sugar
100ml/3 fl oz water • 5 egg yolks
250g/8oz softened butter
400g/14oz raspberry jam
50g/2oz plain cooking chocolate
125ml/4 fl oz whipped cream
16 glacé cherries

Preparation time: 20 minutes
Resting time: 1 day
Baking time: 40 minutes
Final preparations: 1 hour
Analysis per slice, approx, if divided into 16 slices:
• 2390kJ/570kcal • 12g protein
• 33g fat • 56g carbohydrate

Separate the eggs and whisk the whites with the salt and 50g/2oz sugar. Beat the yolks with 5 tbsps warm water and the remaining sugar. Stir in the flour, baking powder and cornflour. • Heat the oven to 150°C/300°F/ Gas Mark 2. Bake the sponge mixture for 10 minutes. Increase the temperature to 180°C/350°F/ Gas Mark 4 and bake for a further 30 minutes. • Switch off the oven and leave for 15 minutes. • Grind the almonds finely. Boil the sugar and water to a syrup. • Beat the egg yolks and add the syrup. Combine with the almonds and butter, stirring well. • Cut the sponge base crossways into three layers. Coat the bottom two layers with raspberry jam and buttercream. • Replace the top layer and cover the surface and sides with buttercream. Press flaked almonds into the sides and sprinkle the surface with grated chocolate. Pipe with 16 whirls of cream, each topped with a cherry.

Chocolate Cream Gâteau

Illustrated right

Quantities for 1 24cm/9¹/₂in tin
4 eggs
Pinch of salt
200g/7oz sugar
100g/4oz flour
100g/4oz cornflour
1 tsp baking powder
¹/₂ packet unflavoured gelatine
400ml/15 fl oz whipping cream
2 tbsps sugar
400g/14oz peach jam
2 tbsps cocoa powder
100g/4oz chocolate vermicelli
100g/4oz candied orange peel

Preparation time: 20 minutes
Baking time: 40 minutes
Resting time: 1 day
Final preparations: 40 minute
Nutritional value:
Analysis per slice, approx, if divided into 12 slices:

• 1800kJ/430kcal • 7g protein
• 17g fat • 61g carbohydrate

Prepare a sponge mix as described in the previous recipe using the eggs, salt, sugar, flour, cornflour and baking powder. Bake at 150°C/ 300°F/Gas Mark 2 for 10 minutes, and at 180°C/350°F/Gas Mark 4 for a further 30 minutes. Leave to rest for 1 day. Cut crossways into three layers. • Dissolve the gelatine in 125ml/4 fl oz hot water. • Whip the cream with the sugar until stiff and stir the dissolved gelatine into it. Place some of the whipped cream into a piping bag. • Spread the two lower sponge layers with jam and cream. Re-assemble the three layers. • Stir the cocoa powder into the remaining cream and spread it over the surface and sides of the cake. Sprinkle with the chocolate vermicelli and dot with whirls of cream, topped with orange peel.

Heavenly Cake

This work of art tastes heavenly

Black Bread Cherry Gâteau

An unusual and delicious cake from Central Europe

Quantities for 1 26cm/10in springform tin	
175g/6oz softened butter	
200g/7oz sugar	
3 eggs	
300g/10oz flour	
2 tsps baking powder	
100g/4oz ground almonds	
3 tbsps vanilla sugar	
1/2 packet unflavoured gelatine	
750ml/1 1/2 pints whipping cream	

Preparation time: 20 minutes
Baking time: 1 hour 40 mins
Final preparations: 20 mins
Nutritional value:
Analysis per slice, approx, if divided into 12 slices:
- 2390kJ/570kcal
- 10g protein
- 40g fat
- 42g carbohydrate

Cream the butter with 150g/5 1/2oz sugar and eggs. Mix together the flour and baking powder and add to the creamed butter. • Heat the oven to 180°C/350°F/Gas Mark 4. Butter the bottom of the tin. • Spoon a quarter of the mixture into the tin and bake for 10 minutes. • Combine the almonds with 2 tbsps vanilla sugar. Spread a quarter of this mixture over the cake base and bake for a further 15 minutes. • Prepare three more layers in the same way. • Bake the last layer for only 20 minutes and cut it into 12 equal segments. Return to the oven for the final 5 minutes. • Dissolve the gelatine in 125ml/4 fl oz hot water. • Whip the cream with the remaining vanilla sugar and the sugar until stiff. Gradually add the whipped cream to the dissolved gelatine. Transfer a third of the cream to a piping bag. Spread the rest of the cream over the three layers and assemble the cake. • Score the top layer into 12 segments. Pipe a large whirl of cream in each segment. • Arrange the 12 cut segments at an angle on the cream whirls.

Quantities for 1 26cm/10in springform tin	
200g/7oz crustless day-old wholemeal rye bread	
150g/5 1/2oz almonds	
6 eggs	
225g/8oz sugar	
1 tsp baking powder	
1 tbsp flour	
2 tbsps rum or kirsch	
400ml/15 fl oz whipping cream	
400g/14oz sour cherries, stoned	

Preparation time: 40 minutes
Baking time: 40 minutes
Nutritional value:
Analysis per slice, approx, if divided into 12 slices:
- 1680kJ/400kcal • 11g protein
- 23g fat • 35g carbohydrate

Cut the bread into cubes and toast them in a dry frying pan, stirring constantly. Leave the bread to cool. • Grind the almonds. Separate the eggs. Beat the egg yolks and slowly add 200g/7oz sugar. • Combine the flour and baking powder. Stir into the beaten eggs, together with the black bread, ground almonds and rum or kirsch. Whisk the egg whites to form stiff peaks and fold into the mixture. • Heat the oven to 200°C/400°F/Gas Mark 6. Butter the tin. • Pour the mixture into the tin and bake for 40 minutes. • Leave the cake to cool. • Whip the cream with the remaining sugar until very stiff. Slice the cake in half crossways to make 2 layers. Spread 2 tbsps of whipped cream over the bottom half and spread the cherries on top, reserving 12 for decoration. Lay the top layer over the cherries and coat the whole cake with two thirds of the whipped cream. Score the top into 12 segments. • Use the remaining cream to pipe decorative whirls onto the surface of the cake. Top each whirl with a cherry, chill in the refrigerator and serve at the earliest opportunity.

Black Forest Gâteau

A classic offering for special occasions – always serve fresh

Quantities for 1 24cm/9¹/₂in tin

100g/4oz plain cooking chocolate • 150g/5¹/₂oz butter

150g/5¹/₂oz sugar

1 tbsp vanilla sugar • 4 eggs

50g/2oz ground almonds

50g/2oz self-raising flour

50g/2oz cornflour

50g/2oz dry breadcrumbs

FOR THE FILLING:

4 tbsps kirsch

¹/₂ packet unflavoured gelatine

500g/1lb 2oz sour cherries

2 tbsps lemon juice

600ml/1 pint whipping cream

2 tbsps sugar

Preparation time: 65 minutes
Baking time: 45 minutes
Resting time: at least 3 hours
Nutritional value:
Analysis per slice, approx, if divided into 12 slices:
• 2180kJ/520kcal • 9g protein
• 35g fat • 39g carbohydrate

Grate 25g/1oz of the chocolate and melt the rest. • Cream the butter with the sugar and vanilla sugar. • Separate the eggs. Combine the almonds, flour, cornflour and breadcrumbs. • Stir the egg yolks and melted, cooled chocolate into the creamed butter. Beat the two mixtures together. Whisk the egg whites until stiff, and fold into the mixture. • Heat the oven to 180°C/350°F/Gas Mark 4. Bake the cake on the lower shelf for 45 minutes. Leave to rest for 3 hours. Slice the cake crossways into three layers. Sprinkle each with the kirsch. • Dissolve the gelatine in 125ml/4 fl oz hot water. Wash and stone the cherries. Simmer them, uncovered, in 125ml/4 fl oz water with the lemon juice for 7 minutes. Leave them to cool, and drain. • Whip the cream with the sugar. Stir all but 12 of the cherries into half the whipped cream, and add the dissolved gelatine a tbsp at a time. • Cover the two lower cake layers with the cherry and cream mixture. Add the final layer and spread with the remaining cream. Decorate with whirls of whipped cream, the cherries and the grated chocolate.

Special Celebration Cakes

Layered celebration cakes iced with lemon cream or royal icing. To save time, bake 2 layers at a time, using 2 springform tins

Boston Cream Pie
Illustrated left

Quantities for 1 26cm/10in tin

FOR THE CAKE MIXTURE:

125g/5oz softened butter
325g/11oz sugar
4 eggs • 250g/8oz flour
2 tsps baking powder
2 tbsps milk

FOR THE FILLING:

3 lemons • 100g/4oz sugar
3 tsps cornflour
500ml/18 fl oz whipping cream

Preparation time: 40 minutes
Baking time: 50 minutes
Nutritional value:
Analysis per slice, approx, if divided into 16 slices:
• 1510kJ/360kcal • 6g protein
• 20g fat • 42g carbohydrate

Cream the butter with 125g/5oz sugar. Separate the eggs. Combine the egg yolks with the flour, baking powder and milk and stir into the creamed butter. • Heat the oven to 200°C/ 400°F/Gas Mark 6. Line the base of the tin. Bake half of the mixture for 15 minutes. Whisk the egg whites with the remaining sugar and beat until stiff but not dry. Cover the baked cake base with half of the whisked egg whites. Bake for a further 10 minutes. Repeat the process using the remaining cake mixture and whisked egg whites. • Leave both bases to cool. • Squeeze the lemons and strain the juice. Mix the juice with 125ml/4 fl oz water and the sugar. Bring to the boil. Stir the cornflour to a paste with 4 tbsps cold water, add to the lemon juice and leave to cool. • Whip the cream until very stiff. Add the cold lemon mixture to the cream a spoonful at a time. Spread half the lemon cream over the bottom half of the cake, replace the upper layer and coat the top and sides with the remainder of the mixture. Serve immediately.

Wedding Cake
Illustrated right

Quantities for 1 26cm/10in tin:

FOR THE CAKE MIXTURE:

250g/8oz softened butter
125g/5oz sugar
1 tbsp vanilla sugar • 4 eggs
150g/5¹/₂oz each flour and cornflour
100g/4oz ground almonds
2 tsps baking powder

FOR THE CREAM FILLING:

125g/5oz butter • 125g/5oz sugar
4 egg yolks • 2 lemons

FOR THE ICING AND DECORATION:

1 egg white
250g/8oz icing sugar
2 tbsps lemon juice
30g/1oz chopped pistachio nuts
16 candied violets

Preparation time: 80 minutes
Baking time: 45 minutes
Nutritional value:
Analysis per slice, approx, if divided into 16 slices:
• 2010kJ/480kcal • 7g protein
• 27g fat • 53g carbohydrate

Cream the butter with the sugar and vanilla sugar. Add four eggs and 4 tbsps water. • Mix together the flour, baking powder, almonds and cornflour. Stir into the creamed butter. • Heat the oven to 180°C/350°F/Gas Mark 4. • Bake for 45 minutes. • Melt the butter and add the sugar and egg yolks. Grate the rind from one lemon and squeeze the juice from both. Add both to the melted butter. Beat in a bain-marie until creamy. • When the cake has cooled, cut into three layers. Spread the bottom and middle layers with the lemon cream and then re-assemble the cake, adding the top slice. • Whisk the egg white until stiff. Mix in the icing sugar and lemon juice. Ice the cake. When the icing has almost set, decorate with piped icing, pistachios and violets.

Raspberry Cream Gâteau

To enjoy this gâteau at its best, leave the final preparations to the last minute and then keep refrigerated

Quantities for 1 26cm/10in springform tin
FOR THE SPONGE:
6 eggs
Pinch of salt
150g/5½oz sugar
175g/6oz flour
75g/3oz cornflour
2 tsps baking powder
FOR THE FILLING AND DECORATIONS:
50g/2oz flaked almonds
½ packet unflavoured gelatine
250g/8oz low-fat quark
Zest of ½ lemon
3 tbsps maple syrup
2 tbsps vanilla sugar
500ml/18 fl oz whipping cream
1 tbsp lemon juice
600g/1lb 6oz raspberries
3 tbsps icing sugar
4 tbsps raspberry jam
2 tbsps raspberry liqueur
25g/1oz chopped pistachio nuts

Preparation time: 30 minutes
Baking time: 30 minutes
Resting time: at least 6 hours
Final preparations: 45 mins
Nutritional value:
Analysis per slice, approx, if divided into 16 slices:
- 1260kJ/300kcal
- 7g protein
- 14g fat
- 22g carbohydrate

Heat the oven to 180°C/ 350°F/Gas Mark 4. Butter the base of the springform tin and sprinkle with breadcrumbs. • Separate the eggs. Whisk the whites with the salt until they are stiff but not dry. Beat the egg yolks and sugar until the sugar has completely dissolved. Pour the whisked eggs on top of the beaten eggs and fold them in. Mix the flour, cornflour and baking powder and sift the mixture over the beaten egg mixture; fold them in. • Pour the sponge mixture into the tin, smooth the surface and

bake on the middle shelf for 30 minutes, or until golden. • Switch off the oven and leave to rest for 5 minutes. Remove from the oven and leave for a further 10 minutes. Unmould the tin onto a cake rack and leave for at least 6 hours. • Toast the flaked almonds in a dry frying pan until golden brown and leave to cool. • Dissolve the gelatine in 125ml/4 fl oz hot water. Combine the quark, grated lemon rind, maple syrup and vanilla sugar. Whip the cream until stiff. Fold 100g/4oz whipped cream into the quark. • Warm the lemon juice with 2 tbsps water. Remove from the heat and add the dissolved gelatine. Gradually add the quark to half of the liquid gelatine. Slowly add the other half of the gelatine liquid to the remaining whipped cream. • Wash the raspberries, dry well and purée 250g/8oz of them with the icing sugar. • Fit a star nozzle to a piping bag and fill with one third of the whipped cream. Mix the

rest of the cream with the puréed raspberries. • Cut the sponge cake in half crossways to make two layers. Stir the raspberry liqueur into the raspberry jam. Brush this over the bottom layer of the cake. Spread the rest of the quark mixture on top, cover with the top half of the cake and press lightly. • Coat the surface and sides of the cake with raspberry cream. Press the flaked almonds into the sides. • Arrange the remaining raspberries on top, dot the edge of the cake with cream whirls and sprinkle each with pistachio nuts. • Refrigerate until ready to serve.

Our tip: To make the torte higher and even more impressive, bake a thin base of shortcrust pastry in the same tin. Brush it with raspberry jam and place the sponge mixture on top.

Dutch Cherry Gâteau

This popular cream cake made with puff pastry should be chilled prior to serving

300g/10oz frozen puff dough
50g/2oz flaked almonds
500g/1lb 2oz dark sweet cherries
4 tbsps sugar
1/2 tsp ground cinnamon
1 tbsp cornflour
2 tbsps redcurrant jelly
100g/4oz icing sugar
1-2 tbsps kirsch
1 packet unflavoured gelatine
750ml/1 1/2 pints whipping cream
1 tbsp vanilla sugar

Preparation time: 20 minutes
Baking time: 30 minutes
Final preparations: 1 1/2 hours
Nutritional value:
Analysis per slice, approx, if divided into 12 slices:
• 1510kJ/360kcal • 4g protein
• 22g fat • 33g carbohydrate

Thaw the dough. • Toast the flaked almonds until light brown. Wash, drain and stone the cherries. Simmer them for 7 minutes in 125ml/4 fl oz water with the ground cinnamon and 2 tbsps sugar. Mix the cornflour with a little cold water and add to the cherry liquid. Bring to the boil then leave to cool. • Heat the oven to 200°C/400°F/Gas Mark 6. • Roll out the dough. • Cut out three circles 26cm/10in in diameter. Rinse a baking sheet in cold water and bake each of the circles for 10 minutes, or until lightly browned. • Coat one cooled pastry layer with redcurrant jelly. Mix the kirsch with the icing sugar and brush it over the jelly to glaze. Leave to dry. • Dissolve the gelatine in 125ml/4 fl oz hot water. • Whip the cream with the remaining sugar and vanilla sugar until stiff. • Mix the dissolved gelatine with 3 tbsps whipped cream and then add to the rest of the whipped cream. • Spread all but 12 of the stewed cherries over the second pastry base and cover with whipped cream. Place the third base on top and cover with a thick layer of cream. Cut the iced layer into 12 segments and arrange them on top of the cream. • Spread the side of the cake with some of the whipped cream and coat it with flaked almonds. Top with whirls of cream and the 12 cherries.

Popular Pastries

Sweet morsels, tartlets and delicious nibbles for teatime and coffee mornings

Fruit-filled Swiss Rolls

These feather-light sponges can be filled with a variety of fruit and cream fillings

Lemon Cream Swiss Roll

In the foreground

Quantities for 1 Swiss roll
4 egg whites
200g/7oz sugar
Pinch of salt
1 tbsp vanilla sugar
8 egg yolks
50g/2oz flour
50g/2oz cornflour
500ml/18 fl oz whipping cream
5 tbsps lemon juice
1/2 lemon, rind grated
2 tbsps icing sugar

Preparation time: 15 minutes
Baking time: 10 minutes
Final preparations: 15 minutes
Nutritional value:
Analysis per slice, approx, if divided into 8 slices:
• 2600kJ/620kcal
• 17g protein
• 42g fat
• 43g carbohydrate

Heat the oven to 200°C/ 400°F/Gas Mark 6. Line a Swiss roll tin with non-stick baking paper. • Whisk the egg whites with 100g/4oz of the sugar, salt and vanilla sugar until they form very stiff peaks. Stir in the egg yolks. Mix the flour and cornflour, and add to the egg mixture, stirring lightly with a whisk. • Pour the sponge mixture into the Swiss roll tin and bake for 10 minutes, or until golden. • Open out a tea towel, sprinkle it with 2 tbsps sugar, invert the sponge on it and cover with a cold, damp cloth. • Whip the cream with the lemon juice and grated rind and sprinkle with the remaining sugar. • Remove the damp cloth. Spread the lemon cream over the sponge. Roll up the sponge with the help of the tea towel. Sift the icing sugar over the Swiss roll.

Raspberry Cream Swiss Roll

In the background

Quantities for 1 Swiss roll
4 eggs • Pinch of salt
150g/5 1/2oz sugar
1 tbsp vanilla sugar
75g/3oz flour • 75g/3oz cornflour
3 tbsps sugar
400ml/15 fl oz whipping cream
200g/7oz raspberries

Preparation time: 15 minutes
Baking time: 8-10 minutes
Final preparations: 15 minutes
Nutritional value:
Analysis per slice, approx, if divided into 8 slices:
• 1680kJ/400kcal • 9g protein
• 22g fat • 44g carbohydrate

Heat the oven to 220°C/ 450°F/Gas Mark 7. Line a Swiss roll tin with non-stick baking paper. • Separate the eggs. Whisk the egg whites with the salt and 75g/3oz sugar until they are stiff. • Beat the remaining sugar and vanilla sugar into the egg yolks. Mix the flour and cornflour and sift over the egg yolk mixture. Fold the stiff egg whites into the flour. Pour the sponge mixture into the Swiss roll tin. • Bake on the upper shelf for 8 to 10 minutes until golden. • Open out a tea towel, sprinkle it with 2 tbsps sugar, invert the sponge on it and cover with a cold, damp cloth. • Whisk the cream with the remaining sugar. Fill a piping bag with half of the cream. Wash the raspberries, dry well, set some aside for the decoration and mix the rest with the whipped cream. Cover the sponge with the raspberry cream and roll it up, using the tea towel to help. Pipe whirls of cream onto the Swiss roll and top with the reserved raspberries.

Belgian Buns

Either a yeast dough or a quark dough can be used here, to make this popular pastry

Quantities for 20 buns
250g/8oz low-fat quark or curd cheese
300g/10oz cold butter
Pinch of salt
1 tsp vanilla sugar
250g/8oz flour
1 tsp baking powder
125g/5oz raisins
50g/2oz ground hazelnuts
1 tsp ground cinnamon
50g/2oz sugar
150g/5¹/₂oz icing sugar
1-2 tbsps lemon juice

Preparation time: 40 minutes
Cooling time: 1 hour
Baking time: 25-30 minutes
Nutritional value:
Analysis per bun, approx:
- 1000kJ/240kcal
- 4g protein
- 14g fat
- 25g carbohydrate

Drain the quark in a sieve. Cut 250g/8oz of the butter into knobs and mix with the quark, together with the salt, vanilla sugar, flour and baking powder. Work the ingredients initially with an electric dough hook and then finish kneading with floured hands. Wrap the dough in aluminium foil and chill for 1 hour. • Roll out the quark dough into a rectangle 40x60cm/ 16x24ins. Melt the remaining butter in a saucepan and then leave to cool. Brush the dough sheet with the melted butter. Wash the raisins in hot water, dry well and mix with the ground hazelnuts, cinnamon and sugar. Spread an even layer over the dough. • Roll up the sheet from the short side and cut into 20 slices, using a knife dipped in cold water. • Heat the oven to 200°C/400°F/Gas Mark 6. • Butter a baking sheet. • Arrange the buns on it and bake on the middle shelf for 25 to 30 minutes. • Beat the icing sugar with the lemon juice to make a thick icing. Brush it over the buns while still warm and leave to cool on a wire rack.

Nut Crescents

These taste best when served very fresh

Nut Cockscombs

Using frozen puff dough is a convenient short cut

Quantities for 12 crescents
20g/1oz yeast
1 tsp sugar
125ml/4 fl oz lukewarm milk
300g/10oz flour
Pinch of salt
1 egg
1 tbsp butter
100g/4oz ground hazelnuts
50g/2oz demerara sugar
Pinch of ground cinnamon
3 tbsps condensed milk
100g/4oz icing sugar
2 tbsps rum

Preparation time: 30 minutes
Rising time: 1¼ hours
Baking time: 20-25 minutes
Nutritional value:
Analysis per crescent, approx:
• 960kJ/230kcal
• 6g protein
• 8g fat
• 33g carbohydrate

Mix the yeast with the sugar and a little warm milk. Leave to rise in a warm place for 15 minutes. • Place half the flour in a bowl with the remaining milk, the starter yeast, salt and egg. Knead to a smooth, workable dough before adding the rest of the flour. Cover and leave for 45 minutes. • Melt the butter and fry the hazelnuts, stirring in the demerara sugar, cinnamon and condensed milk. • Knead the dough again and roll out to a rectangle on a floured surface. Cut out 10 long triangles with narrow bases. Place a spoonful of the nut paste in the middle of each and roll up the dough towards the pointed end. Bend slightly to form crescent shapes. Arrange on a buttered baking sheet, cover, and leave for 15 minutes. • Heat the oven to 200°C/400°F/Gas Mark 6. • Bake the crescents for 20 to 25 minutes, or until goldenbrown. • Combine the rum and icing sugar and brush over the surface of the crescents.

Quantities for 10 cockscombs:
300g/10oz frozen puff dough
150g/5½oz ground hazelnuts
1 tbsp butter
1 egg
100g/4oz sugar

Thawing time: 1 hour
Preparation time: 30 minutes
Baking time: 15-20 minutes
Nutritional value:
Analysis per crest, approx:
• 1210kJ/290kcal
• 5g protein
• 19g fat
• 22g carbohydrate

Lay out five sheets of frozen puff dough and leave to thaw. • Cut the sheets in half then roll each into squares 10x10cm/4x4in. • Lightly fry the ground nuts in the butter and leave to cool. Separate the egg. Whisk the egg white to form stiff peaks and stir in sugar and nuts. • Heat the oven to 220°C/450°F/Gas Mark 7. •

Beat the egg yolk with 1 tsp water. • Spread the nut mixture over the dough squares, leaving a generous margin around the edge. Brush the edges with egg yolk and fold the squares over, pressing the edges together firmly. With a sharp knife, make several cuts in the joined edges. • Rinse a baking sheet in cold water. Bend the nut crests a little to make the cockscomb shape and arrange on the baking sheet. Brush with the remaining egg yolk and bake on the middle shelf for 15 to 20 minutes, or until golden brown.

Traditional Deep-fried Pastries

A deep-fryer or a sugar thermometer are needed to check the temperature of the fat

Dutch Raisin Doughnuts

Illustrated right

Quantities for 26 doughnuts

500g/1lb 2oz flour

45g/1¹/₂oz fresh yeast or 1 sachet dried yeast • 75g/3oz sugar

250ml/8 fl oz lukewarm milk

50g/2oz each candied orange and lemon peel

50g/2oz each raisins and currants

2 tbsps vanilla sugar

Pinch of salt

75g/3oz softened butter

1 orange, rind grated

FOR FRYING:

1kg/2¹/₄lbs vegetable cooking fat

FOR THE ICING:

200g/7oz icing sugar

4 tsps rum or orange liqueur

Preparation time: 40 minutes
Rising time: about 1¹/₄ hours
Frying time: about 1 hour
Nutritional value:

Analysis per doughnut, approx:
- 840kJ/200kcal
- 3g protein
- 9g fat
- 31g carbohydrate

Sift the flour into a bowl and make a well in the centre. Crumble in the yeast and stir in the milk and a little sugar and flour. Cover the starter dough and leave it to rise in a warm place for 15 minutes. • Chop the candied orange and lemon peel finely. Wash the currants and raisins in hot water and leave to dry on a kitchen towel. • Add the rest of the sugar and milk to the starter yeast, together with vanilla sugar, salt, butter and grated rind. Knead with the flour to make a smooth dough. Add the dried fruit, candied orange and lemon to the dough, knead well and leave for 30 minutes, or until it has clearly increased in bulk. • Use a metal spoon to cut 26 pieces from the dough, wrap them in a tea towel

and leave for another 30 minutes.
• Heat the oil in a deep-fryer to 175°C/345°F. • Fry for about 5 minutes on each side, until golden brown. • Stir the icing sugar into the rum or orange liqueur and brush over the doughnuts. Allow the doughnuts to dry on a wire rack and serve warm.

Custard Doughnut Rings

Illustrated left

Quantities for 40 rings

100g/4oz butter • 100g/4oz sugar

1 tbsp vanilla sugar

¹/₂ packet custard powder

2 eggs • 4 tbsps sour cream

450g/1lb flour

1¹/₂ tsps baking powder

FOR FRYING

1kg/2¹/₄lbs vegetable cooking fat

FOR DUSTING

5 tbsps sugar

¹/₂ tsp ground cinnamon

Preparation time: 30 minutes
Frying time: about 1¹/₂ hours
Nutritional value:

Analysis per ring, approx:
- 460kJ/110kcal
- 2g protein
- 5g fat
- 13g carbohydrate

Cream the butter with the sugar, vanilla sugar and custard powder. Stir in the eggs and sour cream. Combine the flour and baking powder, gradually add to the creamed butter and then knead well. • Roll out the dough to a sheet ¹/₂cm/¹/₄in thick and cut out the rings using two circular biscuit cutters, one two inches larger than the other. Heat the oil in the deep-fryer to 175°C/345°F and deep-fry the rings on both sides for 3 to 4 minutes, or until golden brown. Leave to drain on absorbent paper. • Combine the sugar and cinnamon on a plate, and dip the doughnuts in the mixture.

Choux Puffs

Choux pastry is best when fresh

Quantities for 10 choux puffs:
250ml/8 fl oz water
50g/2oz butter
Pinch of salt
125g/5oz flour
3 eggs
200g/7oz icing sugar
2 tbsps rum or lemon juice
FOR FRYING:
1kg/2¼lbs vegetable cooking fat or 1l/1¾ pints oil

Preparation time: 20 minutes
Resting time: 30 minutes
Frying time: about 30 minutes
Nutritional value:
Analysis per puff, approx:
- 1090kJ/260kcal
- 5g protein
- 13g fat
- 29g carbohydrate

Boil the water, butter and salt in a saucepan. Add the flour and stir constantly until the mixture forms a ball and comes away cleanly from the side of the saucepan. Remove the saucepan from the heat and leave to cool. Add the eggs one at a time. The dough should glisten and hang from a wooden spoon in long pointed drops. • Leave the dough to rest for 30 minutes at room temperature. • Heat the fat or oil in a deep-fryer to 175°C/345°F. Cut four 8cm/3in wide strips of greaseproof paper and dip them into the hot fat. • Attach a large star nozzle to a piping bag and pipe a whirl 6cm/2½ins wide and 1½cm/¾in high onto the paper. Dip the whirls into the fat with top side facing downwards. Remove the paper when the whirl slips off. Deep-fry the puffs for about 4 minutes, or until golden brown. Remove them from the fat with a slotted spoon and leave to drain on absorbent paper. • Stir the icing sugar with 2 tbsps water and the rum or lemon juice and dip one surface of the puffs into the icing. Leave to cool and dry on wire racks.

Children's Birthday Favourites

You cannot make too many cakes when there are a lot of hungry mouths to feed!

Marshmallow Cupcakes
Illustrated left

Quantities for 16 marshmallows
4 eggs
Pinch of salt
200g/7oz sugar
1 tbsp vanilla sugar
75g/3oz plain flour
75g/3oz cornflour
1 tsp baking powder
½ packet powdered gelatine
2-3 pieces preserved ginger
400ml/15 fl oz whipping cream
½ lemon, rind grated
200g/7oz plain chocolate icing or couverture
1 orange, rind grated

Preparation time: 30 minutes
Baking time: 15 minutes
Final preparations: 1 hour
Nutritional value:
Analysis per marshmallow, approx:

- 1210kJ/290kcal
- 6g protein
- 15g fat
- 31g carbohydrate

Separate the eggs. Whisk the egg whites with salt until they form stiff peaks. Beat the egg yolks with 3 to 4 tbsps hot water. Sprinkle with the sugar and vanilla sugar. Add the flour, cornflour and baking powder to the egg yolks and then gently fold in the stiff egg whites with a whisk. • Heat the oven to 200°C/400°F/Gas Mark 6. • Place the cupcake cases on a baking sheet and fill with 2 to 3 tbsps of the mixture, leaving plenty of room for the mixture to rise. • Bake for 15 minutes and leave to cool. • To make the cream filling, dissolve the gelatine in 125ml/4 fl oz hot water. Chop the preserved ginger finely. Whip the cream until stiff and mix with the chopped ginger and grated lemon rind. Combine the gelatine with the cream. • Slice the cupcakes in half horizontally and fill with the ginger cream. • Melt the chocolate icing in a bain-marie and ice each cupcake. • Top with a few strands of orange peel cut into julienne strips.

Iced Buns
Illustrated right

Quantities for 12 iced buns
200g/7oz wholewheat flour
100g/4oz fine cornmeal
25g/1oz cornflour
½ tsp vanilla essence
250g/8oz softened butter
100g/4oz honey
200ml/6 fl oz cream
1 egg
200g/7oz thin honey
2 drops of natural lemon essence

Preparation time: 30 minutes
Baking time: 15-20 minutes
Nutritional value:
Analysis per bun, approx:

- 1680kJ/400kcal
- 4g protein
- 24g fat
- 39g carbohydrate

Mix together the flour, cornmeal and cornflour. • Cream 150g/5½oz butter with the honey and add the vanilla. Add the mixed flour, cream and egg a little at a time, stirring well after each addition. Leave for 15 minutes to rest. • Butter a baking sheet. Heat the oven to 180°C/350°F/Gas Mark 4. • Spoon little mounds of the mixture on the baking sheet, well spaced apart, to make 12 small buns. Bake for 15 to 20 minutes, until golden brown. Leave to cool. • Cream the remaining butter and add the honey and lemon essence a little at a time. Ice the flat side of the buns with the honey mixture. • These 'wholefood' iced buns will stay fresh for about four days, but will be at their best after one day.

Delightful Danish

Snails, windmills and crescents are traditional Danish pastry shapes

Copenhagen Snails

In the background

Quantities for 20 snails

FOR THE YEAST PUFF DOUGH:

600g/1lb 5oz flour

30g/1oz fresh yeast or ½ tsp dried

75g/3oz melted clarified butter

75g/3oz sugar • 250ml/8 fl oz milk

2 egg yolks

Pinch each salt and ground cardamom • 250g/8oz cold butter

FOR THE FILLING:

100g/4oz currants

150g/5½oz marzipan

75g/3oz icing sugar • 2 egg whites

1 tsp ground cinnamon

2 tbsps sugar

Preparation time: 2 hours
Baking time: 12-15 minutes
Nutritional value:
Analysis per snail, approx:
• 1380kJ/330kcal • 6g protein
• 17g fat • 38g carbohydrate

Place 500g/1lb 2oz of the flour in a bowl and add the yeast, 1 tsp sugar and half the milk. Leave to rise in a warm place for 30 minutes. • Add the clarified butter and mix well. Roll out a sheet of dough about 1cm/½in thick between two pieces of non-stick baking paper. Combine the cold butter with the rest of the flour; shape into a small slab and chill in the refrigerator. • Knead the sugar, the rest of the milk and the salt and cardamom into the yeast dough. Leave for 30 minutes, then roll out a rectangular sheet double the size of the slab of butter. Lay the butter in the centre of the dough and fold the sides over each other towards the middle. Roll out and fold once more. Refrigerate for 15 minutes. Repeat the process twice more. • To make the filling, rinse the currants, and stir the marzipan with the icing sugar and 1 egg white. • Roll dough into a rectangle 40x55cm/16x21ins and cover with the filling. Sprinkle the sugar and ground cinnamon over the top. Roll up from the long side towards the middle and cut into 2-cm/1-in slices. • Heat oven to 220°C/450°F/Gas Mark 7. • Brush with egg white and bake for 12 to 15 minutes.

Windmills

In the foreground

Quantities for 18 windmills

500g/1lb 2oz wholewheat flour

45g/1½oz fresh yeast or 1 sachet dried yeast • 1 tbsp honey

250ml/8 fl oz milk

1 egg yolk • 200g/7oz butter

150g/5½oz ground almonds

150g/5½ oz rose-hip syrup

Preparation time: 1½ hours
Resting time: about 12 hours
Baking time: 20-25 minutes
Nutritional value:
Analysis per windmill, approx:
• 1210kJ/290kcal • 7g protein
• 17g fat • 26g carbohydrate

Pour 450g/1lb of the flour into a bowl. Make a well in the centre and crumble in the yeast. Stir the honey, milk and about 4 tbsps flour into the yeast. Cover and leave in a warm place for 15 minutes. • Add the egg yolk and 15g/½ oz butter, knead well, cover and refrigerate for 12 hours. • Mix 50g/2oz flour and the remaining butter until smooth. Roll into a 20x20cm/8x8in square. • Roll out the yeast dough and cover one half with the butter. Fold the other half over it and then roll out to the original size. Repeat four times, resting the folded dough, covered in clingfilm, in the refrigerator for 15 minutes between each 'turn'. • Heat oven to 200°C/400°F/Gas Mark 6. • Roll out dough and cut into 12x12cm/5x5in squares. • Mix almonds and rose-hip syrup and spoon a little into the centre of each square. Slit squares at the corners, shape into windmills and bake on a buttered baking sheet for 20 to 25 minutes, until golden.

Palmiers

Served fresh from the oven, they will taste far better than the shop-bought variety

Teatime Puffs

Perfect with tea or coffee when freshly made

Quantities for 30 palmiers

300g/10oz frozen puff dough

100g/4oz sugar

Thawing time: 1 hour
Preparation time: 20 minutes
Resting time: 30 minutes
Baking time: 16-20 minutes
Nutritional value:
Analysis per biscuit, approx:
* 210kJ/50kcal
* 1g protein
* 3g fat
* 7g carbohydrate

Lay out five puff dough sheets next to each other on a sugared, floured work surface and leave to thaw. • Before rolling out, sprinkle the surface with sugar again. Roll out a sheet of dough 20x30cm/8x10in, turning the sheet over frequently. Fold in the long sides of pastry to just meet each other. Sprinkle with a little sugar. Cover the dough and leave to chill in the refrigerator. • Heat the oven to 220°C/450°F/Gas Mark 7. Rinse a baking sheet with cold water. • Cut the length of folded dough into strips as thick as a pencil. Place the strips on a baking sheet allowing plenty of room for expansion. Bake for 8 to 10 minutes, turn over and cook for a further 8 to 10 minutes. • Leave the palmiers to cool on a wire rack.

Our tip: Palmiers taste delicious topped with raspberries and a little sweetened whipped cream. Or try blackberries, cranberry jelly or mango slices. Plain palmiers are delicious with afternoon tea or morning coffee.

Quantities for 16 puffs

300g/10oz frozen puff dough

100g/4oz sugar

100g/4oz chocolate couverture

Thawing time: 1 hour
Preparation time: 30 minutes
Resting time: 15 minutes
Baking time: 16 minutes
Nutritional value:
Analysis per biscuit, approx:
* 540kJ/130kcal
* 1g protein
* 7g fat
* 16g carbohydrate

Lay out five puff dough sheets next to each other on a sugared, floured work surface and leave to thaw. Roll out to a thickness of about 7mm/$\frac{1}{4}$ in. • Use a cutter or a glass 6cm/$2\frac{1}{2}$ins in diameter to make dough circles. On the sugared surface, roll in one direction with the rolling pin, turn over and roll again in the same direction. Rinse a baking sheet with cold water. Place the oval pastry shapes on the baking sheet and leave for 15 minutes. • Heat the oven to 220°C/450°F/Gas Mark 7. • Bake the puffs on the middle shelf of the oven for 8 minutes. Turn them over and bake for a further 8 minutes. • Cool the puffs on another baking sheet. • Melt the chocolate couverture in a bain-marie and dip both ends of each puff in the couverture. Arrange on wire racks and leave until the chocolate has dried.

Our tip: Alternatively, dip the puffs in coffee fondant icing.

Choux Pastries

Pipe in the fillings just before you are ready to serve these delicious morsels

Mocha Cream Éclairs

In the foreground

Quantities for 12 éclairs

FOR THE CHOUX PASTE:

250ml/8 fl oz water
50g/2oz butter
1 tbsp vanilla sugar
Pinch of salt
175g/6oz flour
4 eggs

FOR THE FILLING:

250ml/8 fl oz whipping cream
2 tsps instant coffee granules
1 tbsp sugar

FOR THE ICING:

150g/5¹/₂oz icing sugar
1 tbsp instant coffee granules
2 tbsps rum

Preparation time: 20 minutes
Baking time: 20-30 minutes
Final preparations: 15 minutes
Nutritional value:

Analysis per éclair, approx:
- 1090kJ/260kcal
- 6g protein
- 14g fat
- 26g carbohydrate

Heat the oven to 220°C/450°F/Gas Mark 7. Bring the water to the boil and add the butter, vanilla sugar and salt. Remove from the heat. Add all the flour and stir well. Continue to beat the dough rapidly over a low heat until it comes cleanly away from the sides of the pan. Remove from the heat and stir in 1 egg. Leave to cool and then slowly add the remaining eggs. • Use a piping bag fitted with a large star nozzle to pipe 12 finger-length strips on a baking sheet rinsed in cold water. Leave sufficient space between each strip to allow for expansion. Bake the éclairs in the oven for 20 to 30 minutes, or until golden-brown. • To make the filling, whip the cream with the coffee granules and sugar until stiff. Transfer the cream to a piping bag. • Cut the éclairs in half lengthways and leave to cool. • For the icing, mix the icing sugar with 1 tbsp of hot water, the coffee granules and rum. Ice the top halves of the éclairs and pipe cream over the bottom halves before sandwiching them back together.

Cream Puffs

In the background

Quantities for 40 puffs

125ml/4 fl oz water
50g/2oz butter
Pinch of salt
2 tbsps vanilla sugar
125g/5oz flour
4 eggs
400ml/15 fl oz cream
1 tbsp icing sugar

Preparation time: 30 minutes
Baking time: 20 minutes
Nutritional value:
Analysis per puff, approx:

- 290kJ/70kcal • 2g protein
- 5g fat • 4g carbohydrate

Boil the water in a saucepan and add the butter, salt and 1 tbsp vanilla sugar. Add all the flour and stir well. Continue to beat the dough rapidly over a low heat until it comes cleanly away from the sides of the pan. • Transfer the paste to a bowl and leave to cool. Add the eggs one at a time. • Heat the oven to 220°C/450°F/Gas Mark 7. Butter a baking sheet. • Use a piping bag fitted with a star nozzle to pipe walnut-sized whirls onto the baking sheet. • Bake the cream puffs on the middle shelf for about 20 minutes or until golden brown. At the start, place a cup of water on the floor of the oven and shut the oven door quickly. • Whip the cream with the remaining vanilla sugar until stiff. Cut a slit in the puffs and pipe in the cream. Dust with icing sugar. • For best results serve soon after baking.

Chocolate Nut Triangles

Kept in a tin with tight-fitting lid, they will keep fresh for weeks

Quantities for 20 triangles:
150g/5¹/₂oz softened butter
150g/5¹/₂oz sugar
1 tbsp vanilla sugar
3 eggs
150g/5¹/₂oz flour
75g/3oz cornflour
1 tsp baking powder
25g/1oz cocoa powder
100g/4oz ground hazelnuts
4 tbsps milk
20 whole hazelnuts
200g/7oz chocolate nut paste
200g/7oz chocolate icing

Preparation time: 30 minutes
Baking time: 20 minutes
Final preparations: 15 minutes
Nutritional value:
Analysis per triangle, approx:
• 1200kJ/290kcal
• 5g protein
• 17g fat
• 30g carbohydrate

Heat the oven to 200°C/400°F/Gas Mark 6. Line a baking sheet with non-stick baking paper. • Cream the butter with the sugar and vanilla sugar. Add the eggs one at a time. Mix the flour with the cornflour, baking powder, cocoa powder and ground hazelnuts and stir into the egg and butter mixture, together with the milk. Pour the mixture onto the baking sheet and bake on the middle shelf of the oven for 20 minutes. • Cut the cake into 8cm/3in squares. • Toast the hazelnuts in dry frying pan and rub off the skins in a tea towel. Warm the chocolate nut paste until it is easy to spread. Melt the chocolate icing in a bain-marie. • Coat half of the squares with the nut paste and then place the remaining squares on top. • Halve the sandwiches diagonally and coat with the chocolate icing. Press the nuts into the warm icing.

Oaten Biscuits

A popular biscuit – and not just for children – with a long shelf life

Quantities for 20 biscuits
300g/10oz rolled oats
300g/10oz plain flour
2 tsps baking powder
50g/2oz ground almonds
325g/10oz sugar
3 tsps cocoa powder
1 egg • 1 egg yolk
100g/4oz black treacle or molasses
150g/5¹/₂oz butter
50g/2oz wholegrain oatflakes
3 egg whites • Pinch of salt
1 tbsp vanilla sugar
150g/5¹/₂oz raisins

Preparation time: 1 hour
Baking time: 20 minutes
Nutritional value:
Analysis per biscuit, approx:
• 1300kJ/310kcal • 7g protein
• 10g fat • 49g carbohydrate

Mix all but 15g/¹/₂oz of the butter with 200g/7oz of the rolled oats, the flour, baking powder, almonds, 200g/7oz of the sugar, the cocoa powder, egg, egg yolk and treacle, and knead well. • To make the filling, toast the wholegrain oatflakes in the reserved butter. Whisk the egg whites until they form stiff peaks. Add the remaining sugar and the vanilla sugar. • Wash the raisins in hot water and mix with toasted oatflakes and the remaining rolled oats. Fold in the egg whites • Heat the oven to 180°C/350°F/Gas Mark 4. • Lightly butter a baking sheet. • Roll out the dough on a floured worktop to a thickness of about 5mm/¹/₄in. Use a biscuit cutter or glass to cut 40 circles about 6cm/2¹/₂ins in diameter. • Spoon a little of the filling over half the circles and then cover with the other half. Press down lightly. Place the biscuits on the baking sheet and bake on the middle shelf of the oven for 20 minutes. • Oaten biscuits can be stored in a tin with a tight-fitting lid for two weeks.

Classic Little Sponge Cakes

If real madeleine moulds are unobtainable, use very small paper baking cases

Madeleines
Illustrated left

Quantities for 40 madeleines
250g/8oz softened butter
Grated rind of 1 lemon
250g/8oz caster sugar
250g/8oz flour
6 eggs
Icing sugar (optional)
Clarified butter for the moulds

Preparation time: 45 minutes
Baking time: 10 minutes
Nutritional value:
Analysis per serving, approx:
• 490kJ/120kcal
• 3g protein
• 7g fat
• 11g carbohydrate

Cream the butter with the lemon peel and half the sugar. • Sift the flour into a bowl. • Add the remaining sugar to the eggs and beat to a froth. Add the flour and the butter mixture to the froth, alternately by the tablespoon. • Preheat the oven to 220°C/425°F/Gas Mark 6 . Melt the clarified butter and thoroughly coat the moulds with it. • Fill the moulds two-thirds with the dough. Bake for about 10 minutes on the middle shelf of the oven until golden. • Allow the pastries to cool for a short while in the moulds. Toss them onto a cake rack. • If desired, dust with icing sugar.

Cats' Tongues
Illustrated right

Quantities for 40 tongues
4 eggs
200g/7oz icing sugar, sifted
1 vanilla pod
100g/4oz butter
250g/8oz flour
40g/1½oz flaked almonds
100g/4oz plain chocolate coating
Non-stick baking paper for the baking sheet

Preparation time: 50 minutes
Baking time: 12 minutes
Completion time: 15 minutes
Nutritional value:
Analysis per serving, approx:
• 400kJ/100kcal
• 3g protein
• 4g fat
• 11g carbohydrate

Preheat the oven to 190°C/375°F/Gas Mark 5.

Line the baking sheet with non-stick baking paper. • Beat the icing sugar with the eggs until frothy. • Cut the vanilla pods open lengthways, and scrape out the pith. Add the pod to the egg mixture. • Melt the butter and allow to cool. Fold the flour and the butter into the egg mixture. • Fit a piping bag with a circular nozzle. Fill the bag with the dough. Pipe 8cm/3in lengths onto the baking sheet. The lengths should be a little narrower in the middle than at the ends. Leave enough space between the lengths, as they will expand during baking. • Chop the flaked almonds. Sprinkle them onto the lengths of dough. Bake for about 12 minutes on the middle shelf of the oven until golden. • Cool on a cake rack. • Melt the coating in a hot bain-marie. Brush the undersides of the cats' tongues with the coating. Turn the cats' tongues over so that the coating can set.

Wholewheat Fig Newtons

These Kirsch-flavoured goodies are Fig Newtons with a difference

Quantities for 100 fig newtons
150g/2oz dried figs, diced
2 tbsps rum
2 tbsps kirsch
100g/4oz shelled hazelnuts
200g/7oz wholewheat flour
1 tsp baking powder and 1 tsp cream of tartar, combined
1/2 tsp ground cinnamon
50g/2oz candied lemon peel, diced
50g/2oz candied orange peel, diced
1/2 lemon
100g/4oz softened butter
3 1/2 tbsps clear honey
2 eggs
50g/2oz raw cane sugar
Juice of 1/2 lemon
Butter for the baking sheet

Maceration time: 1 hour
Preparation time: 45 minutes
Baking time: 20-25 minutes
Completion time: 10 minutes
Nutritional value:
Analysis per serving, approx:
- 140kJ/33kcal
- 24g protein
- 36g fat
- 32g carbohydrate

Soak the figs in the rum and kirsch for 1 hour. • Roast the hazelnuts in a dry pan until the skins burst open. • Rub the nuts in a tea-towel to remove the skins. Then coarsely grind the hazelnuts in a spice-grinder. • Preheat the oven to 190°C/375°F/Gas Mark 5. Line half a baking sheet with non-stick baking paper. • Combine the flour with the baking powder, nuts, cinnamon and candied peels. • Cream the butter with the honey. Gradually combine the flour mixture, eggs and figs with the soaking liquid. • Spread the dough over the baking paper to make a 1cm/1/2in-thick sheet. Bake for 20-25 minutes on the middle shelf of the oven until golden-brown. • For the glaze, boil the raw cane sugar with the lemon juice and a little water for just 5 minutes, allow to cool a little and brush some over the slab of dough. • Cut the slab of dough into 2cm/3/4in cubes and allow to cool completely on a cake rack.

Florentines

This popular almond confection tastes even better when home-made

Quantities for 30 Florentines

50g/2oz candied orange peel

50g/2oz candied lemon peel

30g/1oz butter

150g/5½oz flaked almonds, preferably freshly prepared

100g/4oz sugar

2 tbsps vanilla sugar

200ml/6 fl oz cream

60g/2oz flour

200g/7oz plain cooking chocolate

Non-stick baking paper for 2 baking sheets

Preparation time: 30 minutes
Baking time: 35 minutes
Completion time: 20 minutes
Nutritional value:
Analysis per serving, approx:
- 520kJ/120kcal
- 2g protein
- 10g fat
- 12g carbohydrate

Finely chop the candied orange and lemon peel. • Melt the butter in a saucepan. Stir in the flaked almonds, sugar, vanilla sugar, candied orange and lemon peel, cream and flour. Bring to the boil. • Cook over low heat for 3-5 minutes, stirring continuously until thickened. Line 2 baking sheets with non-stick baking paper. • Using 2 teaspoons, place little heaps of the mixture on a baking sheet, well spaced out. Press them into round shapes with the back of a fork. • Place the Florentines on the middle rack of the cold oven. • Heat the oven to 180°C/350°F/ Gas Mark 4, and bake the first batch of Florentines for about 20 minutes. Those in the second batch need only about 15 minutes in the oven. • Allow the Florentines to cool on the baking paper. Then remove the paper and allow them to harden. Melt the chocolate in a hot bain-marie. Apply a thick coating to the underside of the Florentines, or several coats if necessary. Leave them to set.

Tempting Tartlets

The smaller they are, the more irresistable they look

Chocolate Tartlets
In the background

Quantities for 20 tartlets
200g/7oz softened butter
100g/4oz sugar
2 tbsps vanilla sugar • 5 eggs
2 heaped tbsps cocoa powder
1 tsp baking powder
150g/5¹/₂oz flour
50g/2oz potato starch
50g/2oz plain chocolate, grated
100g/4oz ground almonds
1 orange
20 paper baking cases, each 5-6cm/2in diameter
5 tbsps orange liqueur
200g/7oz plain cooking chocolate
100g/4oz candied orange peel, chopped

Preparation time: 30 minutes
Baking time: 20 minutes
Completion time: 15 minutes

Nutritional value:
Analysis per serving, approx:
- 1260kJ/300kcal
- 6g protein
- 21g fat
- 25g carbohydrate

Cream the butter with the sugar and the vanilla sugar. Gradually mix in the eggs. • Mix the cocoa with the baking powder, flour, potato starch, chocolate and almonds. • Preheat the oven to 180°C/350°F/Gas Mark 4. • Wash and dry the orange and grate the rind. Extract the juice and mix both the rind and the juice with the butter-and-egg mixture. • Arrange the cases on the baking sheet. Fill them with the chocolate dough. Bake for about 20 minutes on the middle rack of the oven. • Using a cocktail stick, prick holes in the tartlets and sprinkle the liqueur over them. • Melt the chocolate coating in a bain-marie. Cover or decorate the cooled tartlets with this coating. Sprinkle the candied orange peel over the soft coating and press lightly.

Our tip: Ginger and rum can be used instead of orange juice, orange rind and orange liqueur for flavouring the cakes. Soak the baked cakes in rum, coat with the chocolate and sprinkle with chopped crystallised ginger.

Cherry Tartlets
In the foreground

Quantities for 12 tartlets
100g/4oz butter • 100g/4oz sugar
3 eggs • ¹/₄ tsp salt
Grated rind of 1 lemon
200g/7oz flour
2 tsps baking powder
50g/2oz grated almonds
300g/10oz sour cherries
12 paper baking cases each about 5cm/2in in diameter
3 tbsps icing sugar

Preparation time: 40 minutes
Baking time: 25 minutes
Nutritional value:
Analysis per serving, approx:
- 1000kJ/240kcal
- 6g protein
- 12g fat
- 26g carbohydrate

Cream the butter with the sugar. Fold in the eggs one by one. Mix in the salt and the lemon peel. Combine the baking powder with the flour and almonds. Sift this onto the dough and mix in. • Preheat the oven to 200°C/ 400°F/Gas Mark 6. • Wash the cherries, pat them dry and pit them. Arrange the cases on the baking sheet, line with the dough and fill with the cherries. • Bake for 20 minutes on the middle shelf, then leave in the oven for another 5 minutes after it has been turned off. • Dust with icing sugar when cool.

Sweet Honey Pastries for the Twilight Hour

Imaginative mixtures, the right accompaniment to a fragrant tea

Caramel Honey Biscuits
Illustrated left

Quantities for 40 biscuits
5 tbsps honey
¹/₂ tsp vanilla essence
200ml/6 fl oz cream
100g/4oz butter
250g/8oz wholewheat flour
1 tsp baking powder and cream of tartar, mixed
1 egg
Butter for the baking sheet

Preparation time: 40 minutes
Standing time: 1 hour
Baking time: 15 minutes
Nutritional value:
Analysis per serving, approx:
• 260kJ/62kcal
• 1g protein
• 4g fat
• 5g carbohydrate

Boil the honey with the vanilla for 5 minutes, stirring continuously. • Gradually add the cream and allow to boil for another 5 minutes. • Add the butter and remove from the heat immediately. Stir now and again while the butter is melting and the mixture is cooling. • Combine the flour with the baking powder. Add this to the cooled caramel mixture with the egg, and mix thoroughly. • Cover and leave to stand for 1 hour. • Preheat the oven to 200°C/400°F/Gas Mark 6. Butter the baking sheet . • Using 2 teaspoons, cut out little mounds from the dough. Arrange the mounds on the baking sheet, allowing enough space between them. • Bake for about 15 minutes on the middle shelf of the oven until golden brown. • Allow to cool on a cake rack.
Our tip: These biscuits will taste best if left for about 8 days in an airtight tin for the flavours to permeate.

Vanilla Balls
Illustrated right

Quantities for 50 balls
250g/8oz wholewheat flour
1 tsp baking powder and cream of tartar, mixed
100g/4oz softened butter
3¹/₂ tbsps clear honey
³/₄ tsp vanilla essence
3 egg yolks
Butter for the baking sheet

Preparation time: 40 minutes
Standing time: 30 minutes
Baking time: 10 minutes
Nutritional value:
Analysis per serving, approx:
• 230kJ/55kcal
• 2g protein
• 4g fat
• 4g carbohydrate

Combine the flour with the baking powder. • Cream the butter with the honey and vanilla.

• Gradually mix the flour mixture and the egg yolks with the honey and butter mixture. Cover and leave the dough to stand for about 30 minutes. • Preheat the oven to 200°C/400°F/Gas Mark 6. Butter the baking sheet. • Shape little walnut-size balls from the dough. Arrange them on the baking sheet. Bake for about 10 minutes on the middle shelf of the oven until they turn light golden. • Allow to cool on a cake rack.

Tiny Cakes for a Sweet Treat

These should be made as tiny as possible for the tea table

Rock Cakes
Illustrated left

Quantities for 40 cakes
50g/2oz raisins
50g/2oz dried apricots
50g/2oz shelled hazelnuts
3 tbsps rum
125g/5oz softened butter
125g/5oz sugar
2 eggs
250g/8oz flour
1/4 tsp baking powder
1/4 tsp ground cinnamon
1/4 tsp salt
125g/5oz icing sugar, sifted
1 tbsp lemon juice
Non-stick baking paper for the baking sheet

Preparation time: 40 minutes
Baking time: 15 minutes
Completion time: 15 minutes
Nutritional value:
Analysis per serving, approx:
• 400kJ/95kcal
• 2g protein
• 4g fat
• 13g carbohydrate

Wash the raisins and the apricots in hot water, drain and pat dry. • Cut the apricots into small cubes, and chop the hazelnuts. • Combine the fruit, the nuts and the rum and reserve them. • Cream the butter with the sugar. Gradually add the eggs, flour with the baking powder, cinnamon and salt. Stir for 10 minutes by hand, or for 4 minutes with an electric blender at low speed. Lastly, add the fruit mixture.• Preheat the oven to 200°C/400°F/Gas Mark 6. Line the baking sheet with non-stick baking paper. • Using 2 teaspoons, lift out 40 little mounds and arrange on the baking sheet. Bake for about 15 minutes on the middle shelf of the oven until golden. • Add the lemon juice and a few drops of water to the icing sugar to make a thick icing. •

Lift the rolls from the baking sheet. Arrange them on a cake rack and decorate with the icing while they are still warm.

Currant Cakes
Illustrated right

Quantities for 32 cakes
100g/4oz currants
150g/5 1/2oz butter
100g/4oz sugar
1 tsp vanilla sugar
2 eggs
100ml/3 fl oz milk
250g/8oz flour
1 tsp ground cinnamon
2 tsps baking powder
1/4 tsp salt
32 paper baking moulds, about 3cm/1 1/4in in diameter
Icing sugar (optional)

Preparation time: 40 minutes
Baking time: 20 minutes
Nutritional value:

Analysis per serving, approx:
• 400kJ/95kCal
• 2g protein
• 5g fat
• 11g carbohydrate

Wash the currants thoroughly in hot water and drain well. • Cream the butter with the sugar and the vanilla sugar. • Gradually mix the eggs and the milk with the butter and sugar mixture. • Preheat the oven to 200°C/400°F/Gas Mark 6. Combine the flour with the cinnamon and the baking powder. Sift this onto the butter mixture. Sprinkle on the salt and knead to a dough. Lastly, fold the currants into the dough. • Arrange the paper moulds on the baking sheet and fill two-thirds with the dough. Bake for about 20 minutes on the middle shelf of the oven until golden. • Allow to cool a little on a cake rack. Serve as fresh as possible. Dust with some icing sugar if desired.

Meringues with Green Jelly

You could use lime jelly instead of unflavoured gelatine

Quantities for 30 meringues

3 egg whites

¼ tsp salt

170g/6oz caster sugar

1 tbsp unflavoured gelatine

200g/7oz green grapes

3 kiwi fruits

100ml/3fl oz white wine or apple juice

30g/1oz chopped pistachios

Non-stick baking paper and oil for baking the tray

Preparation time: 45 minutes
Baking time: 2 hours
Completion time: 35 minutes
Nutritional value:
Analysis per serving, approx:
- 200kJ/48kcal
- 2g protein
- 1g fat
- 8g carbohydrate

Preheat the oven to 120°C/250°F/Gas Mark 1. Line 2 baking sheets with non-stick baking paper and lightly brush both pieces with oil. • Beat the egg whites with the salt into stiff peaks. Sprinkle with half the sugar and continue beating until the egg white is stiff and glossy. Gradually beat in the remaining sugar. • Fill a piping bag with the meringue. Pipe 30 spiral bases onto the baking sheets, each measuring 4cm/1½in in diameter. Dot the edges of each meringue with little spots. • Rather than baking, dry them out for 2 hours on the middle and lower racks of the oven. Keep the oven door slightly ajar by wedging the handle of a wooden spoon in the door. Afterwards, leave them to cool on a cake rack. • Cover the gelatine with cold water and leave to soak for 10 minutes. • Wash, halve, peel and seed the grapes. Peel and dice the kiwi fruits. • Put the fruit and the wine or juice into a saucepan and bring to the boil, then remove from the heat. • Dissolve the gelatine in the hot stewed fruit. Cool until the fruit jelly begins to thicken. • Fill the meringues with the fruit jelly and sprinkle with the pistachios.

Little Dainties for Special Occasions

Both these biscuits should be piped on to the baking sheet

Orange Glacé Biscuits
Illustrated left

Quantities for 50 biscuits
90g/4oz butter • 75g/3oz sugar
¹/₄ tsp salt • 3 egg whites
75g/3oz flour
Grated rind of 2 oranges
6 tbsps candied orange peel
5 tbsps icing sugar, sifted
2-3 tbsps orange juice
Butter for the baking sheet

Preparation time: 45 minutes
Baking time: 10 minutes
Completion time: 30 minutes
Nutritional value:
Analysis per serving, approx:
- 148kJ/35kcal
- 1g protein
- 2g fat
- 3g carbohydrate

Cream the butter and the sugar. Add the salt to the egg whites and beat to a stiff foam. • Fold the beaten egg whites into the butter paste. Sift the flour over this mixture, sprinkle with the grated orange rind and fold into the butter paste. • Preheat the oven to 200°C/400°F/Gas Mark 6. Butter the baking sheet and line it with non-stick baking paper. • Fit a slitted nozzle onto a piping bag. Pipe walnut-sized mounds of the mixture onto the baking sheet, ensuring that there is enough space between them, as the mounds will swell considerably. • Bake for about 10 minutes on the middle shelf of the oven. They will be ready when the edges start to darken. • Leave the biscuits to cool on a smooth surface. • Very finely dice the candied orange peel. • Warm the orange juice, and mix just enough with the icing sugar to obtain a fluid icing that is not too runny. • Brush some over the biscuits. • Sprinkle the candied orange peel over the icing before it sets.

Little Cream Meringues
Illustrated right

Quantities for 25 meringues
2 egg whites
¹/₄ tsp salt
150g/2oz sugar
1 tsp vanilla sugar
200ml/6 fl oz cream
4 tsps instant coffee powder
25 chocolate coffee beans
Butter for the baking sheet

Preparation time: 45 minutes
Baking time: 2 hours
Completion time: 15 minutes
Nutritional value:
Analysis per serving, approx:
- 260kJ/62kcal
- 1g protein
- 3g fat
- 7g carbohydrate

Cream the egg whites with the salt. • Sprinkle with 100g/4oz of the sugar and the vanilla sugar and keep beating until the egg white is firm and shiny. • Preheat oven to 100°C/225°F/Gas Mark ¹/₄. Line a baking sheet with non-stick baking paper. • Fit a piping bag with a star-shaped nozzle, and fill with the beaten egg white. Pipe circles of the mixture onto the baking sheet, and shape them into 'nests' 4cm/1¹/₂in in diameter. • Place the sheet onto the middle shelf of the oven. The meringues should not bake, but merely dry out for 2 hours. To do this, wedge the oven door slightly ajar using the handle of a wooden spoon. • Lift the meringues from the paper with a spatula and leave to cool. • Beat the cream with the remaining sugar and the instant coffee powder until firm, then pipe the paste into the meringues using a piping bag fitted with a star-shaped nozzle. Top each meringue with a chocolate mocha bean.

Delicious Marzipan Tartlets

These can be made with raw or cooked marzipan

Marzipan Tartlets
In the foreground

Quantities for 60 tartlets

250g/8oz wholewheat flour
1/4 tsp salt
125g/5oz butter, cut into small pieces
2 egg yolks
1 tbsp lemon juice
2 tbsps raw cane sugar
1/2 tsp ground cinnamon
250g/8oz almonds
3 tbsps set honey
1 1/2 tbsps rosewater
Butter for the baking sheet

Preparation and standing time: 1 1/2 hours
Baking time: 12 minutes
Nutritional value:
Analysis per serving, approx:
- 290kJ/69kcal
- 2g protein
- 5g fat
- 4g carbohydrate

Combine the butter with the flour, salt, egg yolks, lemon juice, sugar and cinnamon. Knead to a smooth dough. • Cover and chill for 1 hour. • To make the marzipan, pour boiling water over the almonds and leave to steep for 10 minutes. Rinse quickly under cold water and remove the skins. • Cut 30 almonds in half lengthways and reserve. • Dry the remaining almonds and grind them finely. Add the honey and the rosewater and knead to an elastic marzipan. • Preheat oven to 200°C/400°F/Gas Mark 6. • Butter the baking sheet. • Lightly dust the work surface with flour. Divide the dough into four. Roll out each piece on a lightly-floured work surface. Use a small biscuit cutter to cut circles from the dough and arrange them on the baking sheet. • Coat each circle with 1 1/2 tsps marzipan and place half an almond on each. • Bake on the middle shelf of the oven for about 12 minutes, or until lightly browned.

Marzipan Tartlets with Pistachios
In the background

Quantities for 40 tartlets

100g/4oz raw marzipan
180g/6oz softened butter
125g/5oz sugar
1/4 tsp salt
3 eggs
150g/5 1/2oz flour
75g/8oz potato starch
1 tsp baking powder
3 tbsps apricot jam
2 tbsps chopped pistachios
Extra-strong aluminium foil for the moulds

Preparation time: 50 minutes
Baking time: 20 minutes
Nutritional value:
Analysis per serving, approx:
- 410kJ/98kcal
- 2g protein
- 6g fat
- 10g carbohydrate

Dice the raw marzipan and add the butter. • Combine with the sugar, salt and eggs. • Combine the flour and the potato starch with the baking powder. Sift this over the mixture. Fold in and then whip for 3 minutes, until creamy, using an electric mixer. • Cut extra-strong aluminium foil into 10cm/4in-wide strips, then into 40 squares. Using a small glass as a template, cut out little moulds about 35mm/1 1/2in in diameter. • Preheat oven to 200°C/400°F/Gas Mark 6. • Fill a piping bag with the dough. Pipe a small portion of dough into each mould. Add 1/4 tsp jam. Pipe another portion of dough into them, but fill only two-thirds full. • Bake on the middle shelf of the oven for about 20 minutes or until golden-brown. • Warm the remaining jam on a low heat, and stir until smooth. Brush some jam over the tartlets while they are still hot and sprinkle with the

Glazed Babas

Miniature rum babas, delicacies from Lorraine

Quantities for 12 babas

15g/¹/₂oz yeast
2 tbsps lukewarm milk
1 tbsp sugar
100g/4oz butter
200g/7oz flour
2 small eggs
¹/₄ tsp salt
100g/4oz currants
125ml/4 fl oz rum

FOR THE GLAZE:

200g/7oz sugar
3 tbsps apricot jam
12 cocktail cherries

Butter for the cup moulds, each 4cm/1¹/₂in diameter and 8cm/3in high

Preparation time: 50 minutes
Standing time: 1¹/₂ hours
Baking time: 20 minutes
Nutritional value:
Analysis per serving, approx:
- 1100kJ/260kcal
- 4g protein
- 9g fat
- 37g carbohydrate

Combine the yeast with the milk. • Melt the butter. • Sift the flour into a warmed bowl. Add the dissolved yeast, eggs, salt and butter. Cover and leave to rise for 1 hour. • Wash the currants in hot water and drain. Pour on half the rum and leave to macerate. • Butter the moulds well. • Mix the currants and their soaking liquid into the dough. Fill the moulds two-thirds full with the dough. Cover and allow to rise for a further 30 minutes. • Preheat the oven to 200°C/400°F/Gas Mark 6. • Bake for 20 minutes on the middle shelf of the oven. Tip the babas out of their moulds and leave to cool. • Boil the sugar in exactly 375ml/14 fl oz water for 5 minutes. Remove from the heat and dip the babas in the syrup until they are saturated; drain them. • Strain the jam through a sieve, warm it, and mix with the remaining rum. Brush some over the babas. • Cut the cherries into quarters and press them onto the babas in star-shapes.

Shortcrust Peanut Whirls

These have an unusual taste, very crunchy and tempting

Quantities for 50 whirls

400g/14oz flour

200g/7oz butter, cut into small pieces

100g/4oz sugar

$^1/_4$ tsp salt

100g/4oz peanut butter

75g/3oz raw cane sugar

2 tsps ground cinnamon

100g/4oz very finely chopped peanuts, unsalted

Non-stick baking paper for the baking sheet

Preparation time: 40 minutes
Standing time: 30 minutes
Baking time: 15 minutes
Nutritional value:
Analysis per serving, approx:
- 200kJ/43kcal
- 1g protein
- 2g fat
- 5g carbohydrate

Sift the flour onto a work surface and make a well in the centre. • Sprinkle the butter onto the edges of the flour. Sprinkle on the sugar and salt. • Turn the peanut butter into the well. With a knife, mix the ingredients together. • Add 6 tbsps ice-cold water to the dough and rapidly knead to an elastic dough. • Divide the dough into two portions. Lightly dust a work surface with flour. Roll each portion of dough into a 15 x 30cm/6 x 12in rectangle. • Sift the raw cane sugar onto the sheets of dough. Sprinkle on the cinnamon and peanuts. Roll up each sheet from the longest side like a Swiss roll and press the ends lightly. Wrap the rolls in foil and refrigerate. • Preheat the oven to 200°C/400°F/Gas Mark 6. Line the baking sheet with non-stick baking paper. • Using a long thin-bladed knife, cut 5mm/$^1/_4$in slices from the dough, dipping the blade into very hot water before cutting each slice. • Arrange the whirls on the baking sheet. Bake for about 15 minutes on the middle shelf of the oven until golden brown. • Allow to cool for a short while, then lift from the baking sheet with a spatula.

Fruit Tartlets

These tartlets are made from a combination of shortcrust dough and choux paste

Quantities for 12 tartlets

FOR THE SHORT PASTRY:

250g/10oz flour	
125g/5oz butter, cut into small pieces	
100g/4oz caster sugar	
1 egg	
1/4 tsp salt	

FOR THE CHOUX PASTE:

50g/2oz flour	
125ml/4 fl oz milk	
50g/2oz butter	
2 eggs	

FOR THE FILLING:

125ml/4 fl oz milk	
1/4 tsp vanilla essence	
2 tbsps flour	
3 tbsps sugar	
1 tsp butter	
1/4 tsp salt	
1 egg	

TO DECORATE:

1 tbsp icing sugar	
75g/3oz blackcurrant jelly	

Butter for 12 tartlet tins, each 8cm/3in in diameter

Preparation time: 1 1/4 hours
Standing time: 2 hours
Baking time: 25 minutes
Completion time: 15 minutes
Nutritional value:

Analysis per serving, approx:
- 1400kJ/330kcal
- 8g protein
- 17g fat
- 37g carbohydrate

To make the shortcrust dough, sift the flour onto a work surface and make a well in the centre. • Sprinkle the butter over the flour. Put the sugar, egg and salt into the hollow and swiftly knead all ingredients to an elastic dough. • Wrap the dough in foil and refrigerate for about 2 hours. • For the choux pastry, sift the flour onto a sheet of paper. • Put the milk and the butter into a saucepan, and bring to the boil. Add the flour in one go and beat until it forms a lump that no longer sticks to the sides of the pan. • Remove from the heat and allow to cool slightly. Then beat in the eggs one by one. • To make the filling, Heat the milk with the vanilla essence. • Beat the flour with the sugar, butter, salt and egg. • Still stirring, mix the hot milk with the flour-and-butter paste, return to the pan and stir for just another 30 seconds. • Pour the filling into a bowl, and add a little sugar to prevent a skin forming while it is cooling. • Preheat the oven to 200°C/400°F/Gas Mark 6. Butter the tartlet moulds. • Roll out the shortcrust dough to a thickness of 5mm/1/4in. Using a serrated pasta wheel, cut out 24 1 x 8cm/1/2 x 3in strips. • Cut out 12 circles of about 11cm/4 1/4in diameter from the remaining dough. Line the tart tins or moulds with the dough circles • Combine the choux pastry with the filling. Fill the tartlets three-quarters full and arrange the shortcrust strips in a cross pattern over each. • Bake for about 25 minutes on the middle shelf of the oven until golden. • Leave the tartlets to cool on a cake rack. • Dust them with icing sugar. • Warm the blackcurrant jelly and pour some into each triangle between the short-pastry strips.

Confectionery

Delicious sweetmeats designed to impress

Successful Sweet-making

Fondant

If you are using the fondant as a glaze or thin icing, then it should be more liquid than an icing used for coating or as a centre for a chocolate. Fondant icing will look more attractive if apricot jam is first spread over the dough.

1 Sieve the jam through a fine sieve. Add a little water and bring to the boil, stirring occasionally with a wooden spoon. Brush the jam over the surface of the dough while both are still warm.

2 Sift some icing sugar and gradually add hot water, drop by drop, until the desired consistency is obtained.

3 Fondant icings and glazes made from egg whites and sifted icing sugar can also be used for patisserie. Stir the egg white and sugar to the desired consistency. Lemon juice or 1 tbsp of melted, cooled butter can be added.

4 Fondant used as a coating or filling for confectionery should be thick. Place the item to be coated on a dipping fork and dip it into the mixture twice. Leave the fondant to cool on greaseproof or non-stick baking paper.

Chocolate coating and icing

Chocolate compound coating can easily be home-made by chopping up cooking chocolate or chocolate cake covering (couverture) into small pieces and melting them in a bain-marie or in a microwave oven. Couverture and chocolate icing are also available ready-made.

1 To make chocolate coating, combine some butter or creamed coconut and icing sugar with melted chocolate and allow the mixture to cool to the required consistency. A nice gloss can be obtained if the coating is allowed to set and then reheated.

2 To make shells for chocolate fondants, pour some melted coating into the cups, and gently swill it around the cup. Leave to dry upside down on a piece of foil.

3 Pour the filling into the set chocolate shell and smooth the top.

4 Reheat the remaining chocolate coating in the bain-marie once again until it is of spreading consistency. Cover the sweet and smooth with a small spatula.

Chocolate truffles

Truffle paste for pralines consists of either chocolate and cream enriched with butter or creamed coconut, or of chocolate and butter. Flavourings are always added, rum being the most popular. A soft creamy truffle mixture is ideal for piping truffle rosettes into paper cases.

1 Either heat up the cream and melt chopped pieces of chocolate in it, or combine the melted chocolate with butter and icing sugar.

2 Beat the warm truffle paste in a metal bowl with an electric beater over water containing ice cubes.

3 Fit a piping bag with a star-shaped nozzle and fill it with the paste. Pipe rosettes into the sweet cases and refrigerate until set.

4 Alternatively, shape the chilled truffle paste into little balls. Dark truffles can be coated with fondant, pale ones can be dipped in chocolate coating or chocolate sprinkles

Crystallised fruit

Fruit keeps longer if sugar coated. Fruit that is dipped once in a clear or fondant syrup is called glacé. Crystallised or candied fruits are those in which the syrup completely saturates the fruit. This is achieved by successive dippings in stronger and stronger concentrations of the syrup.

1 Peel and cut 100g/4oz fruit to confectionery-size. Cover with water, boil for 10 minutes and drain.

2 Combine 100g/4oz glucose syrup (available from chemists) and 400g/14oz sugar with the pineapple juice, and leave for 12 hours. Reduce the sugar solution to a syrup by heating it to 110°C/225°F and pour it over the pineapple while still hot.

3 After 24 hours, pour off the syrup, reheat to 110°C/225°F and pour it over the pineapple again. Repeat this process at least four times.

4 Drain the pineapple and allow to dry in a warm place for about 24 hours. If desired, the pineapple pieces can be dipped in melted chocolate.

Sweetmeats from Around the World

These soft centres are irresistible

Romanian Christmas Candies
Illustrated left

Quantities for 20 candies
100g/4oz plain chocolate coating
50g/2oz unblanched almonds
100g/4oz icing sugar
1 egg white
1-2 tsps rum (54%)
FOR THE FILLING:
50g/2oz plain chocolate coating
2 tbsps butter
1 egg yolk, hard boiled
1 tbsp maraschino
FOR COMPLETION:
25g/1oz milk chocolate
20 sweet cases

Preparation time: 1 hour
Cooling time: 12 hours
Nutritional value:
Analysis per serving, approx:
• 470kJ/110kcal
• 2g protein
• 7g fat • 10g carbohydrate

Break up the coating. Combine with the almonds and grind in a spice grinder. • Sift the icing sugar over the chocolate and almond mixture. Add the egg white and rum. Knead to a smooth dough. • Shape into a 4cm/1½in- diameter roll. Cut 20 thick slices from the roll, and refrigerate. • For the filling, melt the plain chocolate in a hot bain-marie, and allow to cool. • Cream the butter. Crumble the egg yolk with a fork. Mix with the butter, the liqueur and the coating. • Press the chilled squares of chocolate a little flat, and distribute the filling onto each square. Press another square on top of the filling and shape each of them into balls. • Roll the balls in the chocolate chips and press lightly. Put the balls into the sweet cases. Refrigerate and set for 12 hours. Store in a cool place and eat while still fresh.

Merano Nut Creams
Illustrated right

Quantities for 20 pieces
250g/8oz sugar
125ml/4 fl oz water
125g/5oz raw marzipan
70g/3oz icing sugar
40 walnut halves
20 sweet cases
Oil for the greaseproof paper

Preparation time: 40 minutes
Nutritional value:
Analysis per serving, approx:
• 680kJ/160kcal
• 2g protein
• 8g fat
• 21g carbohydrate

Add the sugar to the water. Bring to the boil and stir until the sugar has dissolved. On medium heat, allow the sugar solution to reduce to a light-brown syrup for about 15 minutes. • Knead the raw marzipan with the icing sugar and shape it into a roll. Cut into 20 slices and shape each into an oval. Place a walnut half on either side of each oval. • Oil a sheet of greaseproof paper. • Dip the creams into the sugar syrup several times. Arrange them on the sheet of greaseproof paper and allow to dry. • Put the Merano nut creams into the sweet cases. Store in an airtight jar, but not for too long.

Petits Fours with Fondant Icing

These tiny cakes are the epitome of the baker's art

Quantities for 20 petits fours
FOR THE SPONGE
5 eggs
150g/5¹/₂oz sugar
Grated rind of 1 lemon
¹/₄ tsp salt
75g/3oz flour
50g/2oz potato flour
50g/2oz blanched, ground almonds
FOR THE FILLING AND DECORATION:
400g/14oz raw marzipan
4 tbsps raspberry liqueur
500g/1lb2oz apricot jam
125ml/4 fl oz milk
400g/14oz icing sugar
4 tbsps raspberry jam
10 crystallised violets
30 silver sugar pearls
Non-stick baking paper for the baking sheet

Preparation time: 30 minutes
Baking time: 12 minutes
Standing time: 2 hours

Completion time: 1¹/₄ hours
Nutritional value:

Analysis per serving, approx:
- 1600kJ/380kcal
- 5g protein
- 9g fat
- 65g carbohydrate

Preheat the oven to 200°C/400°F/Gas Mark 6. Line the baking sheet with non-stick baking paper. • Separate the egg whites from the yolks. • Cream the egg yolks with 4 tbsps warm water, the sugar and the lemon peel. • Beat the egg whites with the salt into stiff peaks and fold into the egg yolk mixture. Mix the flour and the potato flour and sift over the mixture. Sprinkle with the ground almonds and fold the ingredients in lightly. • Spread the sponge filling over the baking sheet. Bake for about 12 minutes on the middle shelf of the oven until golden. • Turn the sponge filling out onto a cake rack and immediately remove the baking

paper. Leave to stand for at least 2 hours. • Dice the marzipan, cream it and mix with the raspberry liqueur. • Bring the apricot jam to the boil and strain through a fine sieve. • Cut the cake in half, first across, then lengthways. • Coat all 4 sponge sheets with the apricot jam, then coat 2 of the sheets with the marzipan paste. • Lay the sheets which are coated with only the apricot jam onto those coated with the marzipan paste, so that the uncoated sides of the sheets are uppermost. Cut out an equal number of 3cm/1¹/₄in cubes and triangles from the filled sponge. Then coat them with apricot jam. • Heat the milk. Sieve the icing sugar and add just enough milk for a thick fondant to form. • Strain the raspberry jam through a fine sieve and mix with half the fondant. • Take two forks and put a petit four onto each one. Hold each petit four over a different bowl, each containing the different

coloured fondants. Coat all surfaces except the underside of the cubes with the light-coloured fondant, and the triangles with the pink fondant. Arrange all the petits fours on a cake rack. • Put the remaining portions of icing into separate little cones made from greaseproof paper, and pipe little garlands in alternate colours the thickness of a strand of wool onto the petits fours through the small nozzle. • Put the crystallised violets onto the white petits fours and silver sugar pearls onto the pink ones.

Our tip: Ready-made fondant icing is also available in vanilla, lemon and chocolate flavours.

Puff-pastry Butterflies

If the pastries are to look at all like butterflies you need to follow the shaping directions carefully

Quantities for 22 butterflies
300g/10oz frozen puff dough (5 sheets)
75g/3oz sugar
1 egg yolk
100g/4oz apricot jam
50g/2oz icing sugar

Preparation time: 40 minutes
Baking time: 12 minutes
Completion time: 15 minutes
Nutritional value:
Analysis per serving, approx:
- 420kJ/100kcal
- 1g protein
- 5g fat
- 13g carbohydrate

Remove the puff dough from the packet and thaw at room temperature. • Sprinkle each sheet with sugar and roll out to twice its length. Fold the sheets back to their original shape. Sprinkle the outsides with sugar and press lightly. • Preheat the oven to 250°C/475°F/Gas Mark 9. Rinse the baking sheet under cold water and do not dry. • Whisk the yolk with 1 tbsp water. Coat 4 of the pastry sheets lengthways in the middle with one stroke of the whisked egg yolk. Lay all the coated sheets one on top the other, so that the yolk strips are exactly lined up. Lay the uncoated sheet on top. Using a wooden spoon with a thick handle, press the whole stack together so that a groove is formed in the middle. • Cut the stack across into strips, each 1cm/½in thick. Twist each strip once to form a spiral. Arrange them on the baking sheet. Spread out the fine strips at the side into star-shapes from the centre of the dough to form 'wings'. • Bake for about 12 minutes on the middle shelf of the oven until golden. • Bring the jam to the boil and strain. Coat the butterflies with the jam while they are still warm. Cool on a cake rack and dredge them with sifted icing sugar.

Cream Horns

Make these in the autumn when pomegranates are in season

Quantities for 12 horns

330g/11oz frozen puff dough (5 sheets)
2 egg yolks
2 tbsps single cream
FOR THE FILLING:
250ml/8 fl oz double cream
3 tbsps icing sugar
2 tbsps instant chocolate pudding
3 tbsps juice and seeds of 1 pomegranate
FOR DECORATION:
2 tsps chocolate flakes
2 tsps pomegranate seeds
12 home-made moulds (see "Our tip" below)

Preparation time: 1 hour
Baking time: 12 minutes
Completion time: 30 minutes
Nutritional value:

Analysis per serving, approx:
- 1100kJ/260kcal
- 5g protein
- 20g fat
- 13g carbohydrate

Remove the puff pastry from the packet, and arrange the sheets next to each other. Leave them to thaw at room temperature. • Lightly dust a work surface with flour. Roll out all the thawed pastry to a 5mm/^{1}/$_4$in-thick, 18 x 26cm/7 x 10in rectangle. Using a smooth-edged pasta wheel and a ruler, cut the rectangle lengthways into 12 5mm/^{1}/$_4$in-wide strips. • Preheat the oven to 220°C/425°F/Gas Mark 6. Rinse the baking sheet and the little moulds under cold water but do not dry them. • Whisk the egg whites with the cream. Brush this lengthways over one half of each strip. • Arrange the strips around the moulds so that the uncoated sides of the pastry face outwards. Then wrap the strips around the little moulds in spirals so that each half which has been coated with egg white is overlapped by the following spiral of dough. • Arrange the little moulds on the baking sheet and

bake the horns for about 12 minutes on the middle shelf of the oven until golden-brown. • Pull the little moulds out of the horns while they are still warm. Leave them to cool on a cake rack. • Whip the cream with the icing sugar until firm, and divide into two portions. Mix one portion with the chocolate powder, the other with the juice and pomegranate seeds. • Fit two piping bags with small star-shaped nozzles. Fill one bag with the chocolate cream and the other with the pomegranate cream. Pipe the chocolate cream into six of the horns, and the pomegranate cream into the other six. Cap both ends of each pastry with a rosette. Sprinkle with chocolate flakes or pomegranate seeds, depending on the filling.

Our tip: To make the little moulds, shape pieces of flexible card into cones, each 3cm/1^1/$_4$in in diameter and about 6cm/2^1/$_4$in in length. Then wrap them tightly in

aluminium foil. Should the horns brown before the stated baking time is completed, cover them loosely with non-stick baking paper so that they will still become well-baked inside.

Swiss Squares

These dainty pastries do justice to special occasions

Quantities for 40 squares
FOR THE DOUGH:
8 eggs
125g/5oz icing sugar
2 tbsps vanilla sugar
1/4 tsp salt
40g/1 1/2oz grated cooking chocolate
50g/2oz flour
50g/2oz cocoa powder
65g/2oz ground almonds
75g/3oz butter
FOR THE CREAM:
1 vanilla pod
500ml/16 fl oz milk
40g/1 1/2oz potato starch
3 egg yolks
100g/4oz sugar
250g/8oz butter
3 tbsps kirsch
TO DECORATE:
1 tbsp cocoa powder
50g/2oz flaked milk chocolate
Butter and greaseproof paper for the baking sheet

Preparation time: 40 minutes
Baking time: 35 minutes
Standing time: 15 hours
Completion time: 1 hour
Nutritional value:

Analysis per serving, approx:
- 780kJ/190kcal
- 5g protein
- 14g fat
- 10g carbohydrate

Preheat the oven to 200°C/400°F/Gas Mark 6. Butter a 17 x 25cm/6 1/2 x 10in baking sheet and line with buttered greaseproof paper. • Separate the egg yolks from the whites. • Cream the yolks with the icing sugar and the vanilla sugar. • Beat the egg whites with the salt into stiff peaks. • Mix the chocolate, flour, cocoa powder and ground almonds into the egg white. Fold this into the yolk mixture. • Melt the butter over low heat, but do not allow it to become hot. Trickle it in a thin stream into the dough. • Spread the dough on the baking sheet. Bake for 35 minutes on the middle shelf of the oven. • Allow the sponge to cool on the baking sheet. Turn it out on to a work surface and peel off the greaseproof paper. Leave the dough to stand for 12 hours. • About 4 hours before serving, cut open the vanilla pod lengthways, scrape out the pith, and bring to the boil in 375ml/14 fl oz milk. • Stir into the remaining milk the potato starch, yolks and 50g/2oz sugar. • Remove the boiling milk from heat and discard the halved vanilla pods. Add the remaining sugar and then the yolk mixture and bring back to the boil. • Lower the cream filling to room temperature in a cold bain-marie by stirring frequently. • Cream the butter and allow this also to reach room temperature. • Combine the vanilla cream filling and the kirsch with the butter one tablespoonful at a time. • Cut the sponge across twice. Spread each layer evenly with butter filling right to the edges. • Dust the top layer in strips with cocoa powder. Chill for 3 hours. • Before serving, cut the cake into 3 x 3cm/1 1/4 x 1 1/4in cubes and decorate each cube with the flaked chocolate. Arrange the Swiss Squares in sweet cases to serve.

Deep-fried Pineapple Patties

Serve lukewarm as a dessert, or cold as confectionery

Quantities for 24 sweets

200g/7oz fresh pineapple, peeled, cored and cut into small pieces
50g/2oz desiccated coconut
200ml/6 fl oz cream
30g/1oz semolina
40g/1½oz sugar
2 eggs
6 sheets rice paper
50g/2oz clarified butter

Preparation time: 1 hour
Nutritional value:

Analysis per serving, approx:

- 350kJ/83kcal
- 2g protein
- 6g fat
- 63g carbohydrate

Put half of the pineapple pieces into a saucepan with the desiccated coconut and the cream. Add the semolina and the sugar. Bring to the boil, stirring all the time. • On a low heat, allow to swell to a thick semolina pudding for 5 minutes, stirring. Allow to cool. • Separate the egg whites from the egg yolks. Fold the egg yolks into the semolina. Beat the whites until firm and fold into the semolina pudding. • Soak each sheet of rice paper for ½ minute in a shallow bowl of water. Pat between 2 kitchen towels until the sheets of rice paper are no longer wet, but still malleable. • Take 2 sheets of rice paper at a time and coat with one third of the semolina mixture. Sprinkle on the remaining pineapple cubes. Tightly roll the sheets of rice paper together. • Cut the rolls into slices, each about 15mm/³/₄in thick. • Heat the clarified butter. Fry the slices on both sides until golden. Drain well on absorbent paper. Serve lukewarm or cold, as fresh as possible. Dust with icing sugar if desired.

Surprise Creams

First of all a delight to look at, then a true pleasure when eaten

Strawberry Creams
In the foreground

Quantities for 90 creams
250g/8oz full-flavoured strawberries
250g/8oz icing sugar
250g/8oz plain chocolate coating
90 foil sweet cases
1 tbsp raspberry liqueur
150g/5¹/₂oz white chocolate
2 tbsps cream
100g/4oz raw marzipan
Red food colouring
2 tbsps icing sugar

Preparation time: 1¹/₂ hours
Cooling time: 45 minutes
Nutritional value:

Analysis per serving, approx:
• 170kJ/40kcal • 0g protein
• 2g fat • 6g carbohydrate

Wash the strawberries, drain and remove the hulls. • Put them into a pan and add the icing sugar. On a low heat, simmer for 30 minutes, stirring, until they are reduced to a purée. • Melt the coating in a hot bain-marie. • Take 5 sweet cases at a time, and three-quarters fill with the coating. Swill the coating around so that they are properly lined. Place a piece of aluminium foil under a cake rack. Place the lined sweet cases upside down on the rack and allow the excess coating to drip onto the foil. Refrigerate the cases for 15 minutes. • Stir the strawberry purée in a bowl over a larger bowl of iced water. Mix in the raspberry liqueur. Fill the sweet cases with the purée. • Melt the white chocolate and spread over the purée. Cool, and refrigerate for 30 minutes until the coating has set. • Colour the raw marzipan light red. Add 2 tbsps icing sugar and knead.Shape into 90 miniature strawberries. Place one on each cream.

Liqueur Creams
In the background

Quantities for 75 creams
300g/10oz plain chocolate coating
75 foil sweet cases
150g/5¹/₂oz white chocolate
2 tbsps cream
100g/4oz softened butter
100g/4oz icing sugar, sifted
3 tbsps cherry brandy
1 tsp kirsch
100g/4oz crystallised violets or roses

Preparation time: 1 hour
Cooling time: 30 minutes
Nutritional value:

Analysis per serving, approx:
• 220kJ/52kcal • 0g protein
• 4g fat • 6g carbohydrate

Break up the coating. Melt in a hot bain-marie. • Take 5 sweet cases at a time, and fill three-quarters with the coating. Swill the coating around so that the cases are properly lined. Place a piece of aluminium foil under a cake rack. Place the lined sweet cases upside down on the rack and allow the excess coating to drain off. • Break up the white chocolate. Put into a pan and add the cream. Melt on low heat. • Cream the icing sugar with the butter. Add the chocolate one spoonful at a time, and lastly the cherry brandy and kirsch. Refrigerate this mixture and the lined sweet cases for 30 minutes. • Remove the coating that has dropped onto the sheet of aluminium foil. Reheat with the remaining coating and cool slightly. • Fill the sweet cases two-thirds with the chocolate and liqueur mixture. Cover with the coating. Place 1 crystallised violet onto each cream before the coating sets. • Store in a cool, dry place. Eat within 2 weeks.

Chocolate Confectionery with a Light Topping

Especially delightful creations, though they do not keep long

Peppermint Ice
In the foreground

Quantities for 30 pieces
125ml/4 fl oz cream
250g/8oz white chocolate
100g/4oz butter, cut into small pieces
2-3 tbsps crème de menthe
1-2 drops peppermint oil
30 foil sweet cases
60g/2oz candied angelica

Preparation time: 1 hour
Nutritional value:
Analysis per serving, approx:
• 370kJ/88kcal
• 1g protein
• 8g fat
• 6g carbohydrate

Warm the cream on low heat to 75°C/167°F. • Break up the chocolate. Combine with the cream and melt. Remove from the heat. • Melt the butter in the chocolate and cream mixture.

Then stir in the crème de menthe.
• Season with the peppermint oil. Refrigerate for 45 minutes. • While the mixture is refrigerating, stir vigorously every 15 minutes. • Fit a small star-shaped nozzle onto a piping bag. Fill the mixture into the bag. Pipe rosettes into the foil sweet cases. • Cut the angelica into 30 small lozenges and decorate each cream with them. • Store cold until serving. For better results, store in the ice-cube trough.

Mini-mousses
In the background

Quantities for 20 servings
1 tablespoon unflavoured gelatine
80g/3oz plain chocolate coating
3 eggs
60g/2oz sugar
3 tbsps cream
150g/5½oz raw marzipan, cut into pieces
50g/2oz icing sugar
1 tbsp rum
40g/1½oz white chocolate

Preparation time: 1 hour
Cooling time: 4 hours
Completion time: 20 minutes
Nutritional value:
Analysis per serving, approx:
• 510kJ/120kcal
• 3g protein
• 6g fat
• 14g carbohydrate

Cover the gelatine with cold water and leave to soak for 10 minutes. • Break up the coating. Melt in a hot bain-marie. • Separate the egg whites from the egg yolks. Beat the egg yolks with half the sugar until frothy. • Press out the gelatine. Dissolve in the melted coating. • Gradually add the egg yolk and sugar mixture and the cream to the coating. • Beat the egg whites until stiff. Sprinkle in the remaining sugar. •

Carefully fold the beaten egg white into the chocolate mixture to form a mousse. Refrigerate for 4 hours. • Take the raw marzipan and add the icing and the rum, and knead. • Sandwich the marzipan between 2 sheets of stay-fresh foil and roll out to a 5mm/¼in sheet. Cut out 20 circles, each 4cm/1½in in diameter. • Using a mini ice-cream scoop, cut 20 half-spheres from the mousse, dipping the scoop in water each time. Place a half-sphere on each marzipan circle. • Finly grate the white chocolate over the mini-mousses. Store cold until serving.

Wholefood Confectionery

For those who wish to enjoy confectionery with a clear conscience

High Energy Clusters
Illustrated left

Quantities for 50 clusters

250g/8oz yellow soya beans	
80g/3oz raw cane sugar	
1/2 tsp ground vanilla	
3 1/2 tbsps honey	
50g/2oz butter, cut into small pieces	
2-3 tsps instant coffee powder	
Grated rind of 1 orange	
2 tbsps ground carob, sifted	
30g/1oz finely-grated coconut flakes	

Soaking time: 12 hours
Preparation time: 40 minutes
Cooking time: 2 1/4 hours
Nutritional value:
Analysis per serving, approx:
• 170kJ/40kcal
• 2g protein
• 2g fat
• 4g carbohydrate

Cover the soya beans with water and leave to soak for 12 hours. • Drain well in a sieve and put them into a pan. Add 750ml/1 pint fresh water, 50g/2oz raw cane sugar and the vanilla. Cover the pan and simmer on low heat for about 2 hours until the beans are soft. • Strain the beans and reserve the liquid. • Purée the beans in a blender. Boil the liquid with the honey until the mixture is reduced to a creamy caramel. • Add the butter to the mixture. Combine the honey with the instant coffee powder, bean purée, remaining raw cane sugar, orange rind and sifted carob. • Shape walnut-sized balls from the mixture, and flatten each a little with the palm of your hand. Turn them in the coconut flakes. • These will only keep for a few days.

Sesame Seed Clusters
Illustrated right

Quantities for 40 clusters

200g/7oz clear honey	
2 tbsps butter	
1/2 tsp ground vanilla	
1/2 tsp ground cinnamon	
150g/5 1/2oz unblanched sesame seeds	
Butter for the greaseproof paper	

Preparation time: 30 minutes
Standing time: 1 hour
Nutritional value:
Analysis per serving, approx:
• 170kJ/40kcal
• 1g protein
• 2g fat
• 4g carbohydrate

Put the honey, the butter, the vanilla and the cinnamon into a heavy-based pan. Cook on medium heat for 3-4 minutes, stirring constantly, until the mixture starts to thicken. • Add the sesame seeds and the honey mixture. Continue stirring and allow the mixture to caramelise. This will take another 3-4 minutes. • Lower the heat a little. Continue stirring until the mixture has become a reddish-brown. This will take a further 2-3 minutes. • Remove from the heat, and stir until the frothing ceases. • Butter a large piece of greaseproof paper. • Spread the nut-brittle mixture about 1/2cm/3/4in thick on the greaseproof paper. Leave for 1 hour. Divide the nut brittle into 40 equal pieces, handling it with another piece of greaseproof paper - this will prevent any unsightly fingermarks being made on the nut brittle. • If liked, serve them in sweet cases. They will stay fresh for several weeks if stored in an airtight tin.

Candied Pumpkin

An excellent type of confectionery which can also be made with other kinds of fruit, such as water-melon rind

Quantities for 30 sticks
400g/14oz firm, freshly-peeled pumpkin flesh
350g/11oz demerara sugar
50g/2oz glucose
2 tbsps ground ginger
1 tsp ground cinnamon
1 tsp pimento
1 tsp ground cloves
1 tsp grated nutmeg
150g/5½oz plain chocolate coating

Preparation time: 1 hour
Crystallising time: 3½ days
Completion time: 25 minutes
Nutritional value:
Analysis per serving, approx:
- 340kJ/81kcal
- 0g protein
- 2g fat
- 17g carbohydrate

Cut the pumpkin flesh into sticks, each 4cm/1½in long and 1cm/½in wide. • Put 250ml/8 fl oz of water into a pan, bring to the boil, add the pumpkin sticks, and blanch for 7 minutes. Remove with a slotted spoon and drain. • Add the demerara sugar and the glucose to the remaining stock and mix. • Sprinkle the spices onto the pumpkin sticks. • Leave the stock and pumpkin sticks uncovered at room temperature for 12 hours. • Reduce the stock to a thick syrup – it should register a temperature of 110°C/225°F on a sugar thermometer. Pour this over the pumpkin sticks. • Allow to stand for 24 hours in the syrup. • Pour off the syrup, reduce once again, and pour onto the sticks. Leave to stand for another 24 hours. • Arrange the pumpkin sticks on a cake rack and leave to dry for 24 hours. • Break up the chocolate coating. Melt in a hot bain-marie. Immerse about half of each pumpkin stick in the coating. Allow a little of the excess to drain off. Leave to set on a sheet of aluminium foil or greaseproof paper.

Filled Chocolates with Marzipan and Nuts

Delicious ways of showing your appreciation

Chocolate Nut Creams
Illustrated left

Quantities for 60 creams
500g/1lb2oz plain chocolate coating
125g/5oz shelled walnuts
100g/4oz blanched almonds
50g/2oz pine nuts
150g/5¹/₂oz nougat
50g/2oz icing sugar
2 tbsps amaretto
50g/2oz chopped pistachios
60 foil sweet cases

Preparation time: 1¹/₂ hours
Cooling time: 2 hours
Nutritional value:
Analysis per serving, approx:
• 390kJ/93kcal
• 2g protein
• 6g fat
• 8g carbohydrate

Cut the coating into pieces. Melt in a hot bain-marie. Cool down, then reheat. • Place the foil cases onto a piece of greaseproof paper. • Cover the bases inside each cup with the melted coating, and allow to set. • Grind the walnuts, the almonds and the pine nuts in a spice grinder. • Cut up the nougat into pieces. Stir with the nuts, the icing sugar and the liqueur to a smooth mixture. • Fill the cups with the nut mixture. • Reheat the remaining coating and pour over the nougat mixture. Sprinkle the pistachios over the coating before it sets. Refrigerate the creams for 2 hours until set.

Orange Marzipan Creams
Illustrated right

Quantities for 60 creams
200g/7oz milk chocolate coating
125 ml/4 fl oz cream
25g/1oz creamed coconut
150g/5¹/₂oz blanched almonds
300g/10oz raw marzipan
100g/4oz icing sugar
1 tbsp amaretto
3 tbsps strained marmalade
3 strips candied orange slices
250g/8oz plain chocolate coating
Icing sugar for rolling out

Preparation time: 2 hours
Cooling time: 2¹/₂ hours
Nutritional value:
Analysis per serving, approx:
• 420kJ/100kcal • 1g protein
• 7g fat • 11g carbohydrate

Coarsely chop the milk chocolate coating. • Heat the cream, add the coating and the creamed coconut, and stir until melted together. Cool, and refrigerate for 2 hours. • Roast the almonds in a dry pan until light brown, cool and grate. • Cube the raw marzipan. Knead with the icing sugar and the liqueur. Dust a work surface with icing sugar. Roll out the mixture to a 16 x 18cm/6 x 7in sheet. Coat the surface with the marmalade. • Spread the cold truffle mixture smoothly onto the layer of marmalade. Refrigerate the sheet for 30 minutes. • Cut the candied orange slices into 120 julienne strips. • Melt the plain chocolate coating in a bain-marie. Cool down, and reheat. • Cut the marzipan sheet into 60 2 x 2cm/³/₄ x ³/₄in squares. Put each square onto a dipping spoon. Dip into the coating, remove and allow the excess coating to drip off. Allow to set on a piece of greaseproof paper. • Before the coating sets, garnish each cream with 2 orange strips.

Raspberry Creams

For best results, use large, ripe but firm raspberries

Quantities for 50 creams
200g/7oz ripe raspberries
250ml/8 fl oz raspberry liqueur
200g/7oz milk chocolate coating
50 foil sweet cases
200g/7oz raw marzipan
150g/5½oz icing sugar
1 egg white
1-2 drops red edible colour
75g/3oz plain chocolate
50 foil sweet cases

Marinating time: 3 weeks
Preparation time: 1 hour
Cooling time: 45 minutes
Nutritional value:
Analysis per serving, approx:
• 243kJ/58kcal • 0g protein
• 2g fat • 5g carbohydrate

Carefully wash the raspberries under a gentle stream of water. Drain and dry on a piece of absorbent paper. Put the raspberries into a jar and cover with raspberry liqueur. Close the jar and leave to marinate for 2-3 weeks. • Break up the cooking chocolate and melt it in a bain-marie or double boiler over hot water. Take 5 sweet cases at a time and fill three-quarters full with the coating. Swill the coating around in the sweet cases so that they are completely and not too thinly lined. • Place a sheet of aluminium foil under a cake rack. Place the sweet cases upside down on the cake rack and allow to drain. Refrigerate for 15 minutes. • Drain the raspberries well. Be sure to reserve the raspberry liqueur (it will now be pink in colour and will have a fine aroma). Put the raspberries in the sweet cases, which should be no more than three-quarters full. • Take the raw marzipan, add 50g/2oz icing sugar and knead. Roll out to a thin sheet. Cut out 50 circles. Place one on each of the raspberries. • Combine 100g/4oz icing sugar with the egg white and edible colour. Spread this onto the marzipan. Refrigerate for 30 minutes. • Melt the chocolate in a hot bain-marie, allow to cool, and put one spot onto each cream.

Mozartkugeln

These world famous chocolates taste just as delicious when home-made as they do from the Salzburg factory

Quantities for 50 servings

250g/8oz nougat

150g/5½oz icing sugar, sifted

400g/14oz raw marzipan

2-3 tsps rosewater

250g/8oz plain chocolate coating

Icing sugar for rolling out

Coloured aluminium foil for wrapping

Preparation time: 2 hours
Cooling time: 4 hours
Nutritional value:

Analysis per serving, approx:
- 430kJ/100kcal
- 1g protein
- 5g fat
- 14g carbohydrate

Refrigerate the nougat either for 1 hour, or for 15 minutes in the freezer. • Cut the marzipan into small cubes. Combine with the icing sugar and enough rosewater to form an elastic but not too moist dough. Dust a work surface with icing sugar. Roll out the marzipan to a 4mm/¼in-thick sheet, and a size of about 50 x 25cm/20 x 10in. Cut into 50 rectangles, each measuring 5cm/2in long. • Cut the nougat block into 50 cubes of equal size. With cold hands, roll each one into a ball. Place each one on a marzipan square. Shape the marzipan around the nougat ball, making sure that the ball does not lose its shape. • Refrigerate for 4 hours. • Melt the coating in a hot bain-marie, and allow to cool a little. Put each Mozartkugel onto a dipping fork, dip into the coating, and allow the excess coating to drip off. Place them on a piece of greaseproof paper, and allow to set. • As soon as the coating has set, wrap each Mozartkugel in a piece of aluminium foil. Store in a cool place, but do not refrigerate.

Easy-to-make Confectionery

Popular, attractive and tempting

Marzipan Balls

Illustrated in the first, third and fifth rows

Quantities for 60 balls
250g/8oz unblanched almonds
250g/8oz icing sugar, sifted
1 egg white
1 tsp rosewater
1 tsp rum
1 tsp almond essence
2 tbsps cocoa powder
60 sweet cases

Preparation time: 15 minutes
Drying time: 12 hours
Completion time: 1 hour
Nutritional value:
Analysis per serving, approx:
• 190kJ/45kcal
• 1g protein
• 3g fat
• 5g carbohydrate

Bring about 1l/1¾ pints water to the boil. Add the almonds and steep for 1 minute. • Put the almonds into a sieve and rinse under cold water. Drain, and remove the brown skins. • Lay the almonds on a cloth and leave them to dry for 12 hours. • Finely grind the almonds in a spice grinder or in a blender. Mix the almonds with the icing sugar. • Lightly whisk the egg white. Add the rosewater, the rum, and the almond essence to the almond and icing sugar mixture and gradually add just enough of the egg white to make the mixture malleable and still moist. • Make cherry-sized balls from the marzipan mixture. • Sift the cocoa powder on a plate and coat the balls with it. • Serve in the sweet cases. Store preferably between layers of greaseproof paper in a tin or jar.

Apricot Truffles

Illustrated in the second and fourth rows

Quantities for 55 truffles
150g/5½oz plain chocolate coating
150g/5½oz milk chocolate coating
125ml/4 fl oz cream
2 tbsps butter
20g/¾oz creamed coconut
150g/5½oz dried apricots chopped
3 tbsps apricot brandy
FOR GLAZING AND DECORATING:
100g/4oz chopped pistachios
100g/4oz chopped pine nuts,
400g/14oz plain chocolate coating
Non-stick baking paper

Preparation time: 1¼ hours
Standing time: 3 hours
Nutritional value:
Analysis per serving, approx:
• 430kJ/100kcal
• 2g protein
• 7g fat
• 8g carbohydrate

Coarsely chop both types of coating. • On a low heat, warm the cream to 80°C/176°F. Add all the chocolate coating, butter, and creamed coconut, and stir until melted. Leave to cool, and chill for 2 hours. • Line a large flat dish with non-stick baking paper and chill it. • Cover the apricots with the apricot brandy and soak for 30 minutes. • Purée the apricots in the mixer. Stir the apricots into the chilled cream and chocolate mixture. • Fit a circular nozzle onto a piping bag. Fill the bag with the truffle mixture. Pipe walnut-sized balls onto the chilled dish. Chill the truffles for 1 hour. • Melt the coating in a hot bain-marie. • Allow the coating to cool, but do not let it set. Dip the truffles into the coating, roll them in the chopped nuts, and chill well again, until set.

Crispy Sweet Dainties

Lightly caramelised, with a special flavour

Nut Brittle Sticks
Illustrated left

Quantities for 60 sticks

1 vanilla pod	
250g/8oz blanched ground almonds	
350g/11oz raw marzipan, diced	
400g/14oz icing sugar	
1 tbsp honey	
50g/2oz butter	
125ml/4 fl oz cream	
200g/7oz plain chocolate coating	
creamed coconut for the baking sheet	

Preparation time: 2 hours
Standing time: 4 hours
Nutritional value:
Analysis per serving, approx:
- 460kJ/110kcal
- 1g protein
- 6g fat
- 13g carbohydrate

Preheat the oven to 200°C/400°F/Gas Mark 6. • Cut open the vanilla pod lengthways. Scrape out the pith and reserve. • Spread the almonds onto the ungreased baking sheet. Roast for 10 minutes on the middle shelf of the oven until golden-brown; after the first five minutes, turn them all over. • Put the almonds in a bowl. • Coat the baking sheet and the rolling pin with plenty of creamed coconut. • Sift the icing sugar into a pan. Add the honey and the butter. On low heat allow the mixture to become thick and creamy, until just caramelised. • Warm the cream on low heat. • Remove the caramel mixture from the heat. Add the almonds, the vanilla pith, the marzipan and the cream, stirring. Turn the nut brittle onto the baking sheet and roll out to a 30 x 30cm/12 x 12in sheet. • Allow to cool down. With a very sharp knife, cut into 2 x 5cm/³/₄ x 2in fingers. Cool on a cake rack for 4 hours. • Melt the coating in a hot bain-marie. Lightly oil a sheet of aluminium foil and arrange the fingers on it. Brush the melted coating on to half of each finger. Do this several times, allowing each coating to set before applying the next.

Wholegrain Rice Balls
Illustrated right

Quantities for 50 rice balls

200g/7oz finely-ground brown rice	
30g/1oz raw cane sugar	
¹/₂ tsp ground vanilla	
¹/₂ tsp ground ginger	
¹/₄ tsp ground cloves	
70g/3oz butter, cut into small pieces	
150g/5¹/₂oz honey	
About 50g/2oz millet flakes	
2 tsps cocoa powder	

Preparation time: 40 minutes
Nutritional value:
Analysis per serving, approx:
- 170kJ/40kcal
- 0g protein
- 1g fat
- 7g carbohydrate

Combine the ground rice, raw cane sugar, vanilla, ginger and ground cloves. Turn into a dry pan with a heavy base. Roast at medium heat until the mixture turns light-brown and gives off a pleasant smell. • Add the butter to the honey and the brown rice and mix. • Remove immediately from the heat and add as many millet flakes as the sweet mixture will take. • Divide the rice mixture into two portions. Add the cocoa powder to one portion of the rice mixture, and mix. • As soon as the mixture is cool enough to be touched, shape into walnut-sized balls. Leave to cool completely on a piece of greaseproof paper. • Store in an airtight tin. They will stay fresh for about 2 weeks.

Rum Cream Balls

For a stronger rum flavour, add a few drops of rum essence

Rum Cherries
Illustrated left

Quantities for 50 cherries
50g/2oz cherries, fresh or canned, pitted and drained

about 500ml/16 fl oz rum (45%)

200g/7oz plain cooking chocolate

50g/2oz caster sugar

50 sweet cases

Marinating time: 3 weeks
Preparation time: 1 hour
Setting time: 4 hours
Nutritional value:
Analysis per serving, approx:
- 130kJ/31kcal
- 0g protein
- 1g fat
- 4g carbohydrate

Carefully wash the cherries, making sure that the all the stalks remain intact. Allow them to drain on a cloth. • Prick each cherry with cocktail sticks four times. Put them into a screwtop jar, cover them with sufficient rum, and put the lid on. • Marinate for three weeks in the refrigerator. • Remove the cherries and leave to drain on absorbent paper, and carefully pat dry (the rum can be used for drinks, desserts or other pastries). Cut up the coating into pieces. Melt in a hot bain-marie. • Pour the sugar into a small bowl. • When the coating has cooled but not set, completely immerse each cherry into the coating, then immerse each one half way into the sugar to obtain 'black-and-white' cherries. Allow the coating on the cherries to set by placing them on a fine-mesh cake rack. Arrange the cherries in sweet cases and refrigerate. • They should be eaten within 2 weeks.

Rum Balls
Illustrated right

Quantities for 80 balls
150g/5½oz unblanched almonds

200g/7oz plain chocolate coating

5 tbsps rum (54%)

1 tsp almond essence

1 tsp grated rind of 1 orange

125g/5oz butter

300g/10oz icing sugar

200g/7oz grated chocolate

Preparation time: 1½ hours
Cooling time: 6 hours
Nutritional value:
Analysis per serving, approx:
- 280kJ/67kcal
- 1g protein
- 4g fat
- 7g carbohydrate

Grind the almonds in a spice grinder. • Melt the coating in a bain-marie. Add the rum, almond essence, the orange peel and the grated almonds, and remove from the bain-marie. • Cream the butter. Sift on the icing sugar, and mix in. • Gradually add the chocolate mixture to the creamed butter, mix, and leave to cool. • Place the bowl with the sweet mixture into a larger bowl containing iced water. With 2 teaspoons, cut out small quantities of mixture. Shape into small balls with cool fingers. Roll them in the grated chocolate. • Leave to set for 6 hours in the refrigerator. • If necessary, put them into paper sweet cases. Store in a jar in layers separated by pieces of greaseproof paper.

Nougat Cornets

Show your affection with this popular confection

Quantities for 30 cornets

5 sheets of extra-strong gold foil (from craft suppliers)
40 shelled hazelnuts
4 tbsps cream
100g/4oz plain chocolate coating
200g/7oz nougat
1 tbsp butter

Preparation time: 1½ hours
Cooling time: 1 hour
Nutritional value:
Analysis per serving, approx:
- 330kJ/80kcal
- 1g protein
- 4g fat
- 5g carbohydrate

Preheat the oven to 225°C/437°F/Gas Mark 7. • Take the gold foil and cut out 30 circles, each 6cm/2¼in in diameter. Shape them into pointed cones. • Sprinkle the hazelnuts onto a baking sheet. Roast for 5 minutes in the oven until the brown skins burst open. • Rub the nuts in a dry cloth until all the skins are removed. Cut 15 nuts in half, finely chop the remainder. • Warm the cream on a low heat. Break up the chocolate coating. Add to the cream and melt, stirring. Remove from the heat. • Break up the nougat into small pieces. Add to the butter and the chopped nuts, and gradually combine with the coating. • Place the pan in a bowl of iced water. Whisk the mixture until cold and frothy. • Fit a star-shaped nozzle onto a piping bag. Fill the bag with the nougat mixture. Pipe the mixture into the cornets, rounding off each one with a rosette. Put half a nut onto each rosette. • Refrigerate the cornets for 1 hour. Store in a cool place.

Delightful Nougat Variations

There are many exquisite variations to this base mixture

Nougat with Candied Violets
In the background

Quantities for 24 pieces
30g/1oz pine nuts

30g/1oz pistachios, chopped

100g/4oz crystallised violets

250g/8oz caster sugar

100g/4oz glucose

6 tbsps water

1 egg white

1 drop violet water

Rice paper for the 30cm/12in long loaf-tin (available from Asian delicatessens)

Preparation time: 1 hour
Standing time: 12 hours
Nutritional value:
Analysis per serving, approx:
• 370kJ/88kcal
• 1g protein
• 4g fat
• 18g carbohydrate

Roast the pine nuts in a dry pan, stirring all the time, until light brown. Allow to cool. • Reserve 24 of the crystallised violets, break up the remainder. • Line the loaf-tin with rice paper. • Put the sugar, glucose and water in a pan. Dissolve on a low heat, stirring. Bring to the boil at 120°C/250°F, using a sugar thermometer. Reduce to a thick syrup. • Immediately plunge the pan into cold water in order to arrest the process. • Beat the egg white until firm. While still hot, trickle the syrup onto the beaten egg white. Continue beating until creamy. • Add the pine nuts, chopped pistachios, chopped crystallised violets and violet water, and mix. Pour onto the rice paper in the loaf-tin and spread smooth. Cover with a sheet of aluminium foil and a suitable board. Leave to set for 12 hours. • Tap the nougat out of the tin, roll it around and remove the foil. Cut the block into 4 long, narrow strips. Then cut each of these strips into 6 equal pieces. Garnish each piece with a crystallised violet.

Nougat Chocolates
In the foreground

Quantities for 50 pieces
400g/14oz nougat

200g/7oz raw marzipan, cut into small pieces

50g/2oz icing sugar

2 tbsps ginger marmalade

50g/2oz pistachios

300g/10oz plain chocolate coating

Preparation time: 1½ hours
Standing time: 12 hours
Nutritional value:
Analysis per serving, approx:
• 420kJ/100kcal
• 1g protein
• 5g fat
• 13g carbohydrate

Put the nougat into the ice-cube trough, so that it becomes firm. • Take the raw marzipan, add the icing sugar and ginger marmalade, and knead. • Cut up the nougat into 50 equal cubes. • Sandwich the marzipan between 2 layers of transparent film. Roll out the marzipan to a 2mm/¹⁄sin-thick sheet. Cut into 100 squares, each one the same size as each nougat cube. • Sandwich each nougat cube between two layers of marzipan. • Halve the pistachios lengthways. • Melt the coating in a hot bain-marie and allow to cool a little. • Put the nougat cubes one by one on a fork. Immerse each one in the coating, which should not be too fluid. Arrange on a sheet of greaseproof paper and allow to set. Press a pistachio half onto each cube before the coating has set. Leave for 12 hours to set.

Christmas Fare

Biscuits and pastries for the festive season
and seasonal delicacies from other lands

Striezel and Stollen Cakes

These Continental cakes are eaten around Christmas time

Poppyseed and Walnut Striezel

Illustrated left

Quantities for 1 28cm/11in loaf
200g/7oz wholewheat flour
25g/1oz each buckwheat flour and soya flour
1/2 lemon, rind grated
20g/1/2oz fresh yeast or 1 tsp dried yeast • 175g/6oz clear honey
125ml/4 fl oz milk
150g/5 1/2oz walnuts
125g/5oz freshly ground poppyseeds
Generous pinch of ground cinnamon • 4 tbsps milk
50g/2oz butter
3 tbsps apricot jam

Preparation time: 1 1/4 hours
Baking time: 30 minutes
Nutritional value:

Analysis per slice, approx, if divided into 16 slices:
• 980kJ/230kcal • 6g protein
• 13g fat • 23g carbohydrate

Sift the flours and combine with the grated lemon rind. Make a well in the flours, crumble the yeast into it and stir in 50g/2oz honey, milk and about 1 tbsp of the flour. Cover and leave to rise in a warm place for 15 minutes. • Knead the rest of the flour with the starter yeast and leave for a further 30 minutes. • Reserve a few walnuts for decoration. Grind the remainder for the filling, mixing them with the poppyseeds and ground cinnamon. Add to the milk and remaining honey. Bring to the boil, remove from the heat and add half the butter. Leave to cool, giving the mixture an occasional stir. • Roll the dough out into a rectangle 30x40cm/ 12x15in, cover with the filling and roll up, starting from one of the short sides. Cut in half lengthways. • Heat the oven to 200°C/ 400°F/Gas Mark 6. Butter the tin well. • Wrap the two pieces of dough around each other. Arrange in the tin. Brush the surface with the remaining melted butter and bake for 30 minutes. Test the centre of the cake with a skewer to check whether it is done. Switch off the oven and leave to stand for 10 minutes. Brush the surface with the apricot jam, decorate with the walnuts and leave to cool in the tin.

Quark Stollen

Illustrated right

Quantities for 1 stollen
100g/4oz cornflour
500g/1lb 2oz self-raising flour
200g/7oz sugar • 3 eggs
250g/8oz low-fat quark
200g/7oz sultanas
1 tbsp vanilla sugar
50g/2oz chopped candied citron
1 lemon, rind grated
200g/7oz cold butter
125g/5oz icing sugar
1 tbsp rum

Preparation time: 30 minutes
Baking time: 1 hour
Nutritional value:

Analysis per slice, approx, if divided into 30 slices:
• 880kJ/210kcal
• 4g protein
• 8g fat
• 32g carbohydrate

Mix the flour, cornflour, sugar, eggs and drained quark to make a workable dough. Rinse the sultanas in hot water, dry well and add to the dough, together with the vanilla sugar, candied citron and grated lemon rind. Cut the butter into small pieces and knead into the dough. Heat the oven to 200°C/400°F/Gas Mark 6. • Roll the dough into a rectangle, leaving one side twice as thick as the other. Fold the thick side over the thin side. • Lay the folded dough on a buttered baking sheet and bake for 1 hour. • Stir the icing sugar into the rum and then brush it over the cooled stollen.

Traditional Christmas Stollen

These stollen should be wraped in aluminium foil and stored in a cool place for at least two weeks

Almond Stollen
Illustrated left

Quantities for 2 stollen

42g/1oz fresh yeast or 2 tsps dried yeast • 100g/4oz sugar
200ml/6 fl oz lukewarm milk
500g/1lb 2oz flour
400g/14oz chopped almonds
100g/4oz softened butter
1 egg • Pinch of salt
25g/1oz butter, melted
50g/2oz icing sugar

Preparation time: 50 minutes
Rising time: 1³/₄ hours
Baking time: 45 minutes
Nutritional value:
Analysis per slice, approx, if divided into 40 slices:
• 630kJ/150kcal • 4g protein
• 9g fat • 15g carbohydrate

Crumble the yeast and mix with 1 tsp sugar and the milk. Leave to rise in a warm place for 15 minutes. • Mix half the flour with almonds, butter, the remaining sugar, the egg, salt and starter yeast. Knead in the rest of the flour. If necessary, add a little more flour. Cover the dough and leave for 1 hour. • Shape two rectangles from the dough, leaving one side twice as thick as the other on each rectangle. Fold the thick side over the thin side • Place the two stollen on buttered baking sheets, cover and leave to rise for 30 minutes. • Heat the oven to 220°C/450°F/Gas Mark 7. Put some hot water in an ovenproof dish and place in the bottom of the oven. • Bake the stollen for 45 minutes. After 10 minutes, remove the water and reduce the heat to 200°C/400°F/Gas Mark 6. After 45 minutes, test the centre of the stollen with a skewer. If the skewer emerges cleanly, then the stollen are done. Turn the oven off and leave for 10 minutes. Brush the surface with the melted butter and dust with icing sugar.

Dresden Stollen
Illustrated right

Quantities for 1 stollen

200g/7oz each raisins and currants • 250g/8oz candied peel
200g/7oz chopped almonds
6 tbsps rum
85g/3oz fresh yeast or 2 tbsps dried yeast • 750g/1lb 11oz flour
100g/4oz sugar • 250ml/8 fl oz milk
2 tbsps vanilla sugar
400g/14oz softened butter
Pinch of salt • 1 tsp vanilla essence
100g/4oz icing sugar

Preparation time: 1¹/₂ hours
Baking time: 1¹/₄ hours
Nutritional value:
Analysis per slice, approx, if divided into 40 slices:
• 1000kJ/240kcal • 4g protein
• 15g fat • 31g carbohydrate

Rinse currants and raisins in hot water, dry well. Chop the candied peel and mix with the currants, raisins, almonds and rum. Cover and leave to soak. • Make a well in the flour, crumble the yeast into it and mix with 1 tbsp sugar, a little milk and 1 tbsp of the flour. Leave the starter yeast to rise in a warm place for 30 minutes. • Mix the vanilla sugar with the rest of the sugar, 300g/10oz of the butter and the salt. Sprinkle this around the starter yeast. Knead the starter yeast with the rest of the flour, the remaining milk and the butter mixture. Cover and leave for 30 minutes. • Knead in the soaked fruit and nuts. Roll out dough and make one side twice as thick as the other. Fold the dough in half. Place on a well-buttered baking sheet and leave for a further 30 minutes. • Heat oven to 200°C/400°F/Gas Mark 6. • Bake stollen on the lower shelf of oven for about 15 minutes, then reduce heat to 180°C/350°F/Gas Mark 4 and bake for 1 hour. • Melt the rest of butter and add vanilla essence. Brush the hot stollen with butter, and sprinkle with icing sugar.

Traditional and Modern Biscuits

Little Rascals and Rye Biscuits will become firm favourites

Little Rascals

Illustrated in the centre

Quantities for 60 biscuits

375g/12oz flour
125g/5oz sugar
1 tbsp vanilla sugar
250g/8oz cold butter, cut into small pieces
100g/4oz raspberry jam
100g/4oz icing sugar, sifted
juice of 1 lemon
Non-stick baking paper for the baking sheet

Preparation time: 1 hour
Standing time: 1 hour
Baking time: 10 minutes
Completion time: 30 minutes
Nutritional value:
Analysis per serving, approx:
• 310kJ/74kcal
• 1g protein
• 4g fat
• 10g carbohydrate

Sift the flour onto a work surface. Make a well in the centre. Pour in the sugar and the vanilla sugar. • Sprinkle the butter around the edge of the mound. Knead the ingredients to a dough. Wrap in foil and refrigerate for 1 hour. • Preheat the oven to 200°C/400°F/Gas Mark 6. Line the baking sheet with non-stick baking paper. • Roll out the dough in pieces 5mm/1/4in thick. Cut out circles 3cm/11/4in diameter. • Arrange the biscuits on the baking sheet. Bake for about 10 minutes on the middle shelf of the oven until golden. • Sieve the jam. Warm it on low heat while stirring. • Coat half the biscuits with the jam and lay the uncoated ones on top to make sandwiches. • Add 2 tbsps hot water and lemon juice to the icing sugar, and stir. Spread the icing evenly over the biscuits and leave to set.

Rye Biscuits

Shown on the branches of the Christmas tree

Quantities for 40 biscuits

150g/51/2oz softened butter
1 egg yolk
50g/2oz maple syrup
200g/7oz wholemeal rye flour
1 heaped tbsp ground carob
50g/2oz finely ground almonds
20 almonds for the decoration
Butter and flour for the baking sheet

Preparation time: 45 minutes
Standing time: 1 hour
Baking time: 25 minutes
Nutritional value:
Analysis per serving, approx:
• 280kJ/67kcal
• 1g protein
• 5g fat
• 4g carbohydrate

Cream the butter with the egg yolk and the maple syrup. • Knead the rye flour, ground carob and almonds into the butter mixture. • Shape the dough into a ball. Wrap in greaseproof paper and refrigerate for 1 hour. • Take the almonds intended for the decoration and blanch by covering with boiling water. Leave to stand for a short while, rinse in cold water, and remove the skins. Dab them dry, and halve each one lengthways. • Preheat the oven to 180°C/350°F/Gas Mark 4. Butter the baking sheet and dust with flour. • Shape little walnut-sized balls from the dough. Arrange them on the baking sheet. Flatten each one a little and decorate each with an almond half. • Bake for about 25 minutes on the lower shelf of the oven. • Cool on a cake rack.

Marquesitas de Naranja

If blood oranges are not available for these Spanish biscuits, add a little red colouring to the icing sugar

Quantities for 45 slices
250g/8oz flour
1 tsp baking powder
70g/3oz sugar • 1 egg
125g/5oz butter, cut into dice
100g/4oz ground almonds
25g/1oz desiccated coconut
Grated rind juice of 1 orange
100g/4oz icing sugar
3 tbsps blood orange juice
Non-stick baking paper for the baking sheet

Preparation time: 45 minutes
Standing time: 30 minutes
Baking time: 20 minutes
Completion time: 20 minutes
Nutritional value:
Analysis per serving, approx:
• 320kJ/76kcal
• 1g protein
• 4g fat
• 9g carbohydrate

Combine the flour with the baking powder and the sugar and make a well in the centre. • Pour in the egg. Sprinkle the butter around the edge of the dough, and knead the ingredients together. • Wrap the dough in foil and chill for 30 minutes. • Mix the almonds with the desiccated coconut and the orange peel. Mix in sufficient orange juice until the mixture can be spread easily. • Preheat the oven to 200°C/400°F/Gas Mark 6. Line the baking sheet with non-stick baking paper. • Divide the dough into two portions and roll out two 30 x 30cm/12 x 12in sheets. • Lay one sheet on the baking sheet and coat with the almond mixture. Lay the second sheet over the top. Firmly press the edges and prick the surface several times with a fork. • Bake for about 20 minutes on the middle shelf of the oven until golden. • Cut the cake while still hot into 2 x 5cm/³/₄ x 2in strips. • Stir the icing sugar with the orange juice to make a thin glacé icing, and drizzle over.

Plaited Rum Rings

These require skill to make, but they look delightful and taste delicious

Quantities for 35 rings
300g/10oz flour
100g/4oz cooking chocolate
¹/₄ tsp salt
100g/4oz icing sugar
150g/5¹/₂oz butter, cut into small pieces
1 egg
2 tbsps rum
50g/2oz chopped pistachios
1 yolk for the icing
Butter for the baking sheet

Preparation time: 1 hour
Standing time: 1 hour
Baking time: 15 minutes
Nutritional value:
Analysis per serving, approx:
• 470kJ/110kcal
• 2g protein
• 7g fat
• 11g carbohydrate

Sift the flour onto a work surface. • Finely grate the chocolate. Combine the chocolate and butter with the flour together with salt, icing sugar, egg and rum. Knead the ingredients to an elastic short pastry. Wrap the dough in foil and refrigerate for 1 hour. • Preheat the oven to 200°C/400°F/Gas Mark 6. Butter the baking sheet. • Roll the short pastry into thin pencil shapes, each 15cm/6in long. Take 2 rolls at a time and plait them into little rings. Press the ends together. • Sprinkle the pistachios onto a dish. Whisk the yolk with 1 tsp water. • Brush the yolk over the rings. Lightly press the upper sides of the rings into the pistachios. Bake for about 15 minutes on the middle shelf of the oven. Lift the rings from the baking sheet with a spatula and allow to cool on a cake rack.

Our tip: One variation is to flavour the rings with amaretto and sprinkle them with flaked almonds.

Cashew Horns

These crumbly little horns are typical Austrian biscuits

Chocolate-Coated Batons

You can dip these biscuits in plain or milk chocolate

Quantities for 60 horns
80g/3oz cashew nuts
1x2.5cm/1in piece crystallised ginger
110g/4oz butter, cut into small pieces
125g/5oz flour
80g/3oz raw cane sugar
1/4 tsp salt
Butter for the baking sheet

Preparation time: 45 minutes
Standing time: 1 hour
Baking time: 15 minutes
Nutritional value:
Analysis per serving, approx:
- 420kJ/100kcal
- 1g protein
- 6g fat
- 10g carbohydrate

Finely grind 50g/2oz of the cashews, chop the remaining 30g/1oz and reserve. • Finely chop the ginger. • Combine the butter with the flour, grated nuts, raw cane sugar, salt and ginger and knead to a firm dough. • Shape 4 equal-sized rolls from the dough. Wrap each one in foil and refrigerate for 1 hour. • Preheat the oven to 175°C/347°F/Gas Mark 3. Line the baking sheet with non-stick baking paper. • Cut each roll of dough into equal-sized pieces. Dust your hands with flour, and shape the pieces into horns on a lightly-floured work surface. Make sure that you do not get too much flour into the dough, otherwise the nuts will not bind into the mixture. Lightly press the upper side of the horns into the chopped cashew kernels. Arrange the horns on the baking sheet and bake for about 15 minutes on the middle shelf of the oven until golden. • Leave the horns to cool a little on the tray, then lift off carefully using a spatula. Allow them to cool on a cake rack.

Quantities for 100 sticks
200g/7oz flour
1 tsp baking powder
50g/2oz sugar
100g/4oz butter, cut into small pieces
1 egg
100g/4oz cooking chocolate
Non-stick baking paper for the baking sheet

Preparation time: 1 hour
Standing time: 1 hour
Baking time: 15 minutes
Completion time: 30 minutes
Nutritional value:
Analysis per serving, approx:
- 97kJ/23kcal
- 1g protein
- 1g fat
- 2g carbohydrate

Combine the flour with the baking powder, and sift into a bowl. Sprinkle with the sugar. • Add the butter to the flour with the egg. Mix these ingredients with a wooden spoon, then knead the mixture with your hands to a firm but elastic dough. • Wrap the dough in foil and refrigerate for 1 hour. • Preheat the oven to 200°C/400°F/Gas Mark 6. Line the baking sheet with non-stick baking paper. • Dust your hands with flour. Make pencil-thick rolls from the dough and cut into 5cm/2in lengths. • Arrange the sticks on the baking sheet. Bake on the middle shelf of the oven for 15 minutes until golden. • Leave the sticks to cool on a cake rack. • Melt the chocolate coating in a small saucepan on low heat or in a bain-marie. • Dip each end of the sticks into the coating and leave to harden on greaseproof paper.

Cinnamon Stars

These are classic Christmas biscuits in central Europe

Quantities for 60 stars
300g/10oz unblanched almonds
3 egg whites
1 tsp lemon juice
250g/8oz caster sugar
1 tsp ground cinnamon
1 tbsp vanilla sugar
Icing sugar for rolling out
Non-stick baking paper for the baking sheet

Preparation time: 1¼ hours
Standing time: 30 minutes
Baking time: 25 minutes
Nutritional value:
Analysis per serving, approx:
- 210kJ/50kcal
- 2g protein
- 3g fat
- 5g carbohydrate

Grind the almonds in a spice grinder. • Beat the egg whites with the lemon juice until stiff. Gradually sprinkle in the sugar, and continue beating until the foam is stiff and shiny • Reserve ¾ cup of the beaten egg white for the icing. • Fold the almonds, cinnamon and vanilla sugar into the remaining egg white. Refrigerate for 30 minutes until firm. • Preheat the oven to 150°C/300°F/Gas Mark 2. Line two baking sheets with non-stick baking paper. • Dust a work surface with icing sugar. Roll out the dough to a thickness of 5mm/¼in, lifting it from the surface with a palette knife now and again. • Cut out star-shapes, dipping the cutter in icing sugar each time, so that the dough does not stick to it. Quickly knead together the remaining pieces of dough and roll out once again. • Arrange the stars on a baking sheet. Coat each star evenly with the reserved egg white. Rather than baking them, dry out for about 25 minutes on the lower and middle racks of the oven. After about 12 minutes, change the baking sheets around. Keep in the oven until the biscuits can be lifted easily from the non-stick baking paper.

Macaroons with Dates and Desiccated Coconut

Macaroons are popular in any variation

Coconut Macaroons
Illustrated left

Quantities for 70 macaroons
3 egg whites
1/4 tsp salt
200g/7oz sugar
1 tsp lemon juice
220g/7oz desiccated coconut
100g/4oz chocolate cake covering
70 rice paper circles, each about 4cm/1 1/2in in diameter

Preparation time: 35 minutes
Baking time: 20 minutes
Completion time: 25 minutes
Nutritional value:
Analysis per serving, approx:
- 150kJ/36kcal
- 1g protein
- 1g fat
- 6g carbohydrate

Preheat the oven to 160°C/325°F/Gas Mark 2. Arrange the rice paper circles on a baking sheet. • Beat the egg whites until firm. Gradually mix in the salt, the sugar and the lemon juice. Continue beating until stiff and shiny. • With a whisk, fold the desiccated coconut into the egg white. • Moisten 2 teaspoons, and cut out little mounds and place them on each wafer. • Bake for about 20 minutes on the middle shelf of the oven until light golden. • Cool on a cake rack. • Melt the chocolate cake covering in a hot bain-marie, and allow to cool. Reheat the coating until thick but still liquid. Sprinkle the cake covering over the macaroons and allow to set firmly. Store in a tin.

Date Macaroons
Illustrated right

Quantities for 50 macaroons
250g/8oz dried dates
3 egg whites
180g/6oz caster sugar
1/4 tsp salt
2 tbsps vanilla sugar
75g/3oz ground almonds
75g/3oz hazelnuts
100g/4oz chocolate cake covering
50 rice paper circles, each about 4cm/1 1/2in in diameter

Preparation time: 50 minutes
Baking time: 20 minutes
Completion time: 30 minutes
Nutritional value:
Analysis per serving, approx:
- 260kJ/62kcal
- 2g protein
- 2g fat
- 9g carbohydrate

Preheat the oven to 170°C/325°F/Gas Mark 3. Arrange the rice paper circles on the baking sheet. Stone the dates and cut them into narrow strips. Reserve one-quarter of the strips for decoration. • Beat the egg whites into stiff peaks. Gradually sprinkle with the sugar, salt and vanilla sugar until the egg white is stiff and shiny. • Combine the almonds with the hazelnuts and date strips. With a whisk, fold them into the beaten egg white. • Moisten 2 teaspoons and use them to cut out little mounds from the dough and to put onto each rice paper circle. • Bake for about 20 minutes on the middle shelf of the oven. Cool on a cake rack. • Melt the chocolate cake covering in a hot bain-marie. Top each macaroon with a small quantity of chocolate and 2 date strips.

Grenoble Biscuits

These dainty biscuits belong almost to the realm of petit fours

Quantities for 40 biscuits
120g/5oz flour
50g/2oz sugar
70g/3oz ground hazelnuts
1/4 tsp salt
1/4 tsp ground cinnamon
Grated rind of 1 lemon
1 egg yolk
80g/3oz cold butter, cut into small pieces
FOR GARNISHING:
1 egg white
60g/2oz sugar
50g/2oz ground hazelnuts
40 shelled hazelnuts
Butter for the baking sheet

Preparation time: 40 minutes
Standing time: 30 minutes
Baking time: 12-15 minutes
Nutritional value:
Analysis per serving, approx:
- 310kJ/74kcal
- 2g protein
- 7g fat
- 9g carbohydrate

Combine the flour with the sugar, nuts, salt, cinnamon and lemon peel. Turn onto a work surface and make a well in the centre of the mound. • Pour the yolk into the well. Sprinkle the butter onto the flour. Chop the whole mound with a large knife, then knead with your hands to a dough. • Shape the dough to a roll, 4cm/1½in in diameter. Wrap in clingfilm and refrigerate for 30 minutes. • Preheat the oven to 200°C/400°F/Gas Mark 6. Butter the baking sheet. • Beat the egg white until frothy. Sprinkle in the sugar and continue beating until very firm. Fold the ground nuts into the beaten egg white. • Cut the dough into 40 equal slices. Arrange them on the baking sheet and coat each one with the meringue. Put 1 hazelnut on top of each biscuit. • Bake for 12-15 minutes on the middle shelf of the oven until golden brown. • Cool on a cake rack.

Butter Biscuits, Lovingly Prepared

The dough will be more malleable if stored in a cool place

Butter Biscuits
Illustrated left

Quantities for 60 biscuits
250g/8oz flour • 75g/3oz sugar
1/4 tsp salt • 2 tsps vanilla sugar
1 egg • 125g/5oz butter

FOR THE DECORATION:
150g/5 1/2 oz icing sugar, sifted
2 tbsps lemon juice
2 tbsps white rum
1 tbsp cocoa powder
2 tbsps sugar strands
25g/1oz candied lemon peel,
finely-chopped

Preparation time: 45 minutes
Standing time: 1 hour
Baking time: 10 minutes
Completion time: 45 minutes
Nutritional value:
Analysis per serving, approx:
• 220kJ/52kcal • 1g protein
• 3g fat • 8g carbohydrate

Knead the flour, sugar, salt,
vanilla sugar, egg and butter,
just until they form a firm dough.
Cover with clingfilm and chill for
at least 1 hour. • Preheat the oven
to 200°C/400°F/Gas Mark 6.
Butter the baking sheet. • Divide
the dough into four pieces and roll
out each in turn to a thickness of
3mm/1/4in each. Cut out shapes as
desired. Arrange the shapes on a
baking sheet. Bake for about 10
minutes on the middle shelf until
golden. • Divide the icing sugar
into two portions. Add the lemon
juice to one portion, and the rum
and cocoa to the other. • When
the biscuits have cooled, brush
one half with one type of icing,
and the rest with the other type.
Decorate as illustrated.

Black-and-whites
Illustrated right

Quantities for 80 biscuits
400g/14oz flour
150g/5 1/2 oz icing sugar, sifted
2 small eggs • 2 tbsps rum
200g/7oz butter, cut into dice
1/2 tsp salt
2 tbsps cocoa powder
2 egg whites

Preparation time: 1 hour
Standing time: 1 1/2 hours
Baking time: 12 minutes
Nutritional value:
Analysis per serving, approx:
• 210kJ/50kcal
• 1g protein
• 3g fat
• 6g carbohydrate

Combine the flour with icing
sugar, and divide into two
portions. Add to each portion 1
egg, 1 tbsp rum, half the butter,
and 1/4 tsp salt. Sift the cocoa into
one of the portions. • Knead both
portions. From each portion,
form a ball, and a bar measuring
3 x 3cm/1 1/4x 1 1/4in across. Chill
for 1 hour. • Butter a baking
sheet. • Then roll out both light
and dark balls of dough into
sheets about 5mm/1/4in thick.
Whisk the egg whites, lightly brush
some over the sheets of dough.
Lay one sheet of dough on top of
the other and roll them up like a
Swiss roll. Chill for 30 minutes. •
Preheat the oven to 200°C/
400°F/Gas Mark 6. • Cut
5mm/1/4in slices from the roll of
dough. Bake for about 12 minutes
on the middle shelf. Take the bar
of pale dough, and cut off one
fifth lengthways. Roll this out into
a long sheet and brush with egg
white. • Take the remainder of the
bar of pale dough, and cut into 4
equal lengths. Take the bar of
dark dough and cut into 5 equal
lengths. Coat all sticks with egg
white. • Arrange all the sticks of
dough so that when you look at
the pile from one end you see a
`chequerboard' cross-section.
Wrap the sheet of pale dough
around the sticks. Chill for 30
minutes. • Cut into 5mm/1/4in
slices. Bake for about 12 minutes.

Crispy Squares

These go particularly well with a cup of tea

Lemon Kisses

Delicacies that melt in the mouth

Crispy Squares

Quantities for 70 pastries
125g/5oz softened butter
1 egg yolk
100g/4oz caster sugar
120g/5oz flour
100g/4oz blanched almonds
1 egg
5 tbsps raw cane sugar
Butter for the baking sheet

Preparation time: 40 minutes
Baking time: 10 minutes
Nutritional value:
Analysis per serving, approx:
- 180kJ/43kcal
- 1g protein
- 3g fat
- 4g carbohydrate

Combine the butter with the yolk. Sprinkle on the sugar and beat until frothy. • Sift the flour onto the butter mixture and gradually fold in. • Preheat the oven to 200°C/400°F/Gas Mark 6. Butter the baking sheet. • Turn the dough onto the baking sheet, and press with your fingertips until very flat. It will be enough once the dough covers the baking sheet evenly. • Coarsely chop the almonds. • Whisk the egg and brush onto the dough. Sprinkle the almonds onto the dough and sift the raw cane sugar onto the almonds. • Bake for about 10 minutes on the middle shelf of the oven until golden. • While they are still hot, cut the cakes into 3 x 4cm/1¼ x 1½in rectangles and cool on a cake rack.

Our tip: Instead of using beaten egg yolk to glaze, you can brush the pastries with warmed, strained marmalade before sprinkling with the almonds.

Lemon Kisses

Quantities for 60 kisses
125g/5oz softened butter
100g/4oz caster sugar
2 eggs
125g/5oz flour
125g/5oz potato flour
1 tsp baking powder
2 tbsp rum
100g/4oz icing sugar, sifted
2 tbsps lemon juice
Grated rind of 1 lemon
Non-stick baking paper for the baking sheet

Preparation time: 1 hour
Baking time: 12 minutes
Completion time: 20 minutes
Nutritional value:
Analysis per serving, approx:
- 210kJ/50kcal
- 1g protein
- 2g fat
- 7g carbohydrate

Cream the butter and the sugar with the eggs. • Combine the flour, the potato flour and baking powder. Sift this over the froth. Add the rum and stir with a wooden spoon. Lastly, knead with your hands. • Preheat the oven to 200°C/400°F/Gas Mark 6. Line the baking sheet with non-stick baking paper. Shape little walnut-sized balls from the dough. Arrange them on the baking sheet. Flatten the balls a little and press a hollow in each one with a wooden spoon. • Bake for about 12 minutes on the middle shelf of the oven until golden. Cool on a cake rack. • In a bowl, mix the lemon juice and enough hot water with the icing sugar to form a thick icing. Fill the hollows of each cooled ball with the icing. Sprinkle on the lemon rind before the icing sets.

Our tip: Instead of using lemon juice, use orange juice and grated orange rind for the icing.

Springerle

These little biscuits come from Swabia in Germany. They should be formed using wooden moulds

Quantities for 50 biscuits

500g/1lb 2oz icing sugar, sifted

4 eggs

Grated rind of 1 lemon

500g/1lb 2oz flour

icing sugar and flour for rolling out and for the moulds

Butter and flour for the baking sheet

Preparation time: 1½ hours
Standing time: 24 hours
Baking time: 30 minutes
Nutritional value:
Analysis per serving, approx:
• 400kJ/95kcal
• 2g protein
• 2g fat
• 17g carbohydrate

In a bowl combine the icing sugar with the eggs. With the stirring tool of a hand mixer, beat both ingredients to a pale froth. • Sprinkle with the lemon rind. Sift on the flour. With a wooden spoon, gradually fold the flour in to the froth. Lastly, knead the dough. • Dust a work surface with icing sugar. Roll out the dough to a thickness of 1cm/½in. • Dust the wooden moulds and also the surface of the dough with flour. • Press little pieces of dough into the moulds. Neatly cut away protruding and surplus dough with a knife, and tap out the figures. Brush any excess flour off the figures. • For best results butter 2 baking sheets and dust with flour. • Arrange the figures on the baking sheets. Leave to dry out for 24 hours. • Preheat the oven to 120°C/250°F/Gas Mark 1. • Cover the biscuits with non-stick baking paper. Bake for about 30 minutes on the middle shelf of the oven.

Important: Make sure that the oven door remains closed for the first 20 minutes. • The upper surfaces of the biscuits should remain white with only the undersides turning slightly brown. • When cool, store for 2-3 weeks in a sealed tin, during which time they will soften a little.

Chocolate Fancies for all Ages

Chocolate adds a touch of refinement to any biscuit, whether it is in the dough or as part of the decoration

Chocolate-dipped Fingers
Illustrated left

Quantities for 100 fingers

200g/7oz flour

75g/3oz sugar

1 small egg

100g/4oz butter, cut in dice

100g/4oz plain chocolate cake covering

Non-stick baking paper for the baking sheet

Preparation time: 50 minutes
Standing time: 1 hour
Baking time: 10 minutes
Completion time: 20 minutes
Nutritional value:
Analysis per serving, approx:
• 100kJ/24kcal
• 1g protein
• 1g fat
• 3g carbohydrate

Mix the flour with the sugar and pour onto a work surface. Make a well in the centre and pour in the egg. • Sprinkle the butter onto the flour. Knead to a smooth dough. • Wrap the dough in clingfilm and chill for 1 hour. • Preheat the oven to 200°C/400°F/Gas Mark 6. Line the baking sheet with non-stick baking paper. • Roll out the dough into portions each having the thickness of a pencil. Cut them into 5cm/2in lengths. • Arrange the lengths on the baking sheet. Bake for about 10 minutes on the middle shelf of the oven until light golden. • Cool on a cake rack. • Melt the cake covering in a hot bain-marie. Dip each end of the sticks into the cake covering, and allow any excess coating to drip off. Leave to set on a piece of greaseproof paper.

Chocolate Meringues
Illustrated right

Quantities for 100 meringues

300g/10oz icing sugar

2 egg whites

1/4 tsp salt

1 tbsp lemon juice

3 tbsps cocoa powder

200g/7oz instant chocolate whip

Non-stick baking paper for the baking sheet

Preparation time: 45 minutes
Baking time: 15 minutes
Nutritional value:
Analysis per serving, approx:
• 100kJ/24kcal
• 1g protein
• 1g fat
• 4g carbohydrate

Preheat the oven to 150°C/300°F/Gas Mark 2. Line the baking sheet with non-stick baking paper. • Sift the icing sugar onto a sheet of greaseproof paper. • Cream the egg whites with the salt and the lemon juice. Gradually sprinkle in the icing sugar and continue beating until the froth is stiff and shiny. • Sprinkle the cocoa powder and the chocolate whip over the beaten egg white. Fold in with a wooden spoon. • Fit a small star-shaped nozzle onto a piping bag. Fill the bag with the meringue mixture and pipe hazelnut-sized spots onto the baking sheet. • Rather than baking, dry out for about 15 minutes on the middle shelf of the oven. They will be ready when they can be moved easily on the non-stick baking paper. • Cool and store between layers of greaseproof paper, as they are quite fragile.

Gingerbread Hearts

If you cannot get ammonium carbonate, which is available at Continental delicatessens, use bicarbonate of soda

Quantities for 80 hearts
150g/5¹/₂oz honey
150g/5¹/₂oz maple syrup
200g/7oz butter
500g/1lb 2oz wholewheat flour
Grated rind of 1 orange
1 tsp ground cloves
1 tsp ammonium carbonate
3 tsps water
TO DECORATE:
5 tbsps honey
2 tbsps butter
3 tbsps orange juice
100-200g/4-7oz sugar strands and hundreds-and-thousands
Butter for the baking sheet

Preparation time: 40 minutes
Standing time: 24 hours
Baking time: 12 minutes
Completion time: 20 minutes
Nutritional value:
Analysis per serving, approx:
• 260kJ/62kcal
• 1g protein
• 2g fat
• 9g carbohydrate

On low heat, warm the honey with the syrup and butter until the butter has melted. Allow to cool to room temperature. • In a bowl, mix the flour with the orange peel and the ground cloves. • Combine the honey mixture with the flour. • Dissolve the ammonium carbonate in the water, and knead into the dough. • Cover and leave to stand at room temperature for 24 hours. • Preheat the oven to 180°C/350°F/Gas Mark 4. Butter the baking sheet. • Dust the work surface with flour. Roll out the dough to a thickness of 5mm/¹/₄in. Cut out heart shapes of about 5cm/2in in size. • Bake for about 12 minutes on the middle shelf of the oven until golden. Cool on a cake rack. • Melt the honey with the butter, stir in the orange juice, and brush some over the hearts. Decorate with the sugar strands or hundreds-and-thousands before the icing sets.

Popular Spicy Biscuits

These traditional Christmas offerings can be spiced in many different ways

Aachen Fingers
In the foreground

Quantities for 45 fingers

50g/2oz candied lemon peel, finely cubed • 250g/8oz honey

200g/7oz preserving sugar

50g/2oz butter

1 tbsp ground cinnamon

1 tsp ground cloves

1 tsp ground cardamom

1 tsp coriander

1 tsp ground ginger

500g/1lb 2oz flour

1 tsp bicarbonate of soda

2 tbsps milk

Preparation time: 40 minutes
Standing time: 24 hours
Baking time: 18 minutes
Nutritional value:
Analysis per serving, approx:
• 300kJ/71kcal • 1g protein
• 2g fat • 14g carbohydrate

Warm the honey. Stir in the preserving sugar, butter and spices. Heat until the butter has melted. • Sprinkle with the candied lemon peel. Allow the mixture to cool a little. Sift on the flour and knead. • Dissolve the bicarbonate of soda in the milk. Knead into the dough. • Cover, and leave to stand at room temperature for 24 hours. • Preheat the oven to 180°C/350°F/Gas Mark 4. Butter the baking sheet . • Roll out the dough to a thickness of about 5mm/^{1}/₄in. Cut into 2 x 7cm/^{3}/₄ x 2^1/₂in fingers. • Arrange them on the baking sheet, leaving enough space between each one. Bake for 18 minutes on the middle shelf until golden. • Cool on a cake rack.

Chocolate Gingernuts
In the background

Quantities for 20 gingernuts

100g/4oz chopped almonds

100g/4oz chopped hazelnuts

100g/4oz candied orange peel, finely cubed

100g/4oz candied lemon peel, finely cubed

125g/5oz butter

150g/5^1/₂oz sugar

50g/2oz cooking chocolate

2 eggs

200g/7oz flour

100g/4oz rolled oats

2 tsps baking powder

2 tbsps cocoa powder

1 tsp ground cinnamon

^{1}/₄ tsp ground cloves

^{1}/₄ tsp ground cardamom

^{1}/₄ tsp allspice

^{1}/₄ tsp ground ginger

20 rice paper circles, each 6cm/2^1/₄in in diameter

200g/7oz chocolate cake covering

Preparation time: 45 minutes
Baking time: 25 minutes

Completion time: 15 minutes
Nutritional value:
Analysis per serving, approx:
• 1300kJ/310kcal • 6g protein
• 23g fat • 33g carbohydrate

Preheat the oven to 180°C/350°F/Gas Mark 4. • Cream the butter with the sugar. Grate the chocolate and sprinkle it over the mixture. Add the eggs. • Combine the flour with the rolled oats, baking powder, cocoa powder and spices. Add to the butter and egg mixture with the almonds, nuts, candied orange and lemon peel, and stir. • Arrange the rice paper circles on the baking sheet. Put a portion of dough onto each one. Bake for about 25 minutes on the middle shelf of the oven. • Melt the chocolate cake covering in a hot bain-marie. Dip half of each gingernut into the cake covering. Leave to set on a piece of greaseproof paper.

Cones and Coins with Nuts and Nougat

The smaller their shapes, the more they stimulate the taste buds

Nougat Cones
In the foreground

Quantities for 80 cones
100g/4oz softened butter
200g/7oz nougat
1 egg
2 tbsps vanilla sugar
1/2 tsp ground cinnamon
1/4 tsp salt
300g/10oz flour
1/2 tsp baking powder
100g/4oz plain chocolate cake covering
Butter for the baking sheet
A little sugar for shaping

Preparation time: 40 minutes
Standing time: 3 hours
Baking time: 12 minutes
Completion time: 15 minutes
Nutritional value:
Analysis per serving, approx:
• 190kJ/45kcal
• 1g protein
• 2g fat • 5g carbohydrate

Combine the butter with the nougat. Stir in the egg, vanilla sugar, cinnamon and salt. • Combine the flour with the baking powder. Sift it over the mixture and knead in. • Cover and refrigerate for 3 hours. • Preheat the oven to 200°C/400°F/Gas Mark 6. Butter the baking sheet. • Lightly sprinkle some sugar over a work surface. Roll out pencil-thin strands from the dough and cut into 6cm/2¹/₄in lengths. Bend the lengths into cone shapes. Arrange them on the baking sheet. • Bake for about 12 minutes on the middle shelf of the oven. • Cool on a cake rack. • Melt the cake covering in a hot bain-marie. Dip both ends of each cone into the cake covering. Allow to set on greaseproof paper

Nut Coins
In the background

Quantities for 80 coins
300g/10oz flour
1 egg
150g/5¹/₂oz sugar
1/4 tsp salt
1 tsp baking powder
1/2 tsp ground cinnamon
3 tbsps cocoa powder
150g/5¹/₂oz ground hazelnuts
175g/6oz butter, cut into dice
200g/7oz nut chocolate
Non-stick baking paper for the baking sheet

Preparation time: 30 minutes
Standing time: 2 hours
Baking time: 12 minutes
Completion time: 25 minutes
Nutritional value:
Analysis per serving, approx:
• 220kJ/52kcal
• 10g protein
• 3g fat • 5g carbohydrate

Sift the flour onto a work surface. Make a well in the centre and pour in the egg. • Sprinkle on the sugar, salt, baking powder, cinnamon, cocoa powder and nuts. • Sprinkle the butter onto the flour. Knead the ingredients to a smooth dough. • Roll out 2 portions of dough, each 3cm/1¹/₄in in diameter. Wrap in clingfilm and refrigerate for 2 hours. • Preheat the oven to 200°C/400°F/Gas Mark 6. Line the baking sheet with non-stick baking paper. • Cut the roll into 5mm/¹/₄in slices. Arrange them on the baking sheet. Bake for about 12 minutes on the middle shelf of the oven. Remove immediately from the sheet, otherwise they will continue to bake and become too dark on the undersides. • Melt the nut chocolate in a hot bain-marie. Dip each biscuit halfway into the glaze and dry on greaseproof paper.

Speculeuses

These Belgian favourites can either be made using special wooden moulds or more ordinary shape cutters

Quantities for 120 biscuits

250g/8oz butter, cut into small pieces
250g/9oz caster sugar
100g/4oz unblanched, ground almonds
2 eggs
2 tsps ground cinnamon
1/2 tsp ground cardamom
1/4 tsp ground cloves
1/4 tsp ground mace
1/4 tsp salt
500g/1lb 2oz flour
flour and 150g/5½oz unblanched ground almonds for the moulds and the baking sheet

Preparation time: 1½ hours
Standing time: 1 hour
Baking time: 10 minutes
Nutritional value:
Analysis per serving, approx:
- 240kJ/57kcal
- 1g protein
- 3g fat
- 6g carbohydrate

In a bowl, combine the butter with the sugar, almonds, eggs, cinnamon, cardamom, ground cloves, mace and salt. • Sift the flour onto the butter mixture and knead. Cover, and leave to stand for 1 hour in a cool place. • Dust the moulds with flour. Dust the first baking sheet with flour and sprinkle on some of the ground almonds. Preheat the oven to 190°C/375°F/Gas Mark 5. • Take small quantities of the dough at a time and press into the moulds. Using a piece of fine wire, cut away the remaining dough that protrudes above the mould. Remove the dough shapes from the moulds by tapping the back of the moulds, so that they fall onto the baking sheet. Bake for about 10 minutes on the middle shelf of the oven until golden brown. Those without a mould should roll out their portion of dough to a thickness of about 5mm/¼in, and cut out shapes. • After the biscuits have cooled, store them in a jar with a piece of greaseproof paper between each layer of biscuits, as they are quite fragile.

Louise's Gingernuts

These spicy bicuits come from Nuremberg in Germany

Quantities for 30 gingernuts
200g/7oz unblanched almonds
50g/2oz candied orange peel, finely chopped
2 eggs
200g/7oz sugar
3 tsps ground cinnamon
1/2 tsp ground cardamom
1/4 tsp ground cloves
1/4 tsp ground ginger
1/2 tsp grated rind of 1 lemon
1/4 tsp salt • 100g/4oz flour
1/2 tsp baking powder
30 rice paper circles, 4cm/1 1/2in in diameter
75g/3oz icing sugar, sifted
1 tbsp lemon juice
50g/2oz plain chocolate cake covering
1 tbsp chopped pistachios
1 tbsp almonds

Preparation time: 40 minutes
Standing time: 1 hour
Baking time: 20 minutes
Completion time: 20 minutes
Nutritional value:
Analysis per serving, approx:
• 495kJ/120kcal
• 3g protein
• 6g fat
• 14g carbohydrate

Grind the almonds. • Beat the eggs with the sugar to a white froth. Mix in the spices, lemon peel, candied orange peel and salt. Mix the almonds into the mixture with a wooden spoon. • Combine the flour with the baking powder and sift onto the mixture, and fold in. • Arrange the rice paper circles on the baking sheet. • Put little mounds of the dough onto each circle. Moisten a knife and shape the dough on each circle into a cone. Leave to stand for 1 hour. • Preheat the oven to 175°C/250°F/Gas Mark 3. • Bake for about 20 minutes on the middle shelf of the oven until golden brown. • Add the icing sugar to the lemon juice. • Melt the cake covering in a hot bain-marie. • Coat one half of the gingernuts with the lemon icing and sprinkle on the pistachios. Coat the remaining gingernuts with the chocolate cake covering and sprinkle with almonds.

Colourful Christmas Figurines

Decorate the Christmas tree with a touch of sweet magic

Quantities for 150 figurines
250g/8oz softened butter
200g/7oz sugar
3 eggs
¹/₄ tsp salt
Grated rind of 1 lemon
500g/1lb 2oz flour
FOR THE DECORATION:
250g/8oz icing sugar, sifted
2-3 tbsps lemon juice
Red, green and yellow edible colour
1 egg white
100g/4oz plain chocolate cake covering
Coloured sugar pearls
Non-stick baking paper for the baking sheet
1 sheet card for the templates

Preparation time: 1¹/₂ hours
Standing time: 1 hour
Baking time: 10 minutes
Completion time: 2 hours

Nutritional value:

Analysis per serving, approx:
- 180kJ/43kcal
- 1g protein
- 2g fat
- 6g carbohydrate

Cut 5cm/2in-high shapes out of the card so that they look like Santa Clauses, Christmas trees, angels, comets, stars, etc. Draw lines on the shapes for the later stages of decoration. • Cream the butter with the sugar. Gradually mix in the eggs, salt and lemon rind. • Sift the flour over the butter mixture, and knead. • Wrap the dough in clingfilm and refrigerate for 1 hour. • Preheat the oven to 200°C/400°F/Gas Mark 6. Line the baking sheet with non-stick baking paper. • Divide the dough into five portions. Roll out each portion to a thickness of about 4mm/¹/₄in. Using a template, cut out figures from the dough. With a needle, prick through the template along the decoration lines, so that the lines appear on the dough. With a thick knitting needle make a hole in each shape so that they can be hung up. • Arrange the figures on the baking sheet. Bake for 10 minutes on the middle shelf of the oven until golden. Cool on a cake rack. • For the decoration, heat the lemon juice and add to two-thirds of the icing sugar. Stir until a thick icing forms. Divide this icing into three saucers, and colour each portion with a few drops of different edible colour. • Whisk the remaining icing sugar with the egg white to an elastic icing that can be easily piped. • Take a piece of greaseproof paper and make a simple piping bag with a small nozzle at the end. Fill this with the piping icing. • Melt the cake covering in a hot bain-marie. • Use the red-coloured icing for the hats and coats of the Santa Claus figures, and use the light icing for the fur trimming. Bring out the beard and eyes with the piped icing. • Coat the Christmas-tree shapes with the green-coloured icing, and use the piped icing or the yellow-coloured icing for the candles and stars. Pipe a spot of yellow-coloured icing for the candle flames. • Angels' hair can be made with the yellow-coloured icing, with their wings green and their robes white. The stars and comets can be yellow, with white trimmings. Press sugar pearls onto the white icing before it sets. Arrange the figures on greaseproof paper for the icing to set. • Tie a little ribbon onto each shape. Store between layers of greaseproof paper in an airtight tin.

Pizzas, Quiches and Shaped Pastries

Ideal when entertaining friends, for family
gatherings, picnics and office parties

Favourite Pizzas

You can let your imagination run riot with pizza toppings

Four Season Pizza

illustrated left

Quantities for 2 pizzas:

21g/³/₄oz fresh yeast or 10g/¹/₄oz dry yeast
¹/₂ tsp sugar
125ml/4 fl oz lukewarm water
300g/10oz wheatmeal flour
6 tbsps olive oil • ¹/₂ tsp salt
400g/14oz tomatoes
200g/7oz mushrooms
150g/5¹/₂oz lean, cooked ham
50g/2oz salami • 2 red chillies
4 anchovy fillets
300g/10oz can artichoke hearts
Pinch pepper, salt and rosemary
100g/4 oz grated Parmesan
Olive oil for the baking sheet

Preparation time: 1 hour
Rising time: 1 hour
Baking time: 30 minutes
Nutritional value:
Analysis per pizza, approx:
• 6720kJ/1600kcal
• 86g protein
• 79g fat
• 130g carbohydrate

Mix the fresh yeast with the sugar and water, and allow to rise for 15 minutes. If using dry yeast, blend with the sugar and water and pour onto the flour. • Knead the flour, 4 tbsps oil and the salt into the yeast mixture; cover and allow to rise for 45 minutes. • Peel and slice the tomatoes; slice the mushrooms; cut ham and salami into strips; snip the anchovies and the chillies, and cut the artichoke hearts into slices. • Lightly oil two baking sheets. • Shape the dough into two circles with slightly raised edges, mark each one into four quadrants with a knife, and place on the baking sheets. • Arrange tomatoes, mushrooms, ham with the chillies and the artichokes with the salami on the quarters of the pizza; sprinkle with seasoning, rosemary, anchovies and Parmesan cheese; drizzle oil over the topping. Bake on the centre shelf of a preheated 220°C/425°F/Gas Mark 7 oven for 30 minutes.

Napoletana

Quantities for 2 pizzas:

21g/³/₄oz fresh yeast or 10g/¹/₄oz dry yeast
¹/₂ tsp sugar
125ml/4 fl oz lukewarm water
300g/11oz wheatmeal flour
5 tbsps olive oil • ¹/₂ tsp salt
400g/14oz large tomatoes
1 onion • 1 garlic clove
150g/5¹/₂oz Mozzarella cheese
4 sprigs of basil • 20 black olives
¹/₂ tsp each of dried oregano, black pepper and salt
Olive oil for the baking sheet

Preparation time: 40 minutes
Rising time: 1 hour
Baking time: 30 minutes
Nutritional value:
Analysis per pizza, approx:
• 4620kJ/1100kcal
• 36g protein
• 52g fat
• 120g carbohydrate

Mix the yeast with the sugar and water, and leave to rise for 15 minutes. If using dry yeast, blend the yeast with the sugar and water and pour onto the flour. • Knead the flour, 3 tbsps of the oil and the salt into the yeast mixture, cover and leave to rise for 45 minutes. • Slice the tomatoes, and cut the onions into rings. Crush the garlic. Chop the mozzarella into cubes. Pinch the leaves off the sprigs of basil. • Lightly oil two baking sheets. • Knead the dough thoroughly and shape it into two circles 20cm/8in in diameter, with slightly raised edges; place on the baking sheets. • Arrange the tomatoes, onions and cheese on the base; sprinkle on the olives, basil, garlic and seasoning, and drizzle oil over each pizza. • Bake on the centre shelf of a preheated 220°C/430°F/Gas Mark 7 oven for 30 minutes.

Deep Pan Wholewheat Pizza

This pizza is particularly delicious if you use fresh, rather than dried, mixed herbs

Quantities for 1 baking sheet:

250g/8oz tinned chickpeas
300g/11oz wholewheat flour
42g/1½oz fresh yeast or 21g/¾oz dry yeast
1 tsp honey
125ml/4 fl oz lukewarm water
1 tsp sea salt
9 tbsps olive oil
1 bunch of spring onions
1 green pepper
1 red pepper
1 yellow pepper
100g/4oz black olives
200g/7oz crème fraîche
200g/7oz tomato purée
1 tbsp mixed herbs
½ tsp black pepper
½ tsp sweet paprika
150g/6oz grated pecorino cheese
Butter for the baking sheet

Preparation time: 1 hour
Baking time: 25 minutes
Nutritional value:
Analysis per piece, when cut into 20 slices, approx:
- 1005kJ/240kcal
- 10g protein
- 15g fat
- 15g carbohydrate

Combine the honey, yeast, half the water and 2 tbsps flour. Cover and allow to rise for 15 minutes. • Knead the salt, 3 tbsps oil, the rest of the flour and the yeast starter together, cover and allow to rise for 25 minutes. • Deseed the peppers, then cut the onions into rings and the peppers into strips. Stone the olives and chop them roughly. • Whisk together the crème fraîche, tomato purée, the rest of the water, the remaining oil and the herbs and spices. • Roll out the dough on a greased baking sheet, cover and leave to rise for 15 minutes. • Drain the chickpeas, and spread them over the dough, together with the onions, peppers and olives, then pour the tomato purée mixture over the pizza and sprinkle it with the cheese. • Bake in a preheated 200°C/400°F/Gas Mark 6 oven for 25 minutes.

Hearty Traditional Pies

The secret of a great pie is light pastry

Cheese and Pine Nut Pie
illustrated left

Quantities for 1 26cm/10in pie:
300g/10oz frozen puff pastry
8 preserved vine leaves
1 leek
1 garlic clove
200g/7oz feta cheese
3 eggs
200g/7oz low fat curd cheese
100g/4oz full fat soft cheese
1 tbsp capers
1/2 tsp salt
20g/3/4oz pine nuts
Butter for the pie dish

Preparation time: 40 minutes
Baking time: 50 minutes
Nutritional value:
Analysis per piece, if divided into 12 slices, approx:
• 1000kJ/240kcal
• 11g protein
• 17g fat
• 11g carbohydrate

Defrost the frozen puff pastry. • Wash the vine leaves and pat them dry on kitchen paper. Chop the leek. Finely chop the garlic. • Lay the sheets of pastry one on top of the other and roll them out to the shape of the quiche dish. Line the dish with the pastry and arrange the vine leaves on top. • Work the feta cheese through a sieve and mix into a creamy paste with the eggs, curd cheese, soft cheese, capers, salt, garlic and chopped leek. • Spread the mixture onto the vine leaves and sprinkle on the pine nuts. • Bake on the centre shelf of a preheated 200°C/400°F/Gas Mark 6 oven for 50 minutes; serve hot or cold.

Sauerkraut Pie
illustrated right

Quantities for 1 32cm/12in pie:
350g/11oz floury potatoes
100g/4oz butter
200g/7oz buckwheat flour
30g/1oz soya flour
1 tsp sea salt
1 1/4 tsp baking powder
200g/7oz rindless streaky bacon
4 onions
4 tbsps sunflower oil
1kg/2 1/4 oz sauerkraut, rinsed
200g/7 fl oz sour cream
Pinch of black pepper
1 tsp sweet paprika
4 bay leaves • 1 egg yolk
Butter for the quiche dish

Preparation time: 40 minutes
Cooking time: 40 minutes
Baking time: 35-40 minutes
Nutritional value:
Analysis per piece, if divided into 16 slices, approx:
• 1090kJ/260kcal
• 6g protein
• 19g fat
• 17g carbohydrate

Peel the potatoes and boil until soft, then mash with the butter. Mix the buckwheat flour and potatoes and combine with the soya flour, baking powder and salt, and knead together. • Dice the bacon and onions. • Fry bacon in the oil until crispy, put aside half of the bacon and mix the onion in with the rest; fry until golden. • Chop the sauerkraut. • Whisk the sour cream and spices and combine with the onion and bacon mixture, and the sauerkraut. • Butter the pie dish, pour in the sauerkraut mixture and add the bay leaves. • Roll out the pastry, cut into strips 4cm/2in wide, and lay these across the sauerkraut in a crisscross pattern. • Beat the egg yolk with a little water and use it to glaze the pastry. Press the remaining cubes of bacon into the glaze. • Bake the pie on the centre shelf of a preheated 200°C/400°F/Gas Mark 6 oven for 35 to 40 minutes.

Imaginative Party Food

These striking flans make an unusual party offering

Sweetcorn and Spring Onion Flan
illustrated bottom

Quantities for 1 28cm/11in quiche dish:

200g/7oz wheatmeal flour
100g/4oz cornmeal
1 tsp each of baking powder and dry yeast
125ml/4 fl oz lukewarm water
3 tbsps lemon juice
4 tbsps clarified butter
1/2 tsp salt
1/2 tsp sugar cane granules
150g/51/2oz can sweetcorn
2 bunches spring onions
200g/7oz hard cheese
Butter for the quiche dish

Preparation time: 40 minutes
Rising time: 1 hour
Baking time: 30 minutes
Nutritional value:
Analysis per piece, if divided into 12 slices, approx:

- 920kJ/220kcal
- 10g protein
- 10g fat
- 21g carbohydrate

Mix the flours with the baking powder and yeast and knead with the water, lemon juice, 2 tbsps melted clarified butter, salt and sugar cane granules. Cover and leave to rise in a warm place, until it has doubled in volume – this will take about an hour. • Butter the quiche dish. • Knead the dough again, incorporating the sweetcorn. Roll it out into a circle and line the dish with it. • Trim the spring onions and fry in the remaining clarified butter, stirring frequently, for 4 minutes. Cut them in half lengthwise and scatter on the pastry base. • Cut the ham and cheese into strips and arrange among the onions. • Bake on the bottom shelf of a preheated 200°C/400°F/Gas Mark 6 oven for 30 minutes.

Layered Cheese Flan
illustrated top

Quantities for 1 26cm/11in springform tin:

250g/8oz soft butter
100g/4oz freshly grated Parmesan cheese
4 eggs
350g/11oz wheatmeal flour
1/2 tsp each of salt and sweet paprika
2 tsps baking powder
250g/8oz herby cream cheese
250g/8oz Mascarpone
1 bunch of chives
Butter for the tin

Preparation time: 2 hours
Nutritional value:
Analysis per piece, if divided into 12 slices, approx:

- 2010kJ/480kcal
- 15g protein
- 37g fat
- 21g carbohydrate

Butter the springform tin. • Knead the butter and cheese together, incorporating the eggs gradually. Combine the flour with the salt, paprika and baking powder and mix into the egg and cheese mixture. • Divide the dough into 5 portions and press each one down flat onto the base of the springform tin. Bake each one on the centre shelf of a preheated 200°C/400°F/Gas Mark 6 oven for about 7 minutes until golden. • Leave each pre-baked pastry case to cool. • Mix the herby cream cheese with the Mascarpone. Spread the pastry cases with the mixture and lay one on top of the other. • Spread the remaining cheese mixture round the sides and over the top of the flan. • Chop the chives and sprinkle on the top.

Ratatouille Quiche

A very special quiche, with a rich cream filling

Quantities for 1 28cm/11in springform tin:

FOR THE RATATOUILLE:

350g/11oz aubergines
500g/1lb 2oz courgettes
250g/8oz onions
2 red and 2 green peppers
4 garlic cloves
500g/1 lb 2oz beefsteak tomatoes
6 tbsps olive oil
1 tsp each of salt and freshly ground white pepper
1 bunch each of basil and parsley

FOR THE SHORTCRUST DOUGH:

250g/8oz wheatmeal flour
¹/₂ tsp salt
125g/5oz chilled butter
1 egg yolk

FOR THE FILLING:

125ml/4 fl oz each of cream and crème fraîche
2 eggs
150g/5¹/₂oz freshly grated Gruyère cheese
Butter for the tin

Preparation time: 1 hour
Standing time: 1 hour
Baking time: 45 minutes
Nutritional value:

Analysis per piece, if divided into 12 slices, approx:
- 1760kJ/420kcal
- 12g protein
- 31g fat
- 22g carbohydrate

Cut the aubergines into 2cm/1in cubes and the courgettes into 1cm/¹/₂in slices. Slice the onions in rings. Deseed the peppers and cut into equal-sized narrow strips. Finely chop the garlic. Skin and quarter the tomatoes. • Heat the oil in a casserole and fry the onion rings until lightly browned; add the pepper strips and garlic and fry for 2 minutes, stirring frequently. Add the remaining vegetables, salt and pepper. Cover and simmer over a low heat for 20 minutes. • Chop the herbs. • To make the dough, mix the flour with the salt, tip it onto a work surface and make a well in the centre. • Add the cubed butter to the edge of the flour. Put the egg yolk and 2 tbsps of ice-cold water into the well and knead it quickly to form a smooth, elastic dough. Wrap in aluminium foil and refrigerate for 1 hour. • Cool the vegetables and leave to drain in a sieve. Mix in the chopped herbs. • Whisk the cream with the crème fraîche, eggs and cheese and stir into the ratatouille. • Butter the springform tin. • Roll out the pastry on a lightly floured work surface into a circle slightly larger than the springform tin and line the tin with it, raising the sides to form a 5cm/2in high rim. Pour in the ratatouille and bake the quiche on the centre shelf of a preheated 200°C/400°F/Gas Mark 6 oven for 45 minutes. • Serve hot.

Our Tip: As an alternative, try using organic wholewheat flour for the pastry.

Onion Tart

A variation on the traditional Swiss onion flan

Quantities for 1 28cm/11in quiche dish:

400g/14oz strong plain flour
1 tbsp very fine soya flour
21g/³/₄oz fresh yeast or 10g/¹/₄oz dry yeast
1 tsp honey
100ml/4 fl oz lukewarm water
100g/4oz rindless streaky bacon
4 tbsps sunflower oil
500g/1lb 2oz onions
¹/₂ tsp sea salt • 4 eggs
200g/7oz sour cream
1 tsp caraway seeds
¹/₄ tsp sea salt
2 tbsps chopped chives
Butter for the quiche dish

Preparation time: 1 hour
Rising time: 45 minutes
Baking time: 50 minutes
Nutritional value:
Analysis per piece, if divided into 12 slices, approx:
• 920kJ/220kcal
• 9g protein
• 14g fat
• 15g carbohydrate

Pour the flour on a work surface and make a well in the centre. Crumble the fresh yeast into the centre and drizzle on the honey. If using dry yeast, blend the yeast with the honey. Stir in the dissolved yeast with the water and a little of the flour, cover and leave to rise for 15 minutes. • Dice the bacon and fry in the oil until crispy. • Slice the onions and fry in the bacon fat. • Knead the starter dough with the remaining flour, cover and leave to rise for 20 minutes. • Butter the quiche dish. • Knead the dough again, adding a little more water or white flour if required. • Roll out the dough and line the dish with it, cover and leave to rise for 10 minutes. • Spread the onion mixture over the base of the pastry. Whisk the eggs with the sour cream, caraway seeds and salt, pour onto the onions and bake on the centre shelf of a preheated 180°C/350°F/Gas Mark 4 oven for 50 minutes. • Sprinkle on the chopped chives and serve hot.

Mushroom and Vegetable Quiches

Moist, juicy fillings in crispy shortcrust pastry

Savoy Cabbage and Tomato Quiche
illustrated left

Quantities for 1 28cm/11in springform tin:

250g/8oz wholewheat flour
1 tsp salt
4 eggs
125g/5oz soft butter
400g/14oz tomatoes
300g/10oz Savoy cabbage
1 bunch each of fresh basil and parsley
200ml/7 fl oz cream
125g/5oz freshly grated Cheddar cheese
Pinch each of cayenne and freshly ground nutmeg

Preparation time: 50 minutes
Standing time: 1 hour
Baking time: 40 minutes
Nutritional value:
Analysis per piece, if divided into 12 slices, approx:
- 1300kJ/310kcal
- 11g protein
- 22g fat
- 16g carbohydrate

Knead the flour together with a pinch of salt, 1 egg, the cubed butter and 3 tbsps ice-cold water. Roll out to a 36cm/14in circle and line the tin with it, pressing halfway up the edge of the tin. Refrigerate for 1 hour. • Skin and dice the tomatoes, cutting out the stalk. Cut the cabbage into strips. Remove any large stalks from the herbs and chop. • Combine the tomatoes with the cabbage and herbs and spread on the pastry base. • Whisk the remaining eggs with the cream, cheese, remaining salt and the herbs and pour onto the vegetables. Bake on the centre shelf of a preheated 200°C/400°F/Gas Mark 6 oven for about 40 minutes until golden-brown.

Mushroom and Bacon Quiche
illustrated right

Quantities for 1 28cm/11in springform tin:

100g/4oz wheatmeal flour
150g/5½oz buckwheat flour
1 tsp salt • 4 eggs
125g/5oz soft butter
150g/5½oz rindless streaky bacon
1 large onion
600g/1½lbs mushrooms
1 tbsp lemon juice
1 bunch of chives
200ml/7 fl oz cream
75g/3oz freshly gratedd cheese
pinch of black pepper

Preparation time: 1 hour
Standing time: 1 hour
Baking time: 40 minutes
Nutritional value:
Analysis per piece, if divided into 12 slices, approx:
- 1510kJ/360kcal
- 11g protein
- 28g fat
- 17g carbohydrate

Knead together the flours with a pinch of salt, the egg, cubed butter and 2 tbsps ice-cold water. • Roll the dough out to a 36cm/15in circle and line the tin with it, pressing it up the edge; refrigerate for 1 hour. • Dice the bacon and chop the onion finely. Wipe and slice the mushrooms and drizzle on the lemon juice. • Fry the bacon over a moderate heat until the fat begins to run; add the onions and fry until translucent. • Chop the chives. • Combine the mushrooms with the bacon and chives and spread over the pastry base. • Whisk the remaining eggs with the cream, cheese, pepper and remaining salt and pour over the mushrooms. • Bake in a preheated 200°C/400°F/Gas Mark 6 oven for 40 minutes.

Smoked Salmon Quiche

A real delicacy for those special guests – it can be served hot or cold

Quantities for 1 26cm/11in springform tin:
200g/7oz wheatmeal flour
150g/5oz butter
1 egg
2 tbsps milk
Pinch of salt
300g/10oz thinly sliced smoked salmon
750g/1lb 11oz leeks
4 eggs
6 tbsps crème fraîche
¹/₂ tsp each of salt and freshly ground white pepper
Pinch of nutmeg
1 tsp lemon juice
Butter for the tin

Preparation time: 40 minutes
Standing time: 30 minutes
Baking time: 30-35 minutes
Nutritional value:
Analysis per piece, if divided into 12 slices, approx:
- 1385kJ/330kcal
- 14g protein
- 18g fat
- 15g carbohydrate

Knead the flour, 100g/4 oz of the butter, the egg, milk and salt together to form an elastic dough. Wrap it in aluminium foil and refrigerate for 30 minutes. • Cut the smoked salmon into strips. • Trim the leeks and cut into broad rings. Fry gently in the rest of the butter for 6 minutes. Remove from the heat and leave to cool. • Beat the eggs with the crème fraîche, stir in the leeks and salmon and season with the salt, pepper, nutmeg and lemon juice. • Butter the springform tin. • Roll the dough out in a circle and line the tin with it, pushing it up slightly at the sides. Pour the filling over the dough. • Bake in a preheated 200°C/400°F/Gas Mark 6 oven for 30 to 35 minutes until golden.

Spring Green Quiche

Delicious hot or cold

Quantities for 1 26cm/11in springform tin:
150g/5¹/₂oz wheatmeal flour
150g/5oz butter
150g/5¹/₂oz low fat curd cheese
Pinch of salt
750g/1lb 11oz Swiss chard, turnip tops or spring greens
2 shallots
200g/7oz peeled, cooked prawns
¹/₂ tsp each of salt and freshly ground white pepper
Pinch of nutmeg
¹/₂ tsp grated lemon rind
A little lemon juice
125ml/4 fl oz cream
3 eggs
3 tbsps grated Parmesan cheese
Butter for the tin

Preparation time: 40 minutes
Standing time: 30 minutes
Baking time: 35 minutes
Nutritional value:
analysis per piece, if divided into 12 slices, approx:
- 840kJ/200kcal
- 8g protein
- 14g fat
- 11g carbohydrate

Knead the flour with 100g/4oz of the butter, the curd cheese and salt into a dough. Cover and refrigerate for 30 minutes. • Trim the leaves from the stalks of the greens, and cut the leaves into 1cm/¹/₂in strips. Blanch in boiling salted water for 5 seconds, plunge into cold water and leave to drain. Blanch the stalks for 1 minute. • Chop the shallots and fry in the rest of the butter until translucent. Add the stalks and fry for 3 minutes; combine with the prawns and leaves, and season with the salt and spices. • Butter a springform tin. Roll out the dough and line the tin with it, making a 4cm/2in high rim. Bake blind for 10 minutes in a preheated 200°C/400°F/Gas Mark 6 oven. • Beat the eggs with the cream and Parmesan. Pour the filling over the pastry case, then add the egg-and-cream mixture. • Bake for 35 minutes.

Aubergine and Ham Pie

Hearty country fare, which goes well with dry wine

Minced Beef and Vegetable Quiche

A hearty dish with a hint of the Mediterranean

Quantities for 1 26cm/11in pie:

250g/8oz wheatmeal flour
21g/³/₄oz fresh yeast or 10g/¹/₄oz dry yeast
¹/₂ tsp sugar
125ml/4 fl oz lukewarm milk
600g/1¹/₂lbs aubergines
1 tbsp salt
40g/1¹/₂oz butter • Pinch of salt
200g/7oz uncooked ham
50g/2oz stoned black olives
2 tbsps oil • 3 eggs
100ml/4 fl oz cream
Pinch each of pepper and nutmeg
8 basil leaves
Oil for the springform tin

Preparation time: 1 hour
Rising time: 1¹/₂ hours
Baking time: 45 minutes
Nutritional value:

Analysis per piece, if divided into 12 slices, approx:
• 1090kJ/260kcal
• 10g protein
• 18g fat
• 18g carbohydrate

Make a well in the centre of the flour, crumble in the fresh yeast, sprinkle on the sugar and stir in a little milk. If using dry yeast, blend with the sugar and milk and pour onto the flour. Cover and leave to froth in a warm place for 15 minutes. • Slice aubergines, sprinkle on the salt and leave for 15 minutes. • Melt butter in the remaining milk and knead with the salt, all the remaining flour and the yeast mixture. Cover and leave to rise for 45 minutes. • Cut the ham into strips and slice the olives. Drain aubergines and pat dry. • Fry aubergines in the oil; add ham and olives, fry briefly and leave to cool. • Brush the tin with oil. • Knead the dough, roll it out and line the tin with it; leave to rise for 30 minutes. • Beat the eggs with the cream and spices. • Pour the vegetables and basil onto the pastry and pour over the egg and cream mixture. • Bake in a preheated 200°C/400°F/Gas Mark 6 oven for 45 minutes.

Quantities for 1 26cm/11in springform tin:

125g/5oz wheatmeal flour
75g/3oz cornflour
125g/5oz chilled butter
1 egg yolk
Pinch each of salt and nutmeg
1 large onion • 2 tbsps olive oil
150g/5¹/₂oz minced beef
150g/5¹/₂oz each of aubergines and courgettes
1 small beef tomato
3 garlic cloves
1 tsp each of salt, black pepper and mixed herbs
1 egg white • 4 eggs
250g/8oz Greek yogurt
Olive oil for the tin

Preparation time: 1 hour
Standing time: 45 minutes
Baking time: 30 minutes
Nutritional value:

Analysis per piece, if divided into 12 slices, approx:
• 1090kJ/260kcal
• 11g protein
• 18g fat
• 17g carbohydrate

Knead the flour with the cornflour, butter, egg yolk, 3 tbsps cold water, salt and nutmeg. Chill for 45 minutes. • Chop the onions finely and fry in the oil until translucent. Brown the mince and remove from the pan. • Cut the aubergines and courgettes into 5mm/¹/₄in cubes and fry in the remaining oil for 5 minutes. Skin the tomatoes, chop them roughly and add to the vegetables. Stir in the crushed garlic, season with the salt, pepper and herbs and fry until the liquid has been absorbed. • Combine the vegetables with the minced beef and leave to cool. • Roll out the pastry; line the greased springform tin with it. • Stir the egg white, eggs and yogurt into the vegetables and pour into the pastry case; bake for 30 minutes in a preheated 200°C/400°F/Gas Mark 6 oven.

Paprika Pie à la Pipirrana

Based on a Spanish speciality

Quantities for 1 28cm/11in springform tin:
125g/5oz butter
250g/8oz wheatmeal flour
3 eggs
Pinch of salt
1 large onion
2 yellow and 2 red peppers
150g/5½oz courgettes
2 tbsps olive oil
½ tsp each of salt, black pepper and sweet paprika
Pinch of hot paprika
1 bunch of flat-leaf parsley
100g/4oz grated Cheddar cheese
Olive oil for the springform tin

Preparation time: 50 minutes
Standing time: 30 minutes
Baking time: 35-40 minutes
Nutritional value:
Analysis per piece, if divided into 12 slices, approx:

- 1005kJ/240kcal
- 9g protein
- 16g fat
- 18g carbohydrate

Roughly knead the cubed butter with the flour, 1 egg, 2 tbsps cold water and salt. Refrigerate for 30 minutes. • Chop the onions finely and deseed and dice the peppers. Grate the courgettes coarsely. • Heat the oil and fry the onions until translucent. Add the peppers and fry for a further 5 minutes, then stir in the courgettes, season with the salt and spices and leave to cool. • Brush the springform tin with oil. • Roll out the pastry and line the tin with it. Prick all over with a fork. • Roughly chop the parsley. • Beat the remaining eggs with the cheese; combine with the parsley and vegetables and pour into the tin. • Bake on the bottom shelf of a preheated 200°C/400°F/Gas Mark 6 oven for 35 to 40 minutes.

Oyster Mushroom Quiche

This quiche is at its best served straight from the oven

Quantities for 1 26cm/11in springform tin:

250g/8oz wheatmeal flour
125g/5oz butter
1 egg
Pinch of salt
1 onion
600g/1½lbs oyster mushrooms `
2 tbsps olive oil
200g/7oz cooked ham
2 bunches of chives
½ tsp each of salt and freshly ground black pepper
Pinch each of freshly grated nutmeg and cayenne
½ tsp dried oregano
3 eggs
150g/5½oz crème fraîche
100g/4oz freshly grated Cheddar cheese
Butter for the tin

Preparation time: 1 hour
Standing time: 30 minutes
Baking time: 40 minutes
Nutritional value:
Analysis per piece, if divided into 12 slices, approx:
- 1340kJ/320kcal
- 14g protein
- 23g fat
- 16g carbohydrate

Knead the flour, butter, egg and salt together to form an elastic dough; refrigerate for 30 minutes. • Chop the onions finely. • Wipe the mushrooms and slice thinly. • Fry the onions in the oil until translucent, add the mushrooms and fry for 8 minutes; leave to cool. • Cut the ham into strips and add to the mushrooms. Finely chop the chives and reserve 2 tbsps of them. Add the rest to the mushrooms and season with the salt and spices. • Beat the eggs with the crème fraîche and cheese. • Grease the springform tin with butter. • Roll out the dough and line the tin with it, bringing the sides up 3cm/1in high. • Arrange the mushrooms on the dough base, add the egg-and-cream mixture and bake in a preheated 200°C/400°F/Gas Mark 6 oven for 40 minutes. Serve garnished with the remaining chives.

Vegetable Pie with Cheese Sauce

Cauliflower, broccoli, fennel and tomatoes in a light cheese and oil pastry

Quantities for 1 baking sheet:
FOR THE FILLING:
1 small cauliflower (500g/1lb 2oz)
300g/10oz broccoli
1 fennel bulb
5 tomatoes
250ml/9 fl oz stock
1 small garlic clove
150g/5¹/₂oz Cheddar cheese
50g/2oz butter
4 tbsps flour
250ml/9 fl oz milk
125g/5oz crème fraîche
Pinch each of salt, white pepper and nutmeg
4 tbsps walnuts
FOR THE PASTRY:
150g/5¹/₂oz low fat curd cheese
5 tbsps milk • 6 tbsps oil
1 egg yolk • 1 tsp salt
300g/10oz wheatmeal flour
3 tsps baking powder
Butter for the baking sheet

Preparation time: 1 hour
Baking time: 50-55 minutes
Nutritional value:
Analysis per piece, if divided into 12 slices, approx:
- 1425kJ/340kcal
- 14g protein
- 21g fat
- 27g carbohydrate

Strip the green leaves off the cauliflower and divide into individual florets. Cut the stalks off the broccoli and slice. Cut the stalk off the fennel and cut away the hard outer leaves. Finely chop the feathery green part of the fennel and set aside. Cut the fennel bulb in half and slice thinly. • Divide the tomatoes into eighths, removing the stalks. • Bring the stock to the boil and add the cauliflower florets, broccoli and fennel pieces; simmer for 10 minutes and drain, reserving the stock. • Grate the cheese. • Melt the butter and fry the crushed garlic gently. Add the flour and stir until golden; add the stock and milk gradually. Boil the sauce for a few minutes, stirring continuously. • Stir the crème fraîche and cheese into the sauce. Season with the salt, pepper and nutmeg and add the green fennel. • Chop the walnuts. • To make the pastry, stir together the curd cheese, milk, oil, egg yolk, salt and half the flour. Combine the remaining flour with the baking powder and knead into the dough. • Butter the baking sheet. • Roll the pastry out on the baking sheet, pushing it up the edges. • Arrange the vegetables on the pastry, pour on the sauce and scatter on the nuts. • Slide the pie onto the centre shelf of the cold oven and bake at 200°C/400°F/Gas Mark 6 for 50 to 55 minutes until golden; after 40 minutes reduce the temperature to 180°C/350°F/Gas Mark 4. • Serve hot.

Our Tip: You can use any vegetables you choose, bearing in mind that their flavours should complement each other and provide a good colour contrast.

Stuffed Pinwheels

This tasty snack is good hot or cold

Quantities for 1 26cm/11in springform tin:

FOR THE DOUGH:

400g/14oz wheatmeal flour
21g/³/₄oz fresh yeast or 10g/¹/₄oz dry yeast
Pinch of sugar
4 tbsps lukewarm milk
Pinch of salt
3 tbsps olive oil
200ml/7 fl oz lukewarm water

FOR THE FILLING:

3 medium onions
250g/8oz cooked ham, not too thinly sliced
25g/1oz butter
2 tbsps sesame seeds
1 bunch of parsley
¹/₂ tsp salt
1 tsp freshly ground black pepper
Pinch of ground caraway
1 egg yolk
Butter for the springform tin

Preparation time: 50 minutes
Rising time: 1¹/₂ hours
Baking time: 50 minutes
Nutritional value:

Analysis per piece, if divided into 7 slices, approx:
- 1720kJ/410kcal
- 17g protein
- 17g fat
- 46g carbohydrate

Pour the flour into a bowl and make a well in the centre. Crumble in the yeast, sprinkle on the sugar and stir in the milk. If using dry yeast, blend the yeast with the sugar and milk and pour onto the flour. Cover and leave to rise for 25 minutes. • Knead the starter dough with the remaining flour, the salt, oil and as much lukewarm water as is necessary to form an elastic dough which leaves the bowl clean. Dust the dough with flour, cover and leave to rise for 50 minutes – it should double in volume. • Chop the onions finely. Remove any fat

from the ham and cut into narrow strips. • Heat the butter and fry the onions until translucent; add the ham strips and fry, stirring frequently. Add the sesame seeds and remove from the heat. • Add the chopped parsley to the mixture and season well with the salt, pepper and caraway seeds. • Grease the springform tin with butter. • Knead the dough thoroughly again and, on a lightly floured work surface, roll out to form a 40x50cm/16x20in oblong. Spread the filling on the dough base and roll up from the long side upwards. Cut the roll into 7 equal-sized slices and arrange in the springform tin in a circle with the cut side up. Cover and leave to rise for 15 minutes. • Beat the egg yolk with a little water and brush over the surface. • Bake on the centre shelf of a preheated 200°C/400°F/Gas Mark 6 oven for 50 minutes or until golden-brown.

Our Tip: As an alternative, the pinwheels can be filled with a mixture of 2 parts lightly salted, coarsely chopped peanuts, 1 part fried breadcrumbs and 1 part crisply fried bacon bits. Before baking, brush the pinwheels with melted butter rather than egg yolk.

Soya Quiche

If you use canned beans and peas, you can cut out the soaking and cooking times

Quantities for 1 28cm/11in quiche:

100g/4oz each soya and aduki beans
2 bay leaves
150g/5½oz wholewheat flour
50g/2oz barley flour
25g/1oz millet flakes
25g/1oz soya flour
1¼ tsps baking powder
½ tsp each of sea salt and dried basil
2 pinches of curry powder
1 egg
100g/4oz butter
100g/4oz sour cream
150g/5½oz split peas
3 eggs
150g/5½oz crème fraîche
½ tsp dried rosemary
Butter for the quiche dish

Soaking and cooking time: 14 hours
Preparation time: 45 minutes
Baking time: 30 minutes
Nutritional value:
Analysis per piece, if divided into 12 slices, approx:
- 1385kJ/330kcal
- 15g protein
- 22g fat
- 18g carbohydrate

Soak the beans separately in 500ml/18 fl oz water each for 12 hours. • Simmer the beans in their separate soaking water with 1 bayleaf each – the soya beans should cook for 2 hours and the aduki beans for 1 hour. • Combine the wheat and barley flours with the millet and add the soya flour, baking powder, salt, basil and a pinch of curry. Knead in the egg, cubed butter and sour cream. • Butter the quiche dish. • Roll out the dough and line the bottom and sides of the dish with it. • Drain the beans and remove the bay leaves. Combine the beans and peas and arrange on the pastry base. • Whisk the eggs with the crème fraîche, remaining curry powder and rosemary and pour onto the beans. • Bake on the centre shelf of a preheated 180°C/350°F/Gas Mark 4 oven for 30 minutes.

Savoury Snacks

For late evening, supper, high tea,
cocktail parties and picnics

Pastry Canapés

Their dainty shape makes these canapés particularly appealing

Yeasty Whirls
illustrated left

Quantities for 25 whirls:

21g/³/₄oz fresh yeast or
10g/¹/₄oz dry yeast
125ml/4 fl oz lukewarm milk
Pinch of sugar
250g/8oz wheatmeal flour
Pinch of salt
1 egg yolk • 1 tbsp butter
150g/5¹/₂oz smoked sausage
4 sticks celery
1 tbsp oil
1 tbsp chopped walnuts
Pinch of black pepper
Butter for the baking sheet

Preparation time: 1¹/₄ hours
Rising time: 1 hour
Baking time: 20 minutes
Nutritional value:
Analysis per whirl, approx:
• 375kJ/90kcal
• 3g protein
• 6g fat
• 8g carbohydrate

Dissolve the crumbled fresh yeast or dry yeast in the milk and sugar. Cover and leave to froth at room temperature until it has dissolved. • Combine the flour in a bowl with the salt, add the egg yolk, remaining milk and the butter and knead together with the yeast mixture, until the dough leaves the bowl clean. • Cover and leave to rise at room temperature for 1 hour. • Skin and dice the sausage. Finely chop the celery. • Heat the oil and fry the sausage; add the celery and fry briefly. Dry on absorbent paper, then add the walnuts and season with pepper. • Butter the baking sheet. • Roll out the dough to form a 25x35cm/10x14in rectangle and brush on the filling, leaving a 1cm/¹/₂in wide strip all the way round. Roll the dough up from the short end and cut into 25 pieces. • Lay the coils on the baking sheet and bake on the centre shelf of a preheated 200°C/400°F/Gas Mark 6 oven for 20 minutes or until golden-brown.

Poppy seed Pretzels
illustrated right

Quantities for 30 pretzels:

250g/8oz wheatmeal flour
125g/5oz chilled butter
1 egg yolk
1 tbsp crème fraîche
¹/₂ tsp each of salt, sweet paprika and freshly ground black pepper
3 tbsps black poppy seeds
2 egg yolks
Butter for the baking sheet

Preparation time: 1 hour
Standing time: 40 minutes
Baking time: 15-20 minutes
Nutritional value:
Analysis per pretzel, approx:
• 420kJ/100kcal
• 3g protein
• 7g fat
• 6g carbohydrate

Put the flour in a bowl, cut the butter into knobs and add; then mix in the egg yolk, crème fraîche, salt, paprika and pepper, and knead to form an elastic dough. • Shape into a roll of around 3cm/1in in diameter, cover and refrigerate for 40 minutes. • Butter the baking sheet. • Cut the dough roll into 30 pieces; on a lightly floured work surface shape into 17cm/7in long cylinders and shape these into mini-pretzels. • Pour the poppy seeds onto a plate. Beat the egg yolks with a little water. Brush the egg yolks on the pretzels and turn them gently in the poppy seeds. Arrange them on the baking sheet and bake in a preheated 180°C/350°F/Gas Mark 4 oven for 15 to 20 minutes.

Luxury Cheese Assortment

For anyone who enjoys a nibble – and they are delicious with a clear soup

Quantities for 80 biscuits:

250g/8oz wheatmeal flour

1 tsp baking powder

60g/2oz each of Cheddar, Caerphilly and Camembert cheese

200g/7oz chilled butter

1 egg

Pinch each of white pepper, ground nutmeg and sweet paprika

FOR THE GLAZE AND DECORATION:

1 egg yolk

1 tbsp cream

1 tbsp each of chopped peanuts, pistachios, caraway seeds, poppy seeds and sesame seeds

Greaseproof paper for the baking sheet

Preparation time: 1½ hours
Standing time: 1 hour
Baking time: 10 minutes
Nutritional value:
Analysis per biscuit, approx:
- 185kJ/45kcal
- 1g protein
- 4g fat
- 2g carbohydrate

Sift the flour and baking powder on to a work surface.
• Finely grate the Cheddar and Caerphilly and pass the Camembert through a sieve. Sprinkle the cheese over the flour. Cut the butter into knobs and add to the flour. Break the egg into the centre and sprinkle with the spices. Chop the ingredients, then knead to a smooth shortcrust dough. • Cover and refrigerate for 1 hour. • Line the baking sheet with greaseproof paper. • On a lightly floured work surface roll out the dough in 2 portions to a thickness of 5mm/¼in and either cut out 3cm/1in-sized biscuits or, using a pastry wheel, cut small lozenge shapes. • Beat the egg yolk with the cream. • Lay the first batch of biscuits on the baking sheet, brush with the egg yolk and cream and sprinkle the peanuts, pistachios and poppy, caraway and sesame seeds onto alternate biscuits. • Bake on the top shelf of a preheated 220°C/425°F/Gas Mark 7 oven for 10 minutes until golden.

Ham Crescents

Use the best Italian raw ham, or substitute smoked beef

Quantities for 16 crescents:
500g/1lb 2oz strong plain flour
21g/³/₄oz fresh yeast or
10g/¹/₄oz dry yeast
1 tsp sugar
250ml/9 fl oz lukewarm water
1 tsp salt
2 onions
250g/8oz lean, raw ham
2 tbsps butter
2 tbsps chopped fresh parsley
Pinch of white pepper
1 egg
1 egg yolk
3 tbsps milk
Greaseproof paper for the baking sheet

Preparation time: 1 hour
Rising time: 1 hour
Baking time: 15 minutes
Nutritional value:
Analysis per crescent approx:
• 710kJ/170kcal
• 6g protein
• 5g fat
• 24g carbohydrate

Make a well in the flour, crumble in the yeast and stir in the sugar, a little flour and a little lukewarm water. If using dry yeast, blend with the sugar and water and pour onto the flour. Cover and leave to froth at room temperature for 15 minutes. • Add salt and remaining water to the flour and knead to form a smooth dough. Cover and leave to rise for 30 minutes. • Finely chop onions and ham. • Heat the butter and fry the onions until translucent; add ham and parsley and fry briefly. Remove mixture from the heat, season with the pepper and combine with the beaten egg. • Line the baking sheet with greaseproof paper. • Roll the dough to form 2 circles 36cm/14in in diameter. Cut each circle into 8 triangles; spoon on the filling and shape into crescents by rolling up the triangles. Arrange crescents on the baking sheet and leave to stand for 15 minutes. • Beat the yolk with the milk, brush on the crescents and bake in a preheated 220°C/425°F/Gas Mark 7 oven for about 15 minutes.

Ham and Cheese Diamonds

These are delicious served with wine, and complement vegetable soups well

Quantities for 60 diamonds:
150g/5¹/₂oz wheatmeal flour
150g/5¹/₂oz wholemeal flour
21g/²/₃oz fresh yeast or
10g/¹/₄oz dry yeast
1 tsp sugar
125ml/4 fl oz lukewarm water
2 tbsps butter • ¹/₄ tsp salt
1 onion
1 tsp butter
150g/5¹/₂oz each of cooked and raw ham, fat removed
3 eggs
125ml/4 fl oz single cream
100g/4oz double cream
100g/4oz grated Cheddar cheese
Butter for the baking sheet

Preparation time: 45 minutes
Rising time: 1¹/₂ hours
Baking time: 40 minutes
Nutritional value:
Analysis per diamond, approx:
• 290kJ/70kcal
• 3g protein
• 5g fat
• 4g carbohydrate

Mix the flours in a bowl, make a well in the centre, crumble in the yeast and stir in the sugar and half the water. If using dry yeast, blend the yeast with the sugar and water and pour onto the flour. Cover and leave to froth at room temperature for 15 minutes. Cover and leave to rise for 15 minutes. • Melt the butter in the remaining water and knead with the salt, starter dough and remaining flour. Cover and leave to rise for 45 minutes. • Chop the onions and fry in the butter until translucent. • Cut the ham into strips. • Beat the eggs with the single and double cream; combine with the ham and onion. • Butter half the baking sheet. • Roll out the dough to the size of half the sheet, place it on the sheet and leave to rise for 30 minutes. • Spoon the ham mixture over the dough; sprinkle on the cheese. • Bake on the centre shelf of a preheated 210°C/410°F/Gas Mark 6 oven for 40 minutes; cut into 60 diamonds.

Cashew Biscuits

Lightly spiced with curry

Quantities for 70 biscuits:
150g/5¹/₂oz salted cashew nuts
150g/5¹/₂oz wheatmeal flour
100g/4oz chilled butter
1 tsp curry powder
Pinch of salt
1 tbsp crème fraîche
2 egg yolks
2-3 tbsps grated Parmesan cheese
For rolling out: clingfilm
Greaseproof paper for the baking sheet

Preparation time: 1¹/₂ hours
Standing time: 1 hour
Baking time: 15 minutes
Nutritional value:
Analysis per biscuit, approx:
- 230kJ/55kcal
- 2g protein
- 5g fat
- 2g carbohydrate

Shell the nuts and mix with the flour. Cut the butter into knobs and add to the flour with the curry and salt. Spoon the crème fraîche and 1 egg yolk into the middle. Chop up the ingredients and knead to a smooth, shortcrust pastry. Cover and refrigerate for 1 hour. • Line the baking sheet with greaseproof paper. • Divide the dough into two portions, lay it on clingfilm and roll it out to a thickness of 3mm/¹/sin thick. • Cut out 4cm/2in biscuits with a pastry cutter, or use a pastry wheel to cut lozenge shapes. • Beat the remaining egg yolk with 2 tbsps water. • Lay the biscuits on the baking sheet. Brush them with the egg yolk, sprinkle with the Parmesan and bake on the centre shelf of a preheated 200°C/400°F/Gas Mark 6 oven for 15 minutes or until golden.

Cheese-and-Herb Rolls

Deliciously tangy – ideal for that between-meals snack

Quantities for 32 rolls:
100g/4oz strong plain white flour
100g/4oz wheatmeal flour
50g/2oz freshly grated Parmesan cheese
1 tsp baking powder
1 tsp cream of tartar
Pinch each of sea salt and freshly ground white pepper
¹/₂ tsp each of dried basil, rosemary and thyme
1 tsp dried parsley
3 eggs
100g/4oz butter
Butter for the baking sheet

Preparation time: 40 minutes
Rising time: 40 minutes
Baking time: 15-20 minutes
Nutritional value:
Analysis per roll, approx:
- 270kJ/65kcal
- 3g protein
- 4g fat
- 4g carbohydrate

Combine the flours and pour them into a bowl. Add the cheese, baking powder, cream of tartar, salt, pepper and crushed herbs and mix thoroughly. • Make a well in the centre, add the eggs and, using a fork, stir in a little of the flour. Cut the butter into knobs and add to the flour. Knead the ingredients together to form a smooth dough. Cover and leave to rise for 40 minutes. • Butter the baking sheet. • Mould the dough into a long roll and divide into 32 equal-sized pieces – it is probably best to weigh them. Shape the pieces of dough into small balls, lay them on the baking sheet and bake on the centre shelf of a preheated 200°C/400°F/Gas Mark 6 oven for 15 to 20 minutes until golden-brown. • These rolls will stay fresh in an airtight metal container for up to 1 week.

Three-Cheese Tartlets

These can be frozen and reheated – and they taste like they've been freshly baked

Quantities for 25 tartlets:

500g/1lb 2oz wheatmeal flour
1 packet dry yeast
Pinch of sugar
1 tsp salt
Just under 250ml/9 fl oz lukewarm milk
125g/5oz Brie
125g/5oz feta cheese
250g/8oz low fat curd cheese
1 tbsp butter
1 egg
1 egg yolk
1 bunch of parsley
Butter for the baking sheet

Preparation time: 1 hour
Rising time: 1 hour
Baking time: 20-25 minutes
Nutritional value:
Analysis per tart, approx:
- 840kJ/200kcal
- 7g protein
- 5g fat
- 15g carbohydrate

Knead the flour, yeast, sugar, salt and milk to form an elastic dough. Dust with flour, cover and leave to rise in a warm place, until it has doubled in volume – this should take about 45 minutes. • Purée the Brie and feta cheese, stir in the curd cheese, butter and egg. • Butter the baking sheet. • Knead the dough again; on a floured work surface roll out to a thickness of 4mm and cut out 25 circles of 10cm/4in diameter. Spoon on the filling and bring the edges up 1cm/¹⁄₂in wide over the filling. • Lay the tarts on the baking sheet and brush the edges with the beaten egg yolk. • Cover and leave to rise for 15 minutes. • Bake the tarts on the centre shelf of a preheated 200°C/400°F/Gas Mark 6 oven for 20 to 25 minutes until golden. • Serve the tartlets warm, garnished with the chopped parsley.

Mouthwatering Savouries

These are at their best served hot

Bacon Bakes
illustrated left

Quantities for 50 rolls:
400g/14oz fat bacon
Pinch of dried sage
500g/12oz wheatmeal flour
15g/¹/₂oz butter
1 tsp salt
Just under 300ml/11 fl oz cold water
1 egg yolk
Butter and flour for the baking sheet

Preparation time: 45 minutes
Standing time: 2 hours
Baking time: 12 minutes
Nutritional value:
Analysis per roll, approx:
- 95kJ/95kcal
- 2g protein
- 6g fat
- 7g carbohydrate

Remove the rind from the bacon. Cut the bacon into cubes, mince with the mugwort and cook on a low heat. Strain through a sieve and allow the fat to harden. • Work the flour and butter, salt and water to a stiff dough. Roll it out to a thickness of about 1.5cm/²/₃in, in a 32x42cm/12x16in rectangle. • Spoon the bacon fat onto half of the rolled out dough and fold the other half on top. Leave to stand in a cool place for 30 minutes. • Roll the dough out again to a thickness of 1.5cm/²/₃in, fold together again and leave to stand in a cool place for a further 30 minutes. • Repeat the whole process again twice at half-hourly intervals. • Butter the baking sheet and dust it with flour. • Roll the dough out again to a thickness of 1.5cm/²/₃in and cut out rounds 5cm/2in in diameter. Place them on the baking sheet, brush with the beaten egg yolk and bake in a preheated 200°C/400°F/Gas Mark 6 oven for 12 minutes.

Herb and Cheese Diamonds
illustrated right

Quantities for 1 baking sheet:
200g/7oz rye flour
200g/7oz wheatmeal flour
1 tbsp yeast
2 tbsps sourdough starter mix
About 250ml/9 fl oz lukewarm water
1 tsp honey
1 tsp salt
2 bunches fresh dill
300g/10oz freshly grated Parmesan cheese
3 eggs
300g/10oz crème fraîche
Pinch of white pepper
Lard for the baking sheet

Preparation time: 30 minutes
Rising time: 1³/₄ hours
Baking time: 25 minutes
Nutritional value:
Analysis per slice, if divided into 30 slices, approx:
- 630kJ/150kcal
- 7g protein
- 9g fat
- 12g carbohydrate

Mix the flours with the yeast, sourdough extract, water, honey and salt and knead into a stiff, workable dough. Cover and leave to rise in a warm place, until it has doubled in volume – this will take about 1 hour. • Grease the baking sheet with lard. • Roll the dough out on the baking sheet and prick all over with a cocktail stick. • Pull the leaves off the dill stalks and chop finely. • Combine the Parmesan cheese with the eggs, crème fraîche, pepper and dill and spread over the dough. Cover and leave to rise for 40 minutes. • Bake on the centre shelf of a preheated 200°C/400°F/Gas Mark 6 oven for about 25 minutes.

Tempting Bread Sticks

Delicious with drinks, and you won't pile on the calories!

Beer Sticks
illustrated in background

Quantities for 32 sticks:

200g/7oz rye flour
200g/7oz wholewheat flour
2 tsps caraway seeds
1 tsp sea salt
2 tbsps sourdough starter mix
¹/₂ packet dry yeast
1 tbsp raw cane sugar
200g/7oz lukewarm sour cream or thick-set plain yogurt
5 tbsps wine vinegar
4 tbsps sunflower oil
Butter for the baking sheet

Preparation time: 40 minutes
Rising time: 1 hour
Baking time: 30 minutes
Nutritional value:
Analysis per stick, approx:
• 230kJ/55kcal
• 2g protein
• 2g fat
• 8g carbohydrate

Mix the flours in a bowl with the caraway seeds, salt, sourdough starter mix, dry yeast and raw cane sugar. • Make a well in the centre, add the sour cream, vinegar and oil and knead to a smooth dough. Cover and leave to rise at room temperature for 30 minutes. • Divide the dough into 32 equal-sized pieces – it is probably best to weigh them. Shape them into balls and, on a floured work surface, roll out to 20cm/8in long sticks. • Cover and leave to rise for 30 minutes. • Butter a baking sheet. • Arrange the beer sticks on the baking sheet and bake on the centre shelf of a preheated 200°C/400°F/Gas Mark 6 oven for 30 minutes until crispy and slightly brittle. • Spray with a little cold water and leave to cool on a wire rack. • These bread sticks will stay fresh for at least a week in an airtight metal container.

Grissini
illustrated in foreground

Quantities for 60 grissini:

500g/1lb 2oz wheatmeal flour
1 tsp salt
50g/2oz fresh yeast or 25g/1oz dry yeast
Just under 200ml/6 fl oz lukewarm water
1 tsp sugar
6 tbsps olive oil
FOR THE GLAZE:
Milk
Butter or olive oil for the baking sheet

Preparation time: 40 minutes
Rising time: 1 hour
Baking time: 15 minutes
Nutritional value:
Analysis per stick, approx:
• 145 kJ/35kcal
• 1g protein
• 1g fat
• 6g carbohydrate

Mix the flour and salt in a bowl. Make a well in the centre, crumble the fresh yeast into it and mix in the water, sugar and a little flour. If using dry yeast, blend the yeast with the sugar and water and pour onto the flour. Cover and leave to rise at room temperature for 20 minutes. • Knead the starter dough with the remaining flour and olive oil to form a smooth dough which leaves the bowl clean. Cover and leave to rise for 30 minutes. • On a lightly floured work surface roll out the dough to a thickness of 2cm/1in and cut into 10cm/4in long fingers. Roll into sticks about 20 to 25cm/8 to 10in long. • Grease or oil the baking sheet. • Lay the grissini on the baking sheet, cover and leave to rise for 10 minutes; then brush with milk. • Bake on the top shelf of a preheated 220°C/425°F/Gas Mark 7 oven for 15 minutes until golden.

Cheese Parcels

Instead of feta, try using the mint-flavoured cheese from Cyprus, known as Halloumi

Quantities for 25 parcels:

250g/8oz wheatmeal flour
1 egg
1-2 tbsps lukewarm water
3 tbsps olive oil
Pinch of salt
1 tsp balsamic vinegar
50g/2oz stoned black olives
250g/8oz feta cheese
1/2 tsp each of salt and freshly ground black pepper
1 tsp dried oregano
2 tbsps chopped pistachio nuts
1 egg yolk
100g/4oz melted butter
1 bunch of chives
Butter for the baking sheet

Preparation time: 1 hour
Standing time: 30 minutes
Baking time: 30 minutes
Nutritional value:
Analysis per parcel, approx:
- 545kJ/130kcal
- 4g protein
- 9g fat
- 8g carbohydrate

Put the flour in a bowl. Beat the egg with the water, oil, salt and vinegar, combine with the flour and knead until it is no longer sticky. Cover and refrigerate for 30 minutes. • Chop the olives finely, crumble on the feta cheese and add the salt, pepper, crushed oregano, pistachios and egg yolk. • Butter the baking sheet. • On a floured work surface roll the dough out thinly, to an 80x120cm/32x47in rectangle. If necessary, you can stretch it further, using the backs of your hands. • Brush the melted butter on the rolled out dough. Cut out 25 circles of 8cm/3in diameter and spoon on the filling. Bring the edges up over the filling, pressing together to form little parcels. • Lay the parcels on the baking sheet and bake on the centre shelf of a preheated 180°C/350°F/Gas Mark 4 oven for 30 minutes, basting frequently with the remaining butter. • Wind 1 chive round each cooled parcel as decoration.

Spicy Potato Biscuits

Try frying these instead of baking

Quantities for 40 biscuits:
1kg/2¼lbs floury potatoes
2 garlic cloves
1 bunch of chives
1 tsp salt
Pinch each of ground nutmeg and black pepper
1 tsp dried marjoram
1 egg
100g/4oz wheatmeal flour
100g/4oz freshly grated medium mature Cheddar or Gouda
120g/4½oz chopped sunflower seeds
For the baking sheet and to drizzle: 6 tbsps oil

Cooking time: 30-40 minutes
Preparation time: 40 minutes
Baking time: 25-30 minutes
Nutritional value:
Analysis per biscuit, approx:
- 290kJ/70kcal
- 3g protein
- 4g fat
- 6g carbohydrate

Simmer the potatoes in boiling water for 30 to 40 minutes, peel and, while still hot, press through a sieve. • Finely chop the garlic and chives. • Roughly knead the cooled, mashed potatoes with the garlic, nutmeg, pepper, marjoram, chives, egg, flour and cheese to form a light, workable dough. If necessary, add a little more flour. • Brush the baking sheet generously with oil. • With floured hands, divide the dough into about 40 portions and shape into round, flat biscuits. • Roll both sides of each biscuit in the sunflower seeds and press them in gently. • Lay the potato biscuits on the baking sheet, drizzle a little oil over each one and bake on the centre shelf of a preheated 220°C/425°F/Gas Mark 7 oven for 25 to 30 minutes. • Enjoy the biscuits fresh from the oven.

Bacon and Onion Biscuits

Delicious savoury shortcrust pastry

Quantities for 50 biscuits:
125g/5oz chilled butter
250g/8oz wheatmeal flour
1 egg
Pinch each of salt and ground caraway
1 medium sized onion
100g/4oz streaky bacon
1 tbsp oil
Pinch each of black pepper and ground nutmeg
1 egg yolk
2 tsps caraway seeds
Greaseproof paper for the baking sheet

Preparation time: 1 hour
Standing time: 1 hour
Baking time: 15 minutes
Nutritional value:
Analysis per biscuit, approx:
- 270kJ/65kcal
- 2g protein
- 5g fat
- 4g carbohydrate

Cut the butter into knobs and add to the flour; knead together with the egg, salt and ground caraway seeds. Refrigerate. • Finely chop the onions. Using a sharp knife, remove the rind from the bacon and dice. • Fry the bacon in the oil, add the onions and fry until translucent. • Drain off the fat and leave to cool, then knead the bacon, pepper and nutmeg into the dough. Roll the dough out into a 4cm/2in thick roll, wrap in foil and refrigerate for 1 hour. • Line the baking sheet with greaseproof paper. • Cut the roll of dough into 50 slices. Lay the biscuits on the baking sheet. • Beat the egg yolk with 1 tbsp water, brush over the biscuits. Sprinkle with the caraway seeds. • Bake the biscuits on the centre shelf of a preheated 200°C/400°F/Gas Mark 6 oven for 15 minutes or until golden. • They are at their best served fresh from the oven.

Hearty Snacks for the Gourmet

These can be served hot or cold

Tortilla Squares
illustrated left

Quantities for 20 squares:

300g/10oz similarly sized small potatoes
1 large onion
1 small red pepper
5 tbsps olive oil
1 tsp each of salt and freshly ground black pepper
6 eggs

Preparation time: 1 hour
Cooking time: 25 minutes
Nutritional value:
Analysis per square, approx:
• 335kJ/80kcal
• 4g protein
• 6g fat
• 3g carbohydrate

Peel and chop the potatoes finely; slice the onions into rings. • Deseed the red pepper and dice finely. • Heat 2 tbsps oil in a large pan. Fry the potatoes and onions over a moderate heat for 15 minutes or until soft, turning constantly. • Add the red pepper and fry for 3 minutes, season and leave to cool. • Beat the eggs in a large bowl and add the vegetable mixture. • Heat 2 tbsps oil in the pan, pour in the egg mixture and allow to thicken, shaking the pan frequently so that it does not stick. While the surface is still runny, slide the tortilla onto a plate; use a second plate to help turn it over. Heat the remaining oil in the pan, return the turned tortilla to the pan, uncooked side down and cook for a further 5 to 7 minutes. • Slide onto a plate and cut into 20 squares.

Cornmeal Pie
illustrated right

Quantities for 1 26cm/10in springform tin:

1 medium sized onion
2 garlic cloves
1 tbsp olive oil
1l/1¾ pints beef stock
250g/8oz yellow cornmeal
1 tsp each of salt and freshly ground black pepper
1 bunch of fresh parsley
Butter for the tin

Preparation time: 1 hour
Baking time: 30 minutes
Nutritional value:
Analysis per slice, if divided into 18 slices, approx:
• 250kJ/60kcal
• 1g protein
• 2g fat
• 10g carbohydrate

Finely chop the onion. • Heat the oil in a casserole, fry the onions until translucent, add the crushed garlic and continue to fry until golden. • Add the stock, sprinkle with the cornmeal and simmer gently for 30 minutes, stirring occasionally. Season with the salt and pepper and leave to cool. • Butter a springform tin. • Chop the parsley, add to the cornmeal mixture and tip into the springform tin. • Bake the pie on the centre shelf of a preheated 200°C/400°F/Gas Mark 6 oven for about 30 minutes or until golden-brown. • Cut into 18 pieces and serve hot.

Olive Pinwheels

Absolutely delicious – especially if served fresh from the oven

Quantities for 24 pinwheels:

21g/³/₄oz fresh yeast or 10g/¹/₄oz dry yeast
Pinch of sugar
125ml/4 fl oz lukewarm water
300g/10oz wheatmeal flour
1 tsp salt
3 eggs
6 tbsps olive oil
100g/4oz almonds
150g/5¹/₂ oz black olives
1 bunch of fresh basil
1 garlic clove
200g/7oz low fat curd cheese
Greaseproof paper for the baking sheet

Preparation time: 1 hour
Rising time: 1³/₄ hours
Baking time: 25-30 minutes
Nutritional value:
Analysis per pinwheel, approx:
- 585kJ/140kcal
- 6g protein
- 8g fat
- 10g carbohydrate

Dissolve the crumbled fresh yeast or dry yeast in the water with the sugar, cover and leave to froth at room temperature for 15 minutes. • Knead the flour, salt, 1 egg and oil into the yeast mixture, until it is no longer sticky. Dust the dough with flour, cover and leave to rise for 1 hour, until it has doubled in bulk. • Cover the almonds with boiling water and remove their skins. • Stone the olives and chop finely with the almonds. • Chop the basil and garlic finely. • Combine the curd cheese with the almond and olive mixture, 1 egg and the herbs. • Line the baking sheet with greaseproof paper. • Roll out the dough to a 40x40cm/16x16in square; spoon on the curd cheese mixture, leaving a strip of 2cm/1in at one side clear. • Roll the dough up firmly and, using a sharp, floured knife, cut into 24 pieces. Lay the pinwheels on the baking sheet and press them down gently. • Beat the remaining egg and brush onto the pinwheels; cover and leave to rise for 30 minutes. • Bake in a preheated 200°C/400°F/Gas Mark 6 oven for 25 to 30 minutes.

Spicy Tartlets

Made with frozen puff dough or shortcrust dough

Tomato Tartlets
illustrated left

Quantities for 8 12cm/5in tartlet tins:

300g/10oz frozen puff dough
10 small tomatoes
150g/5¹/₂oz Mozzarella cheese
1 tbsp freshly grated medium mature Cheddar or Gouda cheese
3 eggs
4 tbsps crème fraîche
¹/₂ tsp each of salt, freshly ground black pepper and dried oregano
2 bunches fresh basil

Preparation time: 30 minutes
Baking time: about 15 minutes
Nutritional value:
Analysis per tartlet, approx:
• 1215kJ/290kcal
• 12g protein
• 20g fat
• 15g carbohydrate

Defrost the puff pastry. • Pour boiling water over 8 tomatoes, skin them and cut into eighths. Dice the Mozzarella. Beat the grated cheese with the eggs and crème fraîche; season with the salt, pepper and oregano. Wash and dry the basil, put aside 8 attractive leaves, coarsely chop the others and add to the egg mixture. • Run the tins under the cold tap. • Roll the pastry out as thinly as possible; line the tins with the pastry, pressing it up the sides. • Arrange the tomato eighths in a star shape in the tins, sprinkle on the Mozzarella and pour on the egg mixture. • Arrange the tins on a baking sheet and bake them on the baking sheet on the bottom shelf of a preheated 220°C/425°F/Gas Mark 7 oven for 5 minutes. Reduce the temperature to 200°C/400°F/Gas Mark 6 and transfer to the centre shelf. Bake for a further 8 to 10 minutes until golden-brown. • Garnish with the basil leaves and tomato slices; serve hot or cold.

Leek Tartlets
illustrated right

Quantities for 8 8cm/3in tins:

200g/7oz wheatmeal flour
80g/3oz chilled butter
1 egg yolk
Pinch of salt
3 bunches of chives
250g/8oz full fat curd cheese
1 egg
1 egg yolk
Pinch each of salt and freshly grated nutmeg
¹/₂ tsp ground white pepper
Butter for the tins

Preparation time: 40 minutes
Standing time: 30 minutes
Baking time: 20 minutes
Nutritional value:
Analysis per tartlet, approx:
• 1300kJ/310kcal
• 12g protein
• 22g fat
• 19g carbohydrate

Knead the flour, cubed butter, egg yolk, salt and 2 to 3 tbsps of cold water together to form a smooth dough. Cover and refrigerate for 30 minutes. • Finely chop the chives. Stir the curd cheese into the egg and egg yolk, season with salt, nutmeg and pepper, and add the chives. • Grease the tins with butter. • Roll out the dough as thinly as possible and line the tins with it. Prick the dough base all over with a fork and bake on the bottom shelf of a preheated 200°C/400°F/Gas Mark 6 oven for 5 minutes. Now add the chive mixture to the tartlets and bake for a further 15 minutes on the centre shelf. • Serve warm as a starter, or otherwise cold.

Curd Cheese and Butter Snacks

The filling blends perfectly with the delicate pastry

Saffron Turnovers
illustrated left

Quantities for 40 turnovers:

220g/7¹/₂oz wheatmeal flour	
220g/7¹/₂oz butter	
220g/7¹/₂oz low fat curd cheese	
2 pinches of salt	
1 sachet ground saffron	
1 leek	
2 tbsps butter	
¹/₂ tsp black pepper	
100g/4oz Gorgonzola	
2 egg yolks	
Greaseproof paper for the baking sheet	

Preparation time: 1 hour
Standing time: 45 minutes
Baking time: 15-20 minutes
Nutritional value:
Analysis per turnover, approx:
- 375kJ/90kcal
- 3g protein
- 7g fat
- 4g carbohydrate

Knead the flour with the butter, curd cheese, pinch of salt and saffron. Cover and refrigerate for 45 minutes. • Cut the leek into thin rings and fry in the butter for 5 minutes. Season, leave to cool and combine with the Gorgonzola and 1 egg yolk. • Line the baking sheet with greaseproof paper. • Roll out the dough to a thickness of 5mm/¹/₄in; cut out 40 circles of 7cm/3in diameter and spoon on the filling. Fold up the edges, pressing firmly, and prick each surface once with a fork. • Beat the remaining egg yolk with 1 tbsp water. Brush the crescents with this, place them on the baking sheet and bake on the centre shelf of a preheated 200°C/400°F/Gas Mark 6 oven for 15 to 20 minutes until golden; if possible, serve straight from the oven.

Mini Empanadas
illustrated right

Quantities for 40 empanadas:

250g/8oz wheatmeal flour	
250g/8oz each of butter and low fat curd cheese	
Pinch of salt • 1 onion	
2 preserved chillies	
100g/4oz mushrooms	
1¹/₂ tbsps raisins	
1 hard-boiled egg	
2 tbsps oil	
250g/8oz minced beef	
1¹/₂ tbsps tomato purée	
¹/₂ tsp each of salt, black pepper and dried thyme	
Pinch of cayenne	
2 eggs • 2 tbsps milk	
Greaseproof paper for the baking sheet	

Preparation time: 1¹/₂ hours
Standing time: 45 minutes
Baking time: 25-30 minutes
Nutritional value:
Analysis per empanada, approx:
- 460kJ/110kcal
- 4g protein
- 8g fat
- 5g carbohydrate

Knead the flour with the butter, curd cheese and salt. Cover and leave in a cool place for 45 minutes. • Finely chop the onions and chillies. Wipe the mushrooms and chop finely. Wash the raisins in hot water. Dice the egg. • Fry the onions in the oil until translucent, add the mince and fry. Add the prepared vegetables, raisins, egg, tomato purée and spices, and cook for 10 minutes. • Line the baking sheet with greaseproof paper. • Separate the eggs. • Roll out the dough extremely thinly, cut out 40 7cm/3in squares. Spoon on the filling, brush the edges with the egg white, fold the squares up into triangles and press the edges firmly. • Beat the egg yolks with the milk and brush on the empanadas; bake in a preheated 200°C/400°F/Gas Mark 6 oven for 25 to 30 minutes.

Party Mini Pizzas

Ideal finger food for parties

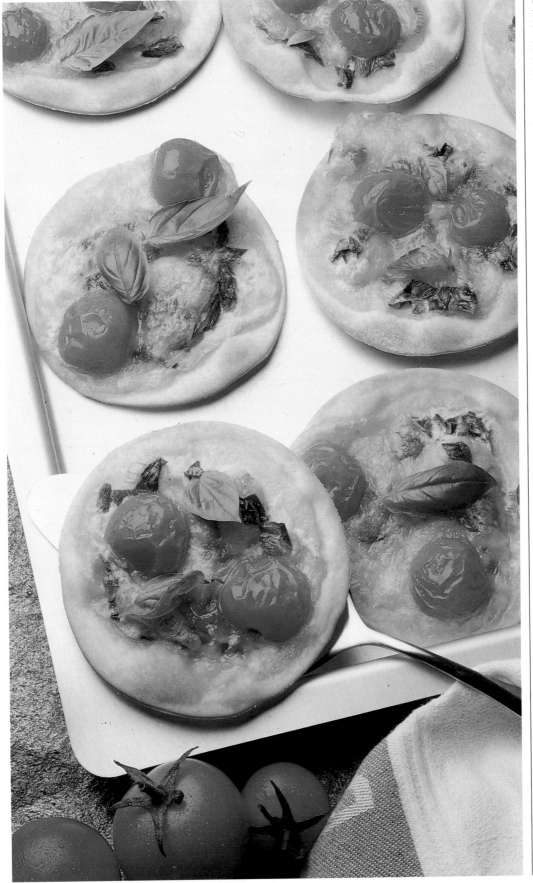

Quantities for 20 pizzas:

250g/8oz low fat curd cheese
1 tsp salt
4 tbsps olive oil
2 eggs
500g/12oz wheatmeal flour
4 small spring onions
1 garlic clove
1 tbsp butter
1 tbsp crème fraîche
50g/2oz peeled, cooked prawns
1 tbsp freshly grated medium mature Cheddar or Gouda cheese
Pinch each of salt and freshly ground black pepper
80g/3oz Mozzarella cheese
20 cherry tomatoes
½ bunch of basil
Greaseproof paper for the baking sheet

Preparation time: 1 hour
Baking time: 10 minutes
Nutritional value:
Analysis per pizza, approx:
- 630kJ/150kcal
- 7g protein
- 5g fat
- 19g carbohydrate

Stir the salt, oil and eggs into the curd cheese; add the flour in spoonfuls, beating well to incorporate after each addition. Roll the dough into a ball and refrigerate. • Finely chop the spring onions. Crush the garlic. • Fry the onions gently in the butter for 5 minutes, add the garlic, stir in the crème fraîche and leave to cool. Combine the prawns with the Cheddar or Gouda, salt, pepper and onions. • Cut the Mozzarella into 10 slices. Halve the cherry tomatoes. Pinch off the basil leaves. • Line the baking sheet with greaseproof paper. • Roll out the pastry as thinly as possible. Cut out 20 10cm/4in circles and place on the baking sheet. • Spoon the onion mixture onto 10 slices and cover the 10 others with 1 slice of Mozzarella and a basil leaf. Season. • Garnish each mini-pizza with 2 tomato halves; bake on the bottom shelf of a preheated 200°C/400°F/Gas Mark 6 oven for 10 minutes. • Serve fresh from the oven.

Loaves, Rolls and Shaped Pastries

Light white bread rolls, substantial wholemeal
buns and delicious traditional baking ideas

Shaping and Decorating

Making fancy breads

You can make all sorts of fancy breads in interesting shapes using simple techniques.

1 Roll out the dough to a thickness of 1cm/½in and cut 25cm/10in long strips. Sprinkle some poppy seeds over the work surface and roll the dough strips up from both ends to meet in the middle.

2 Roll out fingers of dough 25cm/10in long and 2cm/1in thick. Roll each end round into a pinwheel shape in a different direction, until they meet in the middle.

3 Roll up the ends of the dough fingers to form small twists and put one twist on top of another.

4 Roll out 40cm/16in long, thin fingers of dough, leaving the ends a little fatter than the middles. Make a loop, fold each end down and roll it up.

Making creative shapes

A real surprise for your party guests, or an original gift.

1 Shape the dough into 18 equal-sized balls. On a floured work surface, roll 9 of the balls into 15cm/6in long fingers. Shape into rings.

2 Grease the baking sheet or line it with baking paper and place one dough ball in the centre.

3 Lay the rings all round the ball. Roll the other 9 balls into 18cm/7in long fingers and shape into crescents. Place them on the sheet, joining the rings together.

4 Sprinkle the centre roll and the two rows of rings and crescents with seeds of different colours, for instance, alternate sesame with poppy seed, or sesame with caraway and coarse salt.

Making pizza

This flatbread with topping whose popularity is now worldwide, is best made from a yeast dough. Pizzas are usually round, though they can also be baked in rectangular baking sheets.

1 For a Four Seasons Pizza, roll out a circle 20cm/8in in diameter, raising the dough up slightly at the edges. Lay the pizza on an oiled baking sheet and lightly mark out four quarters.

2 Arrange sliced tomatoes, mushrooms, ham, green pepper rings, artichokes and salami on the four quarters.

3 Season with salt, pepper and dried rosemary. Sprinkle with chopped anchovies and freshly grated Parmesan cheese.

4 Drizzle on 1 tbsp olive oil and bake on the centre shelf of the oven until crispy and golden.

Making quiches

These open pies from France use a thin shortcrust dough. The filling is usually based on a savoury custard mixture and can contain a wide variety of ingredients. This is an unusual version because it also has a top crust.

1 For a spinach quiche, roll out two-thirds of well-chilled shortcrust dough on a lightly floured work surface to form a 32cm/13in circle. Butter the bottom and sides of a springform tin. Lift the dough with a rolling pin and place it in the tin.

2 Cook the spinach until wilted, drain it thoroughly and let it cool. Spread half of it over the pastry base. Arrange halved hard-boiled eggs in a circle on top.

3 Cover with the remaining spinach. Beat two egg yolks with 250 ml/8 fl oz single cream and pour this over the spinach.

4 Use the rest of the dough to roll out a 26cm/11in circle. Using the floured rolling pin to help lift the other dough circle, place the lid on top of the filling and press the edges down firmly. Prick with a fork to ensure that the steam escapes evenly during baking.

Kaiser Rolls

These rolls are popular in the United States as well as in Germany

Quantities for 20 rolls:

300g/10oz wheatmeal flour

300g/10oz unbleached strong plain white flour

42g/1½oz fresh yeast or 21g/¾oz dry yeast

3 tsps sugar

350ml/14 fl oz lukewarm water

2 tsps salt

4 tbsps poppy seeds

Butter for the baking sheet

Preparation time: 30 minutes
Rising time: 1½ hours
Baking time: 20-25 minutes
Nutritional value:
Analysis per roll, approx:
- 460kJ/110kcal
- 4g protein
- 1g fat
- 21g/¾oz carbohydrate

Mix the flours, make a well in the centre, crumble in the fresh yeast and stir in 1 tsp of the sugar, half the water and a little flour. If using dry yeast, blend the yeast with the sugar and water and then pour onto the flour. Cover and leave to rise for 20 minutes at room temperature. • Add the remaining water, flour and salt to the starter dough and knead thoroughly for 10 minutes. • Cover and leave to rise in a warm place for 45 minutes. • Butter the baking sheet. • Knead the dough thoroughly again, shape into a roll and cut into 20 equal-sized pieces. On a lightly floured work surface shape the pieces of dough into balls. Lay the rolls on the baking sheet and, using a sharp knife, make a star pattern on the surface. Cover and leave to rise for 25 minutes. • Stir the remaining sugar into 3 tbsps of water and brush this mixture over the rolls. Sprinkle with the poppy seeds. Place a cup of water on the floor of the oven and preheat the oven to 220°C/425°F/Gas Mark 7. Bake on the centre shelf for 20 to 25 minutes or until golden.

French Table Rolls

Classic French breakfast rolls

Quantities for 20 rolls:

500g/1lb 2oz unbleached strong plain white flour

42g/1½oz fresh yeast or 21g/¾oz dry yeast

1 tsp sugar

250ml/9 fl oz lukewarm water

80g/3oz butter

1 tsp salt

Butter for the baking sheet

Preparation time: 45 minutes
Rising time: 1¾ hours
Baking time: 25-30 minutes
Nutritional value:
Analysis per roll, approx:
- 500kJ/120kcal
- 3g protein
- 4g fat
- 19g carbohydrate

Sift the flour into a bowl and make a well in the centre. Crumble in the fresh yeast, sprinkle on the sugar and stir with a little water and flour. If using dry yeast, blend the yeast with the sugar and water and then pour onto the flour. • Dust the starter dough with flour, cover and leave to rise for about 20 minutes, until the surface of the flour shows fine cracks. • Melt the butter in the remaining water – if necessary, warm the water slightly. • Stir the flour into the starter dough. Add the liquid gradually and the salt, and knead into a smooth dough. • Cover and leave to rise until it has doubled in bulk – this should take about 1 hour. • Butter the baking sheet. • Knead the dough thoroughly again and cut it into 20 equal-sized pieces; shape some into round and some into long rolls. Cut a lozenge shape in the long rolls and a single groove in the round ones; dust with a little white flour, cover and leave to prove for 20 minutes. • Bake the rolls on the centre shelf of a preheated 220°C/425°F/Gas Mark 7 oven for 25 to 30 minutes or until golden.

Sweet Wheatgerm Rolls

For a really crispy finish, prepare these rolls on a surface sprinkled with coarse brown sugar crystals

Quantities for 24 rolls:

800g/1lb 12oz wholewheat flour
60g/2oz soya flour
100g/4oz wheatgerm
84g/3oz fresh yeast or 42g/1¹/₂oz dry yeast
4 tbsps Demerara sugar
400ml/14 fl oz lukewarm milk
¹/₂ tsp sea salt
100ml/4 fl oz cream
100g/4oz raisins

FOR THE GLAZE:

Milk
Butter for the baking sheet

Preparation time: 1¹/₂ hours
Rising time: 2 hours
Baking time: 15-20 minutes
Nutritional value:
Analysis per roll, approx:
- 710kJ/170kcal
- 7g protein
- 4g fat
- 28g carbohydrate

Combine the wholewheat and the soya flour with the wheatgerm. • Make a well in the centre of the flours, crumble the fresh yeast into it, sprinkle with the brown sugar and wait 3 to 4 minutes, until the yeast has dissolved. • Mix the milk with the yeast and a little flour, cover and leave to rise at room temperature for 30 minutes. If using dry yeast, blend the yeast with the milk before adding the flour. • Add the salt and cream to the starter dough, blend and knead thoroughly. • Cover and leave for a further hour. • Wash the raisins in hot water and leave to dry. • Butter the baking sheet. • Knead the dough again, adding the raisins and more milk or flour as required. • Divide the dough into 6 equal-sized pieces and divide each of these into 4 further equal-sized pieces. • Roll 4 of the pieces into 30cm/12in long fingers with tapering ends. Brush the fingers with milk and twist the ends into coils, with one end turning to the right and the other to the left. • Halve the next 4 pieces and roll out to 8 small ovals. Brush them with milk and press 2 ovals together. • Halve the next 4 pieces as well, roll out to 8 pencil-thin strands 40cm/16in in length and brush with milk. Wind 2 strands round one another in a spiral shape like a garland. Press the ends firmly together. • Take 4 more pieces of dough and divide them each into 3 pieces. Mould small balls, brush with milk and stick 3 at a time together. • Roll the next 4 pieces out to 30cm/12in long fingers, brush with milk and mould into large marbles. • Divide each of the last 4 pieces into 3 pieces, roll out to 12 long strands, brush with milk and weave into 4 plaits. • Place on the baking sheet, cover and leave to rise for 30 minutes. • Bake on the centre shelf of a preheated 200°C/400°F/Gas Mark 6 oven for 15 to 20 minutes until golden-brown. Spray with a little cold water and leave to cool on a wire rack.

Brioches

In France Brioches are enjoyed fresh from the oven for breakfast and in between meals

Quantities for 20 individual brioche tins 8cm/3in in diameter:

750g/1lb 11oz unbleached, strong plain white flour
42g/1½oz fresh yeast or 21g/¾oz dry yeast
50g/2oz icing sugar
125ml/4 fl oz lukewarm milk
200g/7oz butter
5 eggs
1 tsp salt
FOR THE GLAZE:
2 egg yolks
Butter for the tins

Preparation time: 1 hour
Rising time: 1¾ hours
Baking time: 15-20 minutes
Nutritional value:
Analysis per brioche, approx:
- 1210kJ/290kcal
- 9g protein
- 15g fat
- 30g carbohydrate

Sift the flour into a bowl, make a well in the centre and crumble in the fresh yeast. Stir half the icing sugar and a little milk and flour into the yeast, cover and leave to rise for 15 minutes at room temperature. If using dry yeast, blend the yeast with the sugar and milk and then add to the flour. • Melt the butter and leave to cool. • Stir the eggs into the remaining icing sugar and milk, add the salt and butter, pour the mixture onto the edge of the flour and knead all the ingredients thoroughly with the starter dough. • Cover and leave the dough to rise for 1 hour; it should double in volume. • Grease the tins with butter. • Knead the dough again, shape into a roll and cut into 20 pieces. • Mould each piece into one large and one small ball. Put the larger balls in the tins, make a dip on top of each brioche and press the smaller ball into it. • Beat the egg yolks with 1 tbsp water, brush on the brioches, cover and leave to rise for 30 minutes. • Brush the brioches again with the remaining egg yolk and bake on the centre shelf of a preheated 220°C/425°F/Gas Mark 7 oven for 15 to 20 minutes until golden-brown.

Herbed Scones

These are best served straight from the oven

Yeast Crescents

Vary the quantities of wholemeal and refined flour to suit your tastes

Quantities for 12 scones:

6 tbsps mixed fresh herbs, e.g. cress, marjoram and fresh dill
200g/7oz wheatmeal flour
50g/2oz wholewheat flakes
1 tsp baking powder
1 tsp salt
Pinch of pepper
50g/2oz butter
5 tbsps sour cream or thick-set yogurt
1 egg
Butter for the baking sheet

Preparation time: 30 minutes
Baking time: 15 minutes
Nutritional value:
Analysis per scone, approx:
• 500kJ/120kcal
• 4g protein
• 5g fat
• 13g carbohydrate

Finely chop the herbs. • Butter the baking sheet. • Mix the flour with the wheatflakes, baking powder, salt and pepper. • Cut the butter into cubes and add to the flour. Combine with the sour cream or thick-set yogurt and herbs and knead together. • On a lightly floured work surface roll out the dough to a thickness of roughly 2cm/³/₄in. Cut out 12 circles of about 7cm/2³/₄in diameter and lay them on the baking sheet. • Brush the scones with the beaten egg and bake on the centre shelf of a preheated 225°C/430°F/Gas Mark 7 oven for 15 minutes until golden.

Quantities for 16 crescents:

42g/1¹/₂oz fresh yeast or 21g/³/₄oz dry yeast
500ml/16 fl oz lukewarm water
1 tsp sugar
200g/7oz wholewheat flour
600g/1¹/₂lbs wheatmeal flour
2 tsps salt
3 tbsps condensed milk
4 tbsps coarse salt
Butter for the baking sheet

Preparation time: 30 minutes
Rising time: 1³/₄ hours
Baking time: 35 minutes
Nutritional value:
Analysis per crescent, approx:
• 755kJ/180kcal
• 6g protein
• 1g fat
• 35g carbohydrate

Stir the crumbled fresh yeast or dry yeast with the sugar into 100ml/3 fl oz lukewarm water, cover and leave to froth at room temperature for 15 minutes. • Mix the flours with the salt in a bowl and knead thoroughly with the yeast mixture and the remaining water. • Cover and leave to rise for 1 hour. • Knead thoroughly again, roll out to two circles of 40cm/16in diameter and cut each into 8 equal-sized pieces. Roll each triangle out further, and then roll it up towards the pointed tip. • Butter the baking sheet. Lay the crescents on the sheet, cover and leave to rise for 30 minutes. • Set an ovenproof bowl of cold water in the base of the oven. • Brush the crescents with condensed milk, sprinkle with the coarse salt and bake on the centre shelf of a preheated 225°C/430°F/Gas Mark 7 oven for 30 minutes until golden. After 10 minutes remove the water from the oven and lower the temperature to 200°C/400°F/Gas Mark 6. Once the baking time is up, switch off the oven and leave the crescents there for another 5 minutes.

Creative Party Rolls

These attractively shaped rolls are particularly popular with guests

Quantities for 19 rolls:

800g/1lb 12oz wholewheat flour	
200g/7oz wheatmeal flour	
750ml/26 fl oz lukewarm water	
4 tsps dry yeast	
1 tsp sugar	
1 tbsp salt	
Pinch each of ground coriander and cardamom	

FOR THE DECORATION:

3 tbsps each of poppy seeds and sesame seeds	
Greaseproof paper for the baking sheet	

Preparation time: 1¼ hours
Rising time: 14 hours
Baking time: 35 minutes
Nutritional value:
Analysis per roll, approx:
- 750kJ/180kcal
- 7g protein
- 3g fat
- 33g carbohydrate

Mix the flours in a large bowl and make a well in the centre. • Add the sourdough to the well, mix it with a little water and sprinkle with the sugar and dry yeast. • Sprinkle the salt and spices onto the edge of the flour. Mix all the flours with the remaining water and stir into the sourdough mixture; knead it until the dough is elastic and smooth. • Shape the dough into a ball, dust with flour and cover with a cloth. Leave to rise in a warm place for 3 hours. • Knead the dough thoroughly again; if it is still a little sticky, incorporate a little more wholewheat flour. • Line the baking sheet with greaseproof paper. • On a lightly floured work surface, shape the dough into a long roll about 7cm/3in in diameter. Cut the roll into 13 equal-sized pieces. • Make one round roll and place in the centre of the baking sheet. • Roll the remaining dough into sausage shapes, about 15cm/6in in length.

Mould half of them into rings; press the ends together gently and lay them round the centre roll. Form the other six sausages into crescent shapes and place in an outer circle, so that they join the rings together. They should just touch one another. • Cover the rolls with a cloth and leave to rise for a further 2 hours. • Brush the risen rolls with lukewarm water. Decorate the centre roll and crescent shapes with poppy seeds; sprinkle sesame seeds onto the rings. • Bake the rolls on the centre shelf of a preheated 220°C/425°F/Gas Mark 7 oven for 15 minutes. Reduce the temperature to 180°C/350°F/Gas Mark 4 and bake for a further 20 minutes until golden-brown. • Leave the rolls to cool on the baking sheet for a few minutes, then slide carefully onto a wire rack. • Serve fresh from the oven.

Our Tip: If your baking sheet is too small for this quantity of rolls, divide the dough into 2 pieces and bake two batches, one after the other. If you have neither the time nor inclination to bake the batch as described above, form small, round rolls from the risen dough and arrange them in two 24cm/9 ½in diameter springform tins, spreading out from the centre. Sprinkle some with poppy seeds and some with sesame seeds, and bake at the same temperature as the rolls in the main recipe for 45 minutes.

Buckwheat Rolls

As a tasty alternative to pumpkin seeds, try these rolls with walnuts

Sesame Rye Rolls

Even after two days these rolls taste as if they've been freshly baked

Quantities for 10 rolls:
250g/8oz wholewheat flour
250g/8oz buckwheat flour
42g/1½oz fresh yeast or 21g/¾oz dry yeast
500ml/16 fl oz lukewarm buttermilk
Pinch of sugar
1 tsp sea salt
50g/2oz pumpkin seeds
Butter for the baking sheet

Preparation time: 40 minutes
Rising time: 1½ hours
Baking time: 25 minutes
Nutritional value:
Analysis per roll, approx:
• 880kJ/210kcal
• 8g protein
• 3g fat
• 36g carbohydrate

Measure the flours into a bowl, make a well in the centre, crumble in the fresh yeast and stir with a little buttermilk, the sugar and a little of the flours. If using dry yeast, blend the yeast with the buttermilk and sugar, and add to the flour. • Cover and leave to rise in a warm place for 15 minutes. • Add the remaining buttermilk and salt to the starter dough and knead these together with the remaining flour to form a soft, smooth dough. • Cover and leave to rise for 1 hour. • Set aside 1 tbsp of the pumpkin seeds and chop the rest finely. • Knead the pumpkin seeds into the dough and shape it into 10 equal-sized balls. • Butter the baking sheet. Place the rolls on the baking sheet, cover and leave to rise for a further 15 minutes. • Make deep crosses in the rolls with a wet knife, brush them with cold water, and sprinkle with the remaining pumpkin seeds, pressing them down gently. • Bake the rolls on the centre shelf of a preheated 220°C/425°F/Gas Mark 7 oven for 25 minutes or until golden-brown.

Quantities for 14 rolls:
500g/1lb 2oz wholemeal rye flour
250g/8oz wholewheat flour
42g/1½oz fresh yeast or 21g/¾oz dry yeast
600ml/18 fl oz lukewarm water
Pinch of sugar
1 tbsp sea salt
Pinch each of white pepper and freshly grated nutmeg
150g/5½oz sourdough
FOR THE DECORATION:
3 tbsps raw sesame seeds
Butter for the baking sheet

Preparation time: 20 minutes
Rising time: 1¾ hours
Baking time: 25 minutes
Nutritional value:
Analysis per roll, approx:
• 880kJ/210kcal
• 8g protein
• 2g fat
• 39g carbohydrate

Mix the flours in a bowl. Make a well in the centre, crumble in the fresh yeast, mix in 100ml/3 fl oz of the water, the sugar and a little flour. If using dry yeast, blend the yeast with the water and sugar and then pour over the flour. • Cover and leave to rise in a warm place for 15 minutes. • Knead the remaining flour into the starter dough, add the remaining water, salt, spices and sourdough and work into a smooth dough. Cover and leave to rise until it has doubled in volume – this will take approximately 1 hour. • Grease the baking sheet with butter. • Knead the dough again thoroughly and shape into 14 equal-sized balls. Press down firmly to make them flattish, lay them on the baking sheet and cover. Leave to prove for 30 minutes. • Brush the rolls with cold water, make a shallow cross on the top of each, sprinkle with the sesame seeds and press them in gently. • Bake the rolls on the centre shelf of a preheated 220°C/425°F/Gas Mark 7 oven for about 25 minutes or until golden-brown.

Buckwheat Crispbread

These crispbreads will keep fresh for at least a week in an airtight metal container

Quantities for 25 crispbreads:

200g/7oz buckwheat flour and 200g/7oz rye flour
2¹/₄ tsps baking powder
1 tsp ground caraway seeds
1 tsp sea salt
100g/4oz butter
250g/8oz low fat curd cheese
100ml/3 fl oz milk
Butter for the baking sheet

Preparation time: 40 minutes
Rising time: 45 minutes
Baking time: 20-25 minutes
Nutritional value:
Analysis per crispbread, approx:
• 375kJ/90kcal
• 3g protein
• 4g fat
• 11g carbohydrate

Combine the flours in a bowl. Add the baking powder, caraway seeds and salt. • Cut the butter into cubes and add to the mixture, followed by the curd cheese. Stir all the ingredients together and gradually add the milk. Knead the dough thoroughly, cover and leave to rise for 45 minutes. • Butter the baking sheet. • On a lightly floured work surface, roll out the dough to a thickness of 3mm/¹/₈in. Using a sharp knife or a pastry wheel, cut into 6x10cm/2¹/₂x4in strips. • Lay these on the baking sheet and prick with a fork into regular patterns. • Put the crispbreads into a cold oven on the centre shelf, turn the temperature to 200°C/400°F/Gas Mark 6 and bake for 20 to 25 minutes, until hard and brittle. • Spray them with a little cold water and leave to cool on a wire rack.

Luxury Rusks

These delicious rusks are a teatime favourite

Quantities for a 30cm/12in baking tin:

6 eggs
¹/₂ lemon
8 tbsps maple syrup
¹/₂ tsp ground cinnamon
Pinch salt
300g/10oz wholewheat flour
Butter for the baking tin

Preparation time: 40 minutes
Rising time: 12 hours
Baking time: 45 minutes
Baking toast slices: 8 minutes
Nutritional value:
Analysis per slice, if divided into 26 slices, approx:
• 375kJ/90kcal
• 4g protein
• 4g fat
• 10g carbohydrate

Separate the eggs. • Squeeze the juice from the lemon and finely grate the rind. • Beat the egg yolks with the lemon juice, lemon rind, maple syrup and cinnamon until foaming. •Butter the baking tin. • Whisk the egg whites with the salt until they form stiff peaks. • Add the flour to the egg yolk mixture and fold in the egg whites. • Pour the dough into the baking tin and bake on the bottom shelf of a preheated 200°C/400°F/Gas Mark 6 oven for 45 minutes. • Once it has cooled a little, turn out onto a wire rack and leave to stand for 12 hours. • Cut into 26 slices. Bake on the top shelf of a preheated 150°C/300°F/Gas Mark 2 oven for about 4 minutes each side until golden.

Our Tip: As an alternative to cinnamon, use 1 tsp each ground aniseed and vanilla sugar. Different flavours of syrup can also be used. For a nuttier consistency, incorporate 200g/7oz flour and 150g/5¹/₂oz finely chopped walnuts into the egg yolk mixture.

Wheatmeal or Cornmeal Muffins

Bake these in American muffin tins, English patty pans, or individual foil muffin cups

Wheatmeal Muffins
illustrated rear

Quantities for 1 12-cup muffin tin or 12 individual foil cups:

300g/10oz wheatmeal flour
20g/³/₄oz sugar
2 tsps baking powder
¹/₂ tsp salt
1 egg
125ml/4 fl oz milk
6 tbsps salad oil
1 tbsp sesame seeds
1 tbsp chopped pumpkin seeds
Oil for the tin or cups

Preparation time: 20 minutes
Baking time: 20-25 minutes
Nutritional value:
Analysis per muffin, approx:
• 670kJ/160kcal
• 4g protein
• 6g fat
• 22g carbohydrate

Brush the muffin sheet or aluminium tins lightly with oil.
• Combine the flour, sugar, baking powder and salt in a bowl.
• Add the egg, milk and oil and stir to form a thick dough. • Spoon the dough into the muffin tin or aluminium cups and sprinkle alternately with sesame seeds and pumpkin seeds. • Bake the muffins on the centre shelf of a preheated 200°C/400°F/Gas Mark 6 oven for 20 to 25 minutes or until golden. • Leave to cool on a wire rack and serve as soon as possible after baking.

Cornmeal Muffins
illustrated front

Quantities for 10 cups :

250ml/9 fl oz milk
220g/7oz fine yellow cornmeal
50g/2oz wheatmeal flour
2 tsps baking powder
1 tsp salt
¹/₂ tsp ground aniseed
1 tbsp sugar
2 eggs
50g/2oz soft butter
Butter and dry breadcrumbs for the tins

Preparation time: 20 minutes
Rising time: 10 minutes
Baking time: 20-30 minutes
Nutritional value:
Analysis per muffin, approx:
• 755kJ/180 kcal
• 6g protein
• 8g fat
• 22g carbohydrate

Butter the tins and sprinkle them evenly with breadcrumbs, shaking off the excess. • Bring the milk to the boil. Place the cornmeal in a bowl, pour the boiling milk over it, cover and leave to steep for 10 minutes.
• Mix the flour with the baking powder and add to the cornmeal mixture with the salt, aniseed and sugar. Stir in the eggs and butter.
• Spoon the dough into the cups. Bake the muffins on the centre shelf of a preheated 200°C/400°F/Gas Mark 6 oven for 20 to 30 minutes or until golden-brown. • Cornmeal muffins are at their best when still warm, generously spread with chilled butter.

Jumbles

The sesame seeds can be mixed into the rolls or sprinkled on top before baking, as in the picture

Quantities for 12 rolls:

300g/10oz strong plain white flour
100g/4oz wheatmeal flour
70g/2½oz sesame seeds
1 tsp sea salt
21g/¾oz fresh yeast or 10g/¼oz dry yeast
2 tsps runny honey
250ml/8 fl oz lukewarm milk
Butter for the baking sheet

Preparation time: 40 minutes
Rising time: 1 hour
Baking time: 15-20 minutes
Nutritional value:
Analysis per roll, approx:
- 630kJ/150kcal
- 6g protein
- 4g fat
- 23g carbohydrate

Pour the flours into a bowl. • Toast half the sesame seeds in a dry pan to draw out the flavour. • Mix the flour with the toasted sesame seeds and salt, make a well in the centre and crumble the fresh yeast into it. Add the honey and wait for 2 minutes, until the yeast has dissolved. If using dry yeast, blend the yeast with the honey and then pour this into the flour. • Stir the milk and a little flour into the yeast mixture, cover and leave to rise at room temperature for 15 minutes. • Knead the starter dough thoroughly with the remaining flour until all the liquid has been absorbed. • Cover and leave to rise for a further 25 minutes. • Butter the baking sheet. • Knead the dough again, adding a little water or flour if necessary. • Divide the dough into 12 equal-sized pieces and shape into balls. Sprinkle the remaining sesame seeds on a work surface and roll out the balls on top into 25cm/10in long sausages. Shape these into rings, place them on the baking sheet, gently press them flat, cover and leave to prove for 20 minutes, during which time the rings should increase in volume by one-third. • Bake the rings on the centre shelf of a preheated 200°C/400°F/Gas Mark 6 oven for 15 to 20 minutes until golden-brown. Remove from the oven, spray with cold water and leave to cool on a wire rack.

Party Batch

Your guests will be delighted by these delicious, quick-and-easy rolls

Quantities for 2 batches (20 rolls in each):
1kg/2¼lbs strong plain flour
42g/1½oz fresh yeast or 21g/¾oz dry yeast
1 tsp sugar
500ml/16fl oz lukewarm water
2 tsps salt
FOR THE DECORATION AND GLAZE:
125ml/4 fl oz milk
3 tbsps pumpkin seeds
3 tbsps raw peanuts
3 tbsps sesame seeds
2 tbsps coarse salt
Butter for the baking sheet

Preparation time: 1 hour
Rising time: 2 hours
Baking time (per batch): 20 minutes
Nutritional value:
Analysis per roll, approx:
• 420kJ/100kcal
• 3g protein
• 2g fat
• 19g carbohydrate

Sift the flour into a bowl and make a well in the centre. Crumble in the fresh yeast, add the sugar, 8 tbsps of water and a little of the flour, and stir to form a dough. If using dry yeast, blend the yeast with the sugar and water and then add to the flour. • Dust the dough with a little flour, cover with a cloth and leave to rise in a warm place (about 22°C/70°F), until fine cracks appear on the surface of the flour – this should take about 20 minutes. • Take the starter dough, mix it with the remaining flour and lukewarm water, and the salt, and knead into a light, elastic dough which leaves the bowl clean. • Brush the surface of the dough with a little water, cover and leave to rise in a warm place for a further 45 minutes, by which time it should have doubled in bulk. • Now knead the dough thoroughly again and leave to rise for a further 15 minutes. • Butter two baking sheets. • Shape the dough into two large, equal-sized rolls and cut each roll into 20 equal-sized slices. • Form these into balls and set 20 balls close to each other on each baking sheet. • Chop the pumpkin seeds and peanuts. • Brush the rolls with the milk and decorate them alternately with the pumpkin seeds, peanuts, sesame seeds and coarse salt. • Cover each batch with a cloth and leave to rise in a warm place for 30 minutes. • Bake one after the other, on the centre shelf of a preheated 200°C/400°F/Gas Mark 6 oven for about 20 minutes until golden-brown. • Use a spatula or palette knife to slide them carefully onto a wire rack and leave to cool.

Our Tip: The seeds and nuts used to decorate the rolls can be varied according to individual preference. They also look and taste good with chopped sunflower seeds and poppy seeds, for example, or white poppy seeds and nigella.

Tangy Aniseed Rolls

A pleasant change for the breakfast table

Crispy Bacon Crowns

As an alternative to caraway, try decorating the rolls with poppy seeds

Tangy Aniseed Rolls

Quantities for 12 rolls:

500g/1lb 2oz wheatmeal flour
1 packet dry yeast
Pinch of sugar
1 tsp salt
1 tsp ground aniseed
250ml/9 fl oz lukewarm milk
100g/4oz softened butter
1 egg
1 tbsp condensed milk
1 tbsp each of peeled, chopped almonds and pistachios
Butter for the baking sheet

Preparation time: 20 minutes
Rising time: 1 hour
Baking time: 20-25 minutes
Nutritional value:
Analysis per roll, approx:
• 1000kJ/240kcal
• 7g protein
• 10g fat
• 32g carbohydrate

Combine the flour in a bowl with the yeast, sugar, salt and aniseed. • Add the milk, butter and egg and knead together to form a smooth dough. • Dust the dough with flour and cover. Leave to rise in a warm place for 45 minutes. • Butter the baking sheet. • Knead the dough again, shape into a roll and divide into 12 equal-sized pieces. • Shape the pieces into rolls, lay them on the baking sheet and cover. Leave to rise for a further 15 minutes. • Brush the rolls with the condensed milk; decorate six with the chopped almonds and the rest with the chopped pistachios. Bake the aniseed rolls on the centre shelf of a preheated 200°C/400°F/Gas Mark 6 oven for 20 to 25 minutes until golden.

Crispy Bacon Crowns

Quantities for 12 rolls:

500g/1lb 2oz wheatmeal flour
1 packet dry yeast
Pinch of sugar
1/2 tsp salt
250ml/9 fl oz lukewarm milk
100g/4oz softened butter
1 egg
1 onion
200g/7oz rindless streaky bacon rashers
1/2 tsp dried thyme
1 tbsp condensed milk
1 tsp caraway seeds
Butter for the baking sheet

Preparation time: 30 minutes
Rising time: 1 hour
Baking time: 20 minutes
Nutritional value:
Analysis per roll, approx: •
1380kJ/330kcal
• 8g protein
• 20g fat
• 32g carbohydrate

Mix the flour with the yeast, sugar and salt. • Add the milk, butter and egg; knead everything together thoroughly. Cover and leave to rise in a warm place for 45 minutes. • Peel the onions and dice finely. • Cut the bacon into narrow strips and dry fry until the fat begins to run. Add the onion cubes and fry for 2 minutes, then add the crushed thyme. Leave to cool. • Butter the baking sheet. • Knead the dough again, divide into 12 equal-sized pieces, spread them out flat and place the bacon mixture on top. Bring the edges of the dough up round the filling and press firmly. • Arrange the rolls on the baking sheet smooth side up, cover and leave to rise for 15 minutes. • Now make a cross in the top of each roll, brush with condensed milk, sprinkle with the caraway seeds and bake in a preheated 200°C/400°F/Gas Mark 6 oven for 20 minutes.

Wholegrain Rolls

Refined flour combinations have long been an essential element of these popular breakfast rolls

Wheatmeal Rolls
illustrated left and right

Quantities for 12 rolls:

350g/11oz wholewheat flour

150g/5¹/₂oz fine wheatmeal flour

42g/1¹/₂oz fresh yeast or
21g/³/₄oz dry yeast

1 tsp acacia honey

125ml/4 fl oz each of lukewarm milk and lukewarm water

Pinch of sea salt

2 pinches each of ground aniseed and coriander

FOR THE DECORATION:

3 tbsps cracked wheat

Butter for the baking sheet

Preparation time: 30 minutes
Rising time: 1¹/₂ hours
Baking time: 25 minutes
Nutritional value:

Analysis per roll, approx:
- 630kJ/150kcal
- 6g protein
- 1g fat
- 28g carbohydrate

Combine the flours and make a well in the centre. Crumble in the fresh yeast and pour the honey over it. If using dry yeast, blend the yeast with the honey and then pour this into the flour. • Mix the milk with the water, pour a little of the liquid onto the yeast and incorporate with a little of the flour. Cover and leave to rise for 15 minutes. • Add the salt, spices and remaining liquid to the flour and knead together with the starter dough, until the dough leaves the bowl clean. • Cover and leave to rise, until it has doubled in bulk – this should take about 1 hour. • Butter the baking sheet. • Knead the dough again, then cut into 12 equal-sized pieces and shape into rolls. • Lay them on the baking sheet and brush with lukewarm water. To decorate, sprinkle with the cracked wheat, cover and leave to prove for 15 minutes. • Bake the rolls for 25 minutes in a preheated 220°C/425°F/Gas Mark 7 oven until golden-brown.

Caraway Rolls
illustrated centre

Quantities for 12 rolls:

350g/11oz wholewheat flour

150g/5¹/₂oz wholemeal rye flour

42g/1¹/₂oz fresh yeast or
21g/³/₄oz dry yeast

1 tsp sugar

250ml/9 fl oz-375ml/14 fl oz lukewarm water

2 tsps salt

¹/₂ tsp ground caraway seeds

FOR THE DECORATION:

3 tbsps caraway seeds

Greaseproof paper for the baking sheet

Preparation time: 30 minutes
Rising time: 1¹/₂ hours
Baking time: 25 minutes
Nutritional value:

Analysis per roll, approx:
- 545kJ/130kcal
- 5g protein
- 1g fat
- 26g carbohydrate

Mix the flours and make a well in the centre. Crumble in the fresh yeast, stir in the sugar and a little water and flour, cover and leave for 15 minutes. If using dry yeast, blend the yeast with the sugar and water and then pour onto the flour. • Add the salt and ground caraway seeds to the flour, gradually stir in the remaining water and knead it all together with the starter dough, until the dough leaves the bowl clean. • Cover and leave to rise until it has doubled in volume – this should take about 1 hour. • Line the baking sheet with greaseproof paper. • Knead the dough again, cut into 12 equal-sized pieces and shape into balls. Lay the rolls on the baking sheet, make a shallow cross on the surface, brush them with lukewarm water and sprinkle on the caraway seeds. • Cover and leave to rise for 15 minutes. • Bake the rolls in a preheated 220°C/425°F/Gas Mark 7 oven for 25 minutes until golden-brown.

Bread from Your Own Oven

Speciality loaves, wholemeal loaves, white loaves and slightly sweetened loaves

Shaping and Decorating

Making loaves

Crusty bread can be made into just about any shape you require. You can shape it by hand or simply bake it in a loaf tin, a cake tin or even a tall mould like a large coffee tin. Basket bread, a popular Continental product, has a groove-like pattern on its surface. This is achieved by shaping the dough into a round or oval, and then leaving it to prove in a floured bread-basket made of cane. The loaf is then slid on to the greased baking sheet to be baked. Bread can also be baked in a brick (an unglazed earthenware crock), in flowerpots, in a cast iron pan or a cake tin.

To make a farmhouse loaf, shape the risen dough into a ball with floured hands, flatten it slightly, cover and leave to rise for another 30 minutes. Before baking, brush the loaf with water or milk. Dip a sharp knife in water and use it to cut a chequered pattern on the surface.

Making plaited loaves

Plaited loaves always look attractive and in many cultures they are the classic bread for special occasions. If you have the time and patience, make 8 to 10 small plaits from the dough. You can then make a whole garland of plaits, starting with a single large plait and pressing the ends firmly together. The pictures show you how to produce a double plait – the finished product looks complicated, but it is actually quite straightforward to make.

Make a yeast dough using strong, plain white flour. Knead it and leave it to rise until doubled in bulk. Weigh the dough and divide it into 2 portions, one twice as heavy as the other.

Different sorts of rolls

Rolls have all sorts of different names, there are bridge rolls and kaiser rolls, sandwich and cloverleaf rolls, caraway and salt fingers. They usually consist of a yeast dough, made with milk, water or salt; sometimes eggs are added. If you want a golden-brown crust, brush the rolls prior to baking with lukewarm water, milk, beaten egg or egg yolk. Rolls made with refined flour, wholegrain flour and combined flours can be sprinkled with poppy seeds or sesame seeds, ground coriander, caraway, sunflower and pumpkin seeds, linseed, nigella or coarse salt, or a mixture of these. Rye rolls are good topped with chopped walnuts or freshly grated Cheddar cheese.

Divide the yeast dough into 50g/2oz pieces. With floured hands, shape the pieces into balls, place on a greased baking sheet, cover and leave to rise for 15 minutes. Brush with lukewarm water and dust with a little flour. Make one diagonal incision and leave to rise for a further 15 minutes.

Light brioches

This Parisian speciality has become well known outside France and Switzerland. Brioches, large and small, are now enjoyed at breakfast tables the world over. Brioches require a buttery yeast dough, which makes the finished product light and crumbly. You can buy special brioche tins but you can also use vol-au-vent cases; bright paper cases are ideal for mini-brioches as they can then be served as they are. For normal sized brioches you should proceed as follows:

Make yeast dough from 500g/12oz flour, 30g/1oz yeast, 50g/2oz sugar, 125ml/4 fl oz lukewarm milk, 3 eggs, 200g/7oz soft butter and a generous pinch of salt. Roll it out on a floured work surface to form a long roll. Divide this into 20 pieces.

Alternatively, shape the dough into an oval loaf, brush it with beer, sprinkle with caraway seeds and make three or four incisions in the surface. Cover and leave to rise for 30 minutes. The earlier the incisions are made in the shaped bread, the more they will expand during baking.

Another method is to knead the dough again thoroughly after it has proved once, shape it into an oblong loaf and place in a greased loaf tin. Brush the surface with water, milk or beaten egg and, using a razor blade, make a cut $^{1}/_{2}$cm/$^{1}/_{4}$in cut all the way down the centre. Cover and leave to rise in the tin for 30 minutes.

Divide each portion into 3 pieces and roll by hand into sausage shapes on a floured work surface. Weave the sausages into plaits and press the ends together.

Set the smaller plait on the larger and press them gently together. Beat 1 egg yolk with 2 teaspoons water. Line the baking sheet with greaseproof or baking paper and place the plait on the tray. Brush it with egg yolk, cover and leave to rise. Brush with a little more egg yolk and bake until golden.

For caraway or salty fingers, roll out the risen and thoroughly kneaded dough to a thickness of 1cm/$^{1}/_{2}$in and a diameter of 25cm/10in. Cut diagonally into 4 or 8 pieces. Roll up the triangles from the base to the apex, leave to rise for 15 minutes, brush with beaten egg and sprinkle on caraway seeds or coarse salt.

To make cloverleaf rolls, divide the dough into 60g/2oz pieces and divide each of these into three. With wet hands, shape the pieces into balls and cluster them together in groups of three. Leave the cloverleaf rolls to rise for 15 minutes, then brush with a mixture of egg yolk and milk and sprinkle with poppy seeds or grated cheese.

Cut off one quarter of each piece of dough and, with floured hands, shape it into balls. Set the larger ball in the greased tins and make a small indentation in the top. Brush the indentation with beaten egg yolk and set the smaller ball on top.

Cover with a cloth and leave to rise in a warm place for 15 minutes. Bake on the centre shelf at 220°C/425°F/Gas Mark 7 for 15 to 20 minutes until golden-brown.

Coarse Mixed Grain Bread

All of these grains are obtainable at health food shops. Try combining different grains, while keeping the same proportions of wheat flour

Quantities for 2 loaves:

250g/8oz cracked wheat
150g/5¹/₂oz porridge oats
2 tbsps sourdough
1 sachet dry yeast
750ml/1¹/₄ pints water
100g/4oz rye flakes
350g/11oz wholemeal rye flour
350g/11oz wholewheat flour
1 tsp salt
Butter for the baking sheet

Preparation time: 40 minutes
Rising time: 13 hours or overnight
Baking time: 1³/₄ to 2 hours
Nutritional Value:
Analysis per slice, if divided into 60 slices, approx:
- 185kJ/45kcal
- 2g protein
- 0g fat
- 9g carbohydrate

To make the starter, combine the cracked wheat and oats with the sourdough, the dry yeast and 250ml/9 fl oz lukewarm water. Leave in a warm place for 12 hours. • Soak the rye flakes in 8 tbsps hot water for 12 hours or overnight. • Combine the rye and wholewheat flours with the salt, the soaked rye and the remaining water and knead this into the starter. If the dough is too soft, add more wholewheat flour. Cover the dough and leave to rise for at least 45 minutes. • Butter a baking sheet. • Flour your hands and shape the dough into two long loaves and place them on the baking sheet. Brush the loaves with a little water and bake on the bottom shelf of a preheated 225°C/450°C/Gas Mark 8 oven for 30 minutes. Then reduce the temperature to 180°C/350°F/Gas Mark 4 and bake for a further 1¹/₄ to 1¹/₂ hours. • Cool on a wire rack.

Norwegian Country Bread

A tangy, dark bread for lovers of wholefood

Quantities for 2 x 900g/2lb loaf tins:

FOR THE STARTER DOUGH:

500g/1lb 2oz rye flour

42g/1½oz fresh yeast or 21g/¾oz dry yeast

500ml/18 fl oz lukewarm buttermilk

1 tbsp golden syrup

FOR THE BREAD DOUGH:

200g/7oz wholewheat flour

75g/3oz golden syrup

2 tsps sea salt

1 tbsp ground cardamom seed

Butter for the tins

Preparation time: 50 minutes
Rising time: 4 hours
Baking time: 1 hour 5 minutes
Nutritional value:
Analysis per slice, if divided into 30 slices, approx:
- 335kJ/80kcal
- 3g protein
- 1g fat
- 17g carbohydrate

To make the starter dough, pour the rye flour into a bowl and make a well in the centre. Add the yeast to the buttermilk, stir with the golden syrup and pour into the well and mix with a little of the flour. • Sprinkle some more flour on top. Cover and leave to rise in a warm place for 1 hour or until foaming and slightly risen. • To make the bread dough, add the wholewheat flour to the starter dough. Add the golden and stir well. Add the salt and cardamom seeds and knead to a workable, slightly moist dough, adding more water if necessary. Leave to rise for 3 hours or until doubled in bulk. • Butter the baking sheet. Divide the dough into two pieces and put it in the buttered tins. Smooth over the tops. Cover with a damp cloth and leave to prove until the dough has increased in bulk by about one-third. This will take about an hour. • Bake the bread on the bottom shelf of a preheated 200°C/400°F/Gas Mark 6 oven for about 50 minutes. It should be golden-brown and come away from the tin on all sides. If the bread browns too quickly, cover it with greased baking paper after 40 minutes. • Turn the oven off and leave the bread to rest for 15 minutes. • Remove the bread from the tins, spray it or brush it all over with cold water and leave to cool on a wire rack. The flavour of the bread will take 24 hours to develop fully, by which time the bread will be easy to slice.

Our Tip: Stored in a cool and well-ventilated place, this bread will stay fresh for up to a week. It is most delicious spread simply with butter, but cheese, cream cheese with herbs, Cheddar cheese with radishes or chopped gherkins, ham, salami or smoked salmon also make good toppings. If you prefer bread that is less sweet, replace the 75g/3oz golden syrup with 75g/3oz bitter chocolate. You can sprinkle the loaves with caraway seeds or brush them with an egg yolk mixed with 3 tbsps water before baking.

Rye Bread in a Roasting Bag

Baking in a roasting bag gives this bread a very special aroma

Quantities for 1 loaf:

500g/1lb 2oz wholewheat flour

1.2kg/2 lb 11 oz rye flour

120g/4oz sourdough or starter (see page 8)

7g/¹/₄oz dry yeast

1l/1³/₄ pints lukewarm water

1 tbsp salt

1 tsp golden syrup or honey

¹/₂ tsp each crushed aniseed, fennel and coriander seed

6 tbsps sunflower seeds

FOR THE DECORATION:

1 tbsp rye flakes

¹/₂ tbsp crushed dill

Preparation time: 40 minutes
Rising time: 13-14 hours
Baking time: 1¹/₂ hours
Nutritional value:
Analysis per slice, if divided into 30 slices, approx:
- 710kJ/170kcal
- 5g protein
- 2g fat
- 36g carbohydrate

To make the starter, combine half the rye flour, the sourdough or starter, the dry yeast and the lukewarm water. • Put the rest of the rye flour in a large bowl, make a well in the centre and pour in the yeast mixture. • Cover and leave to rise in a warm place for at least 12 hours. • Add the salt, golden syrup or honey, spices and sunflower seeds to the yeast mixture. Work in the remaining flour and knead to a workable dough. If necessary, add a little more lukewarm water. • Shape the dough into a ball, return it to the bowl, cover with a damp cloth and leave to rise in a warm place for about 1¹/₂ hours. The dough should ferment and air bubbles should form. • Knead the dough thoroughly once again, wet your hands and shape it into three long loaves. Brush with a little water. Combine the coarsely-ground rye and spices and sprinkle these over the dough. • Slide the dough into roasting bags. Seal the bags tightly but use a needle to pierce holes in the top of the bag to allow steam to escape. • Place the breads on a cold baking sheet and bake on a low shelf in a preheated 230°C/450°F/Gas Mark 8 oven for 1¹/₂ hours. • Remove the breads from the bags and cool on wire racks. Wait at least 12 hours before slicing, to allow the flavour of the spices to develop.

Our Tip: Even when thoroughly kneaded, a dough made of wholemeal flours should always be somewhat sticky. Since the amount of liquid needed for making bread varies with the quality of the flours, you may need to add more liquid or flour. Experience will tell you when you have exactly the right consistency.

Bread made from high-gluten American flours will always need additional liquid.
This bread can also be baked in oiled, square baking tins or loaf tins. If using loaf tins, make a long gash down the centre of each loaf and sprinkle with sesame seeds before baking.

Caraway Seed Rye Batch

The rising time includes making the sourdough and starter. Save about 25g/1oz of each mixture for the next batch and the rising time will be halved.

Quantities for 1 batch:

FOR THE SOURDOUGH:
250g/8oz rye flour

15g/¹/₂oz sourdough mix

500ml/18 fl oz lukewarm water

FOR THE STARTER DOUGH:
250g/8oz rye flour

250ml/9 fl oz lukewarm water

FOR THE BREAD DOUGH:
350g/11oz wholewheat flour

250g/8oz rye flour

1 tbsp caraway seeds

1 tbsp sea salt

FOR THE WORK SURFACE:
1 tbsp caraway seeds

1 tbsp wholemeal rye flour

1 tsp salt

Butter for the baking sheet

Preparation time: 50 minutes
Rising time: 38 hours
Baking time: 1¹/₄ hours
Nutritional value:
Analysis per slice, if divided into 40 slices, approx:

- 375kJ/90kcal
- 3g protein
- 1g fat
- 17g carbohydrate

To make the sourdough, combine the rye flour, sourdough and water. • Cover and leave to rise in a warm place for 24 hours. The dough should then be clearly fermented: i.e., the surface will resemble dark foam. • For the starter dough, combine the rye flour with the sourdough and water. Cover, and leave the dough to rise at about 24°C/75°F for a further 12 hours. The fermentation should by now be even more apparent; the dough will foam slightly and smell sour. • For the bread dough, combine the wheat and rye flours with the sourdough, caraway seeds and salt and knead to a workable dough. • Butter the baking sheet. • Mix the caraway seeds, flour and salt on a work surface. Place the dough on top and shape into a ball, pressing the seeds into the dough on all sides.
• Place the ball of dough on the baking sheet, flatten the top a little, cover with a damp cloth and leave to rise until it has increased in bulk by about one-third. This will take about 2 hours. • Bake the bread on the bottom shelf of a preheated 200°C/400°F/Gas Mark 6 oven for about 1 hour until golden-brown. Turn the oven off and leave the bread to rest in the oven for 15 minutes. • Now spray the loaf all over with cold water and leave to cool on a wire rack.

Our Tip: Leave the bread for 24 hours before slicing. If stored in a cool and well-ventilated place it will remain fresh for up to a week. It is best spread with butter and sprinkled with chives, but it is also delicious with herb-flavoured soft cheese or cream cheese garnished with chopped green or red peppers or cucumber.

Plain White Bread

This golden-brown crusty bread can be made as a batch or a loaf

Quantities for 1 batch or 1 24cm/10in loaf tin:

42g/1½oz fresh yeast or 21g/¾oz dry yeast
1 tbsp sugar
500ml-750ml/1-1¼ pints lukewarm water
1.3kg/2lb 15oz strong plain flour
3-4 tsps salt

FOR THE GLAZE:

2 tbsps milk
2 tbsps stout or malt beer
Butter for tin and baking sheet

Preparation time: 40 minutes
Rising time: 3 hours
Baking time: 50 minutes for the tin, 35-40 minutes for the batch
Nutritional value:
Analysis per slice, if divided into 40 slices, approx:
• 460kJ/110kcal
• 4g protein
• 0g fat
• 24g carbohydrate

Crumble the fresh yeast and blend the fresh or dry yeast with the sugar and 100ml/4 fl oz lukewarm water. Cover and leave to froth in a warm place for 15 minutes. • Sift the flour into a large bowl. Add the dissolved yeast, salt and remaining water. Knead the dough well until it leaves the bowl clean and is smooth and elastic. Cover and leave to rise in a warm place for 2 hours or until doubled in bulk. • Butter the baking sheet and loaf tin. • Knead the dough again and divide in two. Half fill the tin with dough and smooth the surface using a wet metal spatula or palette knife. Shape the remaining dough into a long batch, about 6cm/2in in diameter, and place on the baking sheet. Cover and leave both loaves to prove for a further 45 minutes. The dough in the tin should almost have reached the top of the tin by this time. • Place an ovenproof dish of cold water in the base of the oven. • Using a sharp knife, make a long, ½cm/¼in deep cut lengthways in the dough in the loaf tin and brush the top with milk. Make 4 or 5 cuts across the top of the batch and brush with the malt beer or stout.
• Bake the bread on the centre shelf of a preheated 220°C/425°F/Gas Mark 7 oven for 45 minutes. After 10 minutes remove the water from the oven and reduce the temperature to 200°C/400°F/Gas Mark 6. • Take the batch out of the oven after 35-40 minutes and leave to cool on a wire rack. • Bake the loaf tin for a further 10 minutes and leave to rest in the oven for 5 minutes after the oven has been switched off. • Remove from the tin and leave to cool on a wire rack. • This white bread tastes best when eaten straight from the oven. White bread that has been stored in a cool place can be reheated briefly in the oven or made into toast.

Golden Plaits

Delicious for breakfast with butter and jam

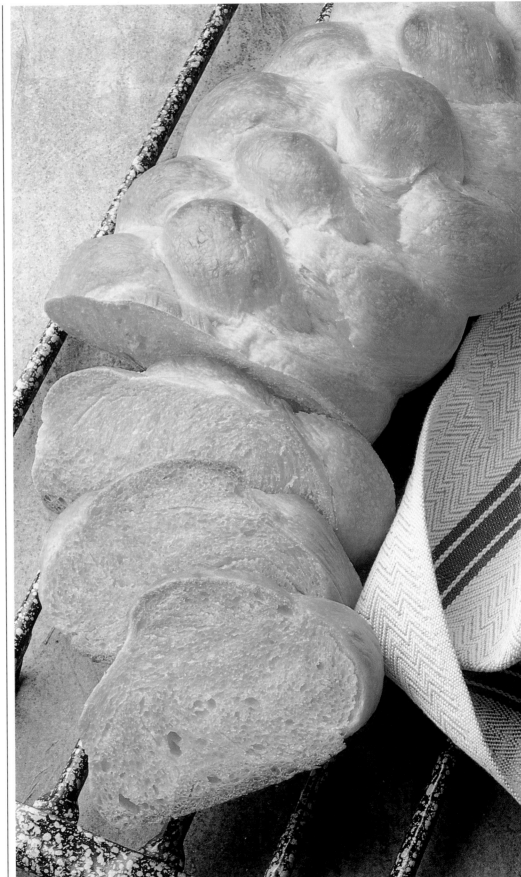

Quantities for 2 plaits:

21g/³/₄oz fresh yeast or 10g/¹/₄oz dry yeast
1 tbsp sugar
600ml/1 pint lukewarm milk
1kg/2¹/₄lbs strong plain white flour
2 tsps salt
100g/4oz soft butter
2 tbsps condensed milk
Butter for the baking sheet

Preparation time: 40 minutes
Rising time: 1³/₄ hours
Baking time: 40 minutes
Nutritional value:
Analysis per slice, if divided into 30 slices, approx:
- 630kJ/150kcal
- 4g protein
- 4g fat
- 25g carbohydrate

Blend the yeast and sugar with 125ml/4 fl oz milk. Cover and leave to froth in a warm place for 15 minutes. Add the yeast mixture to the flour, the remaining milk, salt and butter and knead to a workable dough.
• Cover and leave to rise in a warm place for 1 hour. • Knead the dough again and divide into 6 portions. Place on a lightly floured surface and shape each portion into a 50cm/20in long strip. Lay 3 strips together and make into a plait. Repeat for the second plait. Butter the baking sheet, place the plaits on it, cover and leave to rise for 30 minutes. • Place an ovenproof dish of cold water on the floor of the oven. • Brush the plaits with the condensed milk and bake on the centre shelf of a preheated 200°C/400°F/Gas Mark 6 oven for 40 minutes. Remove the dish of water from the oven after 10 minutes. • Cool the plaits on a wire rack and serve very fresh.

Our Tip: For a more intricate plait, use 4 strips of dough.

Wholemeal Curd Cheese Bread

A delicious breakfast-time bread.

Quantities for 1 loaf:

600g/1lb 5oz wheat grains
42g/1½oz fresh yeast or 21g/¾oz dry yeast
1 tbsp clear honey
100ml/4 fl oz lukewarm water
2 tsps sea salt
500g/1lb 2oz low fat curd or cottage cheese
2 tbsps sunflower oil
Butter for the baking sheet

Preparation time: 30 minutes
Rising time: 1 hour
Baking time: 50 minutes
Nutritional value:

Analysis per slice, if divided into 30 slices, approx:

- 335kJ/80kcal
- 5g protein
- 1g fat
- 13g carbohydrate

Grind half the wheat grains to fine flour; grind the other half coarsely. Combine in a large bowl. • Make a well in the centre and crumble in the fresh yeast; pour on the honey and wait 2 minutes for the yeast to dissolve. • Add the lukewarm water to the yeast and mix, incorporating a little flour to form a wet starter dough. If using dry yeast, blend the yeast with the honey and water before pouring into the well. Sprinkle a little flour on the starter dough, cover and leave to rise in a warm place at about 22°C/70°F until cracks can clearly be seen. This will take about 20 minutes. Add the salt, curd cheese and oil to the starter dough and knead all ingredients with all the flour to a workable dough. Cover and leave to rise again in a warm place for 20 minutes. • Butter the baking sheet. • Knead the dough thoroughly again. If it is too firm, add a little more water; if it is too soft, add a little more wholewheat flour. • Shape the dough into a ball, place on the baking sheet and flatten until it is 20cm/8in thick. • Cover and leave to rise for a further 20 minutes until the loaf has increased in bulk by about one-third. • Bake the bread on the centre shelf of a preheated 200°C/400°F/Gas Mark 6 oven for about 40 minutes until golden-brown and leave to rest for 10 minutes with the oven switched off. • Place the bread on a wire rack, spray all over with a little cold water and leave to cool. • One hour later, the bread will be ready to serve. It is best served fresh with butter and honey or jam or mild cheese.

Our Tip: The crust of wholemeal bread is never as smooth as that of bread made with refined flour and should always be sprayed or brushed with cold water before being allowed to cool. Bakers used to use fat, compact brushes for this purpose. A plant spray with a fine nozzle is an excellent substitute. The water can also be brushed on. Spraying or brushing bread with cold water makes it easier to slice once cool and gives it an appealing, golden-brown glaze.

Wheaten Loaves

A mixture of wholemeal and wheatmeal (partial extraction) flours, plus wheatgerm form the basis for this delicious breads

Hand-shaped Wheaten Bread

illustrated left

Quantities for 2 loaves:

1.5kg/3lbs organic wholemeal flour

1 tsp salt

84g/3oz fresh yeast or 42g/1¹/₂oz dry yeast

250g/8oz wheatmeal flour

1 tsp sugar

2 tbsps wheatgerm

500ml/18 fl oz lukewarm water

4 tbsps milk

Baking paper for the baking sheet

Preparation time: 30 minutes
Rising time: 1 hour 45 minutes
Baking time: 50 minutes
Nutritional value:
Analysis per slice, if 2 loaves divided into 50 slices, approx:
• 460kJ/110kcal
• 4g protein
• 1g fat
• 22g carbohydrate

Combine the wholemeal flour and salt in a bowl, cover and leave in a warm place. • Crumble the fresh yeast over the flour, mix with the sugar, a little water and the flour. If using dry yeast, blend with the sugar and water and pour this over the flour. Cover and leave to rise in a warm place for 30 minutes. • Knead the wheatmeal flour, wheatgerm and the remaining water into the yeast mixture. Knead the dough until smooth and elastic and then leave to rise in a warm place for 45 minutes. • Line the baking sheet with baking paper. • Knead the dough with floured hands. Shape it into two loaves. Place them on the baking sheet, cover and leave to prove for 30 minutes. • Place a dish of cold water on the oven floor. • Make four cuts across the tops of the loaves and brush with milk. Bake on the bottom shelf of a preheated 220°C/425°F/Gas Mark 7 oven for 50 minutes or until golden-brown.

Wheatmeal Loaf

illustrated right

Quantities for 1 30cm/12in loaf:

750g/1lb 11oz wholewheat flour

750g/1lb 11oz wheatmeal flour

2 tbsps wheatgerm

63g/2¹/₂oz fresh yeast or 32g/1oz dry yeast

500ml/18 fl oz lukewarm water

1 tsp salt

1 tbsp melted butter

Oil for the tin

Preparation time: 30 minutes
Rising time: 14 hours
Baking time: 50 minutes
Nutritional value:
Analysis per slice, if divided into 30 slices, approx:
• 670kJ/160kcal
• 6g protein
• 1g fat
• 31g carbohydrate

Combine the flours in a bowl, add the wheatgerm and make a well in the centre. Crumble the fresh yeast into the well. Add 400ml/14 fl oz water and a little flour and mix to a dough. If using dry yeast, blend the yeast with the 400ml/14 fl oz water, add a little flour and pour into the well. Sprinkle a little flour on top and leave to rise in a warm place for 12 hours. • Mix the milk with the rest of the water and the salt and combine with this starter and the rest of the flours to form a workable dough. Cover and leave to rise for 1 hour. • Knead the dough thoroughly again, place in the oiled tin and leave to rise for a further hour. • Make a 5mm/¹/₄in deep cut lengthways in the dough and brush the top with the melted butter. Preheat the oven to 230°C/450°F/Gas Mark 8. Place a cupful of water in the base of the oven. Bake the bread on the bottom shelf for 50 minutes.

Flatbreads from the Orient

These exotic flatbreads are broken, not sliced. Perfect accompaniments to a Turkish kebab or Indian curry.

Turkish Flatbreads
illustrated rear

Quantities for 2 flatbreads:

500g/1lb 2oz strong plain flour
1 packet dry yeast
1 tsp salt
1 tsp sugar
100ml/4 fl oz olive oil
250ml/9 fl oz lukewarm water
2 tbsps sesame seeds
Oil for the baking sheet

Preparation time: 30 minutes
Rising time: 1 hour
Baking time: 15-20 minutes
Nutritional value:
Analysis per flatbread, approx:
• 5880kJ/1400kcal
• 29g protein
• 57g fat
• 180g carbohydrate

Combine the flour, dry yeast, salt, sugar and oil. • Slowly add the water. Knead the dough until it is smooth and shiny and leaves the bowl clean. Cover and leave to rise in a warm place for 45 minutes. • Knead the dough well on a lightly floured work surface, shape into 2 balls and roll each out to an oval 1cm/¹/₂in thick. • Place the flatbreads on the greased baking sheet, cover and leave to rise for 15 minutes. • Brush the flatbreads with water, prick all over with a fork, sprinkle with the sesame seeds and bake in the centre of a preheated 250°C/480°F/Gas Mark 10 oven for 15-20 minutes until honey-coloured.

Indian Flatbreads
illustrated front

Quantities for 10 small flatbreads:

500g/1lb 2oz floury potatoes
2 medium onions
1 tbsp butter or vegetable ghee
1 bunch of parsley
600g/1lb 5oz wheatmeal flour
¹/₂ tsp ground cumin
Pinch of cayenne pepper
1 tsp salt
3 tbsps sunflower oil
250ml/9 fl oz water
100g/4oz clarified butter or vegetable ghee

Preparation time: 1 hour
Baking time: 1¹/₄ hours
Nutritional value:
Analysis per flatbread, approx:
• 1680kJ/400kcal
• 10g protein
• 13g fat
• 64g carbohydrate

Boil the potatoes for 30-35 minutes until cooked; peel and mash while still hot. • Chop and fry the onion in the butter until translucent. • Chop the parsley and combine with the mashed potato, flour, spices, salt and oil. Slowly add the water and then add the cooled onion. • Divide the dough into 12 equal portions and roll out into rounds 15cm/6in in diameter on a lightly floured work surface. • Fry the flatbreads in the clarified butter or ghee in a frying pan over a medium heat for 5 minutes on each side. • Keep the flatbreads warm by covering with aluminium foil and placing in a preheated 75°C/170°F oven until they are all cooked. Serve hot with meat or fish.

Vegetable Panettone

A savoury variation on the famous Italian Christmas cake-bread

Quantities for 1 panettone tin or 1 tall 1.5l/2¹/₂ pint tin:
21g/³/₄oz fresh yeast or 10g/¹/₄oz dry yeast
1 tsp sugar
Pinch of saffron
250ml/9 fl oz warm milk
1 tbsp butter
1 tsp salt
1 egg
400g/14oz wheatmeal flour
50g/2oz skinned, ground almonds
100g/4oz each of carrots and broccoli spears
¹/₂ red pepper
Butter for the tin

Preparation time: 40 minutes
Rising time: 1¹/₂ hours
Baking time: 45 minutes
Nutritional value:
Analysis per slice, if divided into 16 slices, approx:
- 454kJ/130kcal
- 5g protein
- 4g fat
- 21g carbohydrate

Crumble the fresh yeast and mix the fresh or dry yeast with the sugar and 3 tbsps lukewarm water. Cover and leave to rise in a warm place for 15 minutes. • Soak the saffron in the milk, melt the butter in the mixture and stir in the salt, egg, flour, ground almonds and the yeast mixture. Knead to a workable dough. Cover and leave to rise for 40 minutes. • Wash and trim the vegetables, blanch for 3 minutes, drain and cool. Chop finely and add to the dough. Butter the tin, fill it with the dough, make some diagonal cuts in the top of the dough and leave to rise for another 30 minutes. • Bake the panettone on a low shelf in a preheated 220°C/425°F/Gas Mark 5 oven for 45 minutes. After 5 minutes reduce the temperature to 180°C/350°F/Gas Mark 4. • Remove from the tin, leave to cool on a wire rack and serve with butter.

Herbed Oaten Bread

Buttermilk can be used instead of full cream milk

Wheaten Toast Bread

This bread is also delicious eaten fresh

Quantities for 1 loaf:

400g/14oz wheatmeal flour
120g/4oz oats
1 packet dry yeast
1 tsp sugar
2 tsps celery salt
1 bunch each of fresh dill weed, parsley and chives
750ml/1¼ pints lukewarm full cream milk
1 tbsp condensed milk
Butter for the baking sheet

Preparation time: 30 minutes
Rising time: about 1 hour
Baking time: 30-40 minutes
Nutritional value:
Analysis per slice, if divided into 30 slices, approx:
- 290kJ/70kcal
- 2g protein
- 1g fat
- 13g carbohydrate

Mix the flour, oats, yeast, sugar and celery salt together. •

Finely chop the herbs and add to the flour mixture together with the milk. Knead until the dough leaves the bowl clean. • Cover and leave to rise until the dough has almost doubled in bulk – this will take about 40 minutes. • Turn the dough out onto a lightly floured surface and knead well. Shape the dough into a long loaf and smooth the top with your hands. Butter the baking sheet, place the dough on it and cover and leave to rise for 20 minutes. • Make 4 ½cm/¼in cuts across the top of the loaf, brush with the condensed milk and bake on the centre shelf of a preheated 200°C/400°F/Gas Mark 6 oven for 30-40 minutes until golden-brown.

Quantities for 2 25cm/10in baking tins:

21g/¾oz fresh yeast or 10g/¼oz dry yeast
1 tbsp sugar
500ml/18 fl oz lukewarm milk
800g/1lb 12oz wheatmeal flour
2 tsps salt
50g/2oz soft butter
Butter for the tins

Preparation time: 40 minutes
Rising time: 2 hours
Baking time: 40 minutes
Nutritional value:
Analysis per slice, if divided into 40 slices, approx:
- 375kJ/90kcal
- 3g protein
- 2g fat
- 15g carbohydrate

Crumble the fresh yeast and mix the fresh or dry yeast with the sugar and 100ml/4 fl oz milk. Cover and leave to froth in a

warm place for 15 minutes. • Sift the flour into a bowl. Add the yeast mixture, the remaining milk, salt and butter and knead to a workable dough. Cover and leave to rise in a warm place for 1 hour. • Butter the baking tins. • Knead the dough again, divide into 2 portions, place in the tins, smooth the top, cover and leave to rise for a further 45 minutes. • Make one long ½cm/¼in cut along the length of the loaf and bake on the bottom shelf of a preheated 200°C/400°F/Gas Mark 6 oven for 30 minutes. • Remove the bread from the tins and leave for 10 minutes in the oven after it has been switched off. • Leave to cool on a wire rack.

Special Breads

If you like experimenting with new recipes, you will enjoy trying some of these special breads

Courgette and Apple Bread
illustrated left

Quantities for 1 30cm/12in loaf:

300g/10oz courgettes
1 medium-sized apple
300g/10oz wheatmeal flour
3 tsps baking powder
5 eggs
100ml/4 fl oz olive oil
1 tsp salt
150g/5½oz freshly grated Cheddar cheese
50g/2oz pumpkin seeds
Butter for the tin

Preparation time: 20 minutes
Baking time: 1 hour 10 min
Nutritional value:
Analysis per slice, if divided into 30 slices, approx:
- 540kJ/130kcal
- 6g protein
- 9g fat
- 8g carbohydrate

Butter the loaf tin. • Coarsely grate the courgette and apple. • Combine the flour, baking powder, eggs, oil, salt, cheese and grated courgette and apple to form a wet dough. Add the pumpkin seeds. • Put the dough in the loaf tin and bake in a preheated 200°C/400°F/Gas Mark 6 oven for 50 minutes. • Reduce the heat to 180°C/350°F/Gas Mark 4 and continue to bake for a further 20 minutes. Leave the bread to cool in the tin, then loosen the edges all the way around using a knife and turn the bread out onto a wire rack.

Our Tip: This apple and courgette bread is very tempting served with raw ham, tomato salad, tzatziki (or cucumber raitha) and wine.

Portuguese Corn Bread
illustrated right

Quantities for 1 30cm/12in tin:

42g/1½oz fresh yeast or 21g/¾oz dry yeast
Pinch of sugar
200ml/7 fl oz lukewarm water
250g/8oz cornmeal
1 tsp salt
200ml/7 fl oz boiling water
1 tbsp olive oil
250g/8oz wheatmeal flour
Butter for the tin

Preparation time: 30 minutes
Rising time: 1¼ hours
Baking time: 40 minutes
Nutritional value:
Analysis per slice, if divided into 25 slices, approx:
- 315kJ/75kcal
- 2g protein
- 1g fat
- 15g carbohydrate

Crumble the fresh yeast, sprinkle the fresh or dry yeast with the sugar and mix with the water. Cover and leave to froth until the cornmeal mixture (see below) has cooled. • Mix 200g/7oz of the cornmeal with the salt and boiling water and leave to cool for 10 minutes. • Add the yeast mixture, the remaining cornmeal, the oil and the wheatmeal flour to the cornmeal mixture and mix well. Knead the dough until soft and elastic, cover and leave to rise for 30 minutes, then knead well and, if necessary, add a little more wheatmeal flour. • Put the dough in the greased baking tin, cover and leave to rise for a further 30 minutes. • Brush the bread with water and bake in a preheated 200°C/400°F/Gas Mark 6 oven for 40 minutes until golden-brown.

Sweet Yeast Bread

Freshly baked and served with butter and honey, this bread is as good as any cake

Quantities for 1 loaf:

42g/1¹/₂oz fresh yeast or 21g/³/₄oz dry yeast
1 tbsp sugar
200ml/7 fl oz lukewarm milk
100g/4oz currants
4 tbsps rum
650g/1lb 7oz strong, plain white flour
75g/3oz butter
100g/4oz sugar
1 egg
Pinch of salt
100g/4oz chopped hazelnuts
3 tbsps milk
Butter for the tin

Preparation time: 40 minutes
Rising time: 2¹/₄ hours
Baking time: 25-30 minutes
Nutritional value:
Analysis per slice, if divided into 40 slices, approx:
- 460kJ/110kcal
- 3g protein
- 4g fat
- 17g carbohydrate

Dissolve the yeast and sugar in 100ml/4 fl oz milk, cover and leave in a warm place to froth. • Wash the currants in hot water, pat them dry and soak them in the rum. • Mix the flour with the yeast mixture and the remaining milk. • Melt the butter and add to the dough together with the sugar, egg, salt, hazelnuts, currants and rum. Knead well until the dough leaves the bowl clean. • Cover and leave the dough to rise in a warm place for 1¹/₂ hours. • Butter the baking sheet. • Knead the dough again and divide it into 2 portions. Place them on a lightly floured work surface and roll each into a 50cm/20in strip. Twist the strips of dough around each other in a spiral formation and place on the baking sheet. • Cover and leave to rise for another 30 minutes. • Place an ovenproof dish of cold water in the base of the oven. • Brush the dough with the milk and bake in the centre of a preheated 220°C/425°F/Gas Mark 7 oven for 25-30 minutes. • After 10 minutes remove the dish of water from the oven and reduce the temperature to 200°C/400°F/Gas Mark 6.

Greek Easter Bread

A traditional delicacy which is worth eating all year round

Swedish Christmas Bread

Lemon zest can be substituted for bitter orange peel when Seville oranges are not in season

Greek Easter Bread

Quantities for 1 loaf:

600g/1lb 5oz strong plain flour
42g/1½oz fresh yeast or 21g/¾oz dry yeast
100g/4oz sugar
7 tbsps lukewarm water
Pinch of salt
Zest of one lemon
50g/2oz candied lemon peel, finely chopped
½ tsp ground aniseed
125g/5oz soft butter
7 tbsps lukewarm water
5 hard-boiled eggs painted with red food colouring
Olive oil • 1 egg yolk
2 tbsps sesame seeds
Butter for the baking sheet

Preparation time: 45 minutes
Rising time: 3½ – 4½ hours
Baking time: 40-45 minutes
Nutritional value:
Analysis per slice, if divided into 20 slices, not including the eggs:
- 880kJ/210kcal
- 5g protein
- 10g fat
- 29g carbohydrate

If using fresh yeast, crumble the yeast and mix it with 125g/5 oz of the flour, 1 tsp sugar and the water. If using dry yeast, blend the yeast with 1 tsp sugar, the water and 125g/5 oz of the flour; make a well in the centre of the rest of the flour and pour the yeast mixture into it. Leave to rise for 15 minutes. • Add the other ingredients up to and including the milk; knead the dough well and leave to rise for 3-4 hours. • Knead the dough thoroughly again and divide into 3 equal portions and 1 larger portion; shape these into strips. Make the three equal strips into a plait; place the thicker strip on top and press down gently. • Make little hollows in the dough for the eggs. Rub the eggs with oil and press into the plait. • Cover and leave to prove for 20 minutes. • Brush the plait with the beaten egg, sprinkle with the sesame seeds and bake in a preheated 180°C/350°F/Gas Mark 4 oven for 40-45 minutes.

Swedish Christmas Bread

Quantities for 1 wide, 30cm/12in tin of 2.5l/4½ pint capacity:

750g/1lb 11oz wholemeal rye flour
500g/1lb 2oz wholewheat flour
60g/2oz fresh yeast or 30g/1oz dry yeast
500ml/18 fl oz buttermilk
50g/2oz golden syrup
½ tsp salt
2 tsps grated Seville orange peel
¼ tsp each cardamom and coriander seeds, crushed
50g/2oz raisins
2 tbsps golden syrup
Butter for the tin

Preparation time: 30 minutes
Rising time: 2 hours
Baking time: 30 minutes
Nutritional value:
Analysis per slice, if divided into 40 slices, approx:
- 545kJ/130kcal
- 4g protein
- 1g fat
- 26g carbohydrate

Mix the flours together in a large bowl and make a well in the centre. Crumble the fresh yeast. into the well • Warm the butter, milk and syrup, stirring constantly. Mix about 250ml/9 fl oz of this mixture with the yeast and a little flour. If using dry yeast, blend the yeast with 250ml/9 fl oz of the liquid before pouring it into the well and mixing with a little flour. • Cover the starter dough and leave it to rise for 15 minutes. • Add the salt, spices and remaining buttermilk to the flour and starter dough and knead thoroughly until the dough leaves the bowl clean. Cover and leave to rise for 1 hour. • Wash the raisins in hot water and pat dry. • Knead the dough again and incorporate the raisins. Butter the tin, place the dough in it, cover loosely and leave to rise until doubled in volume. • Heat the syrup with 1 tbsp water. • Cut the top of the dough in a grid pattern, brush with the syrup and bake on a low shelf in a preheated 220°C/425°F/Gas Mark 7 oven for 50 minutes.

Index

Index

Recipes Listed by Type of Dough

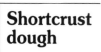

Yeast Puff Dough

Puff and Strudel Pastry

Sour Dough

Wholefood Recipes

Acknowledgements

AUTHORS

Annette Wolter
Cornelia Adam
Elke Alsen
Dagmar Freifrau von Cramm
Marey Kurz
Hannelore Mähl-Strenge
Annedore Meineke
Brigitta Stuber

PHOTOGRAPHY

Susi and Pete Eising
Rolf Feuz and Karin Messerli
Odette Teubner

Translated into English by UPS Translations
Edited by Josephine Bacon